BECOMING A GRAPHIC & DIGITAL DESIGNER

A GUIDE TO CAREERS IN DESIGN

Cover image: Rick Landers
Cover design: Rick Landers
This book is printed on acid-free paper.

For general information about our other products and services, please contact
our Customer Care Department within the United States at
(800) 762–2974, outside the United States at (317) 572–3993 or
fax (317) 572–4002.

Wiley publishes in a variety of print and electronic formats and by
print-on-demand. Some material included with standard print versions
of this book may not be included in e-books or in print-on-demand.
If this book refers to media such as a CD or DVD that is not included
in the version you purchased, you may download this material at
http://booksupport.wiley.com. For more information about Wiley
products, visit www.wiley.com.

Library of Congress Cataloging-in-Publication Data:
ISBN 978-1-118-77198-3 (pbk); ISBN 978-1-119-04470-3 (ebk); ISBN
978-1-119-04496-3 (ebk)

Printed in the United States of America
10 9 8 7 6 5 4 3 2 1

BECOMING A GRAPHIC & DIGITAL DESIGNER

A GUIDE TO CAREERS IN DESIGN

STEVEN HELLER & VÉRONIQUE VIENNE

We dream of a life that fills us with Inspiration, and we dream of a love that even time will lie down & be still for.

FIFTH EDITION

Contents

◉ Online Content

This book has a companion website, which can be found at: www.wiley.com/go/heller5e

The companion website contains exclusive online video interviews.

If your access code is not working, or you have not received one, please contact Wiley Customer Service at http://support.wiley.com for assistance.

Foreword

This is not your grandmother's graphic design. Nor is it your older brother's or sister's. The rate of speed at which the practice moves is cyclonic. All you have to do is look around to see that the world of design involves media that were inconceivable when grandmas were starting their careers.

– From the Preface of 4th Edition

This brand new edition represents a brand new era of graphic design, which is part graphic, almost entirely digital, and decidedly transitional. One of the proposed titles for this book was *Becoming an Integrated Designer* because traditional graphic and relatively new digital design are indeed merging into one practice. Likewise, it could have been called *Becoming an INTEGRAL Designer* because it is integral for practioners to be prepared for the present and the future, having fluency in a variety of media and platforms—those that exist now and those yet to be discovered.

Building on the past successes of *Becoming A Graphic Designer* with Teresa Fernandez and *Becoming a Digital Designer* with David Womack, this new edition addresses the demands of starting a design career in the early twenty-first century. This new volume is not a revision but, rather, a complete restructuring of form and content. All the interviews were done specifically for this edition, and the international coverage is unique as well. Starting with a new definition of *design* as a multiplatform activity that involves aesthetic, creative, and technical expertise, this edition will guide the reader through print and digital design, emphasizing the transitional and improvisational methods so prevalent today. Through over 80 interviews and essays that address inspiration, theory, and practice, the reader will come to understand that field once narrowly known as "graphic design" is much richer and more inviting of thinkers, managers, and makers.

Traditional graphic design and typography platforms (i.e., print) are important yet now comprise a smaller portion of this book. After all, many of the print platforms are now gone, near obsolescence, or subsumed. Digital is, however, an umbrella term for all manner of graphic design, information design, interaction design, and user experience, where the computer is the tool of today. Every "communication designer" must be able to use digital tools whether he or she designs for print magazines or iPhone apps. Also, since the 4th edition, the fact of design entrepreneurship—or "start-up" culture—is now reaching new levels of ubiquity and accessibility. Education is changing to better integrate new technologies: graphic, typographic, product, interaction, branding, and other subgenres. This excerpt from the previous edition still resonates:

Becoming a Graphic & Digital Designer is not going to teach the neophyte how to use the computer. Scores of books and thousands of courses offer basic, intermediate, and advanced instruction. Rather, this book is an introduction—a navigational guide, if you like—to what in recent years has become a complex profession comprising many print, film, and electronic genres. In the music business, it is not enough to play a few chords on the guitar; it is useful to be proficient in R&B, folk, reggae, punk, hip-hop, and so forth. Likewise, graphic design is not simply about the exclusive practice of editorial, book, advertising, or poster design; all these forms can (and even should) be practiced by individuals depending on their relative skill, expertise, and inclination. More important, with the recent development of desktop publishing as well as computer-driven multimedia, the field has expanded to such an extent that entirely new divisions of labor, unprecedented collaborations, and specializations have emerged. This book describes both traditional and new disciplines.

And this quote from Milton Glaser in the previous edition balances the reality of being a designer and an artist with the disciplines necessary to practice effectively:

One of the great problems of being a designer is that you get parochialized and you find yourself increasingly narrowed, doing more and more specialized things that you've done a hundred times before. For me, the way out was to broaden the canvas, to try to do things that I was not very experienced doing, to try to develop a range of activities so that I couldn't be forced into a corner and left to dry. While that is not the solution for everyone, that is a consideration people must at least examine before they embark on a course, for once they have mastered the professional requirement, it may no longer have any interest in it for them.

So, you learn the "lay" of the present landscape and perhaps the future, too. Advice through interviews with designers, design managers, and design educators, each with a distinct practice, will help the navigation. There are so many options for employment today in so many different venues that it is easy to lose track of why one becomes a designer in the first place—to make inventive, imaginative, and useful things that will have value to both the user and the maker.

Glossary
Job Opportunities

The field is changing quickly, and with this comes an entire glossary of new job titles. This is a selection of some of them, but don't be surprised if you come across others in your job hunt.

Job Divisions

Graphic designers are employed in virtually all kinds of businesses, industries, and institutions. Here are some of the typical terms used interchangeably for "in-house design department." (The words *group* and *team* are also commonly used).

Different companies are organized differently, depending on their focus and goals. A large corporation may distinguish package design from promotion design, or editorial design from advertising design; a smaller business may keep all design activities under one umbrella, such as Design Department.

Likewise, proprietary or independent design firms, studios, or offices — design businesses that service large corporations and small businesses — may or may not distinguish among design functions, such as having a print design department separate from a multimedia design department, or promotion and collateral separate from editorial departments.

Art Department

Art and Design Department

Art Services Department

Design Department

Design Services Department

Creative Services Department

Creative Group

Graphics Group

Interaction Group

Research and Development Department

User Experience Group

Job Titles

The titles given to specific jobs and tasks throughout the design field vary according to the hierarchy of the specific company, institution, or firm. For example, an art director for one company may be a design director at another; a senior designer at one may have different responsibilities than a senior at another. Starting from the top, here are typical job titles as used by in-house art departments in publishing, advertising, corporations, and proprietary design firms and agencies.

The managerial level, where jobs may or may not involve hands-on design work in addition to the oversight of the designers:

Creative director

Design director

Corporate art director

Creative service manager

Design manager

Brand strategist

The support level, which involves working directly with the seniors in both design and production capacities:

Junior designer

Assistant designer

Deputy art director

Associate art director

Assistant art director

Production artist

Art associate

The creative or design level, which involves directly serving clients. These titles embody different responsibilities, depending on the organizational hierarchy of the particular business:

Senior designer

Designer

Senior art director

Art director

Graphics editor

Entry level

Assistant designer

Junior designer

Intern (This category is temporary—a stepping-stone, perhaps—and is often unpaid.)

New Jobs

Since this book was first published, interaction design has become a dominant career choice for designers. Although communication is the common denominator between the graphic designer and interaction designer, there are profound differences. For more detailed information, see *Becoming a Digital Designer* by Steven Heller and David Womack (Wiley, 2004). In addition to familiar titles, like "art director," new jobs in this field (see page xi for list of titles) include the following:

Information architect

Interaction designer

Service designer

Web designer

UX (user experience designer)

Freelancer

Freelancers, as opposed to principals of proprietary studios or firms, do not manage businesses with additional employees (although they may hire assistants as needed). They often take on individual, finite freelance projects either on the premises of the client or in their own studios. Freelancers usually do not use titles but, rather, advertise themselves as "Jane Doe, Graphic Designer," or "John Doe, Design Production."

Job Seeking

Social media have revolutionized our interpersonal and professional interactions. Now, not only are graphic designers expected to have a well-crafted resume and online portfolio, but they must also be part of networks like Facebook and LinkedIn. Increasingly, message apps like Twitter, Instagram, and Pintrest are promotional tools for designers.

Of all the new social and professional networks, LinkedIn is quickly becoming a way of connecting with future employees for an increasing number of recruiters and hiring managers. In a segment on NPR, Yuki Noguchi wrote, "Not having a profile on the social networking site LinkedIn is, for some employers, not only a major liability but also a sign that the candidate is horribly out of touch." Monica Bloom, a design industry recruiter for Aquent in Los Angeles, says that it is essential for graphic designers seeking employment to have a LinkedIn profile—more so than Facebook, although that is debatable.

And what about a designer's Google factor? Take a minute, open your Web browser, and do a search on your own name. What comes up? Are there any pictures that come up when your name is searched that you wouldn't want a future employer or coworker to see? What about things you may have said online? Prospective employers, like prospective blind dates, use the Web as reference. So be sure that you are aware of what others might find when they search for you in digital space. As the design industry has become more and more digital, the portfolios are more interactive. Samples alone are not enough. Linking to successful projects increases credibility. While, in most cases, designers should still bring a physical copy of their portfolio to a job interview, an increasing amount of legwork is done when designers have their work posted online at all times for anyone interested to see.

Since many recruiters, headhunters, and employers reach out first to their online contacts with job openings, it pays to get on board all major networking and portfolio websites. There are many portfolio-hosting services, which gives designers an opportunity to circulate their work online for little or no cost. Check out Coroflot.com, Behance.com, DesignObserver.com, and CreativeHotlist.com for portfolio hosting and job notifications. Some employers also use Facebook and Twitter to announce job openings. Be sure your profiles and portfolios are up to date and professional.

When posting online or sending portfolio samples as an email attachment, it is easiest if the files are PDFs and not more than 2 MB in size. In many cases, if the attachment is larger, it will take too long to open online or clog up the recipient's inbox if e-mailed.

The Optimum Portfolio

Portfolios are now mostly online either on your own site or on a service, and/or stored on your tablet or laptop. You can have an analog version, but the days of bulky books and oversized cases are over. There are specific requirements for each discipline, but, on average, the idea is to show no more than 15 examples.

Entry Level

Most entry-level portfolios include a high percentage of school assignments and often one or two redesigns of existing magazines or fantasy magazines. This work exhibits original thinking, unfettered by the constraints of a real job, and yet the solutions are realistic.

Junior/Senior Designer

By this stage, portfolios should include a large percentage of published (online or printed) work. The junior may continue to include school projects, but the senior should jettison them. The samples should be of high quality. Not everything that has been published rates showing in a portfolio. Through these samples, the important thing is to show your taste, talent, and expertise.

First Impressions

Often your first impression will be made through a letter or e-mail sent to a potential employer. This is an opportunity to let them know who you are. So your letter should be simple and straightforward. Avoid flourishes and eccentricities. Be professional. This is an example of how familiarity can be too cute (note the critical annotations):

Hello
(To start, this is too informal; stick to "Dear Ms. Jones")

I'm sure by now, you've received my little mailer from sunny . . ., where I was working for . . . . . studio. I've since returned to the good ol' US of A and I am looking for full-time employment! (Never assume anything. Never send your work separate from your introductory letter. And watch out for sayings like "good ol' US of A." It may be fine in speech, but in a letter, it is an annoying affectation.)

I'm looking to work in a place where I can implement all of my creative and professional skills to create high-quality work. That's why you've received a little mailer from me—You've been hand-picked! You're obviously talented, and I'd love the opportunity to work with you.
(YOU'VE BEEN WHAT?!!? Never suggest that you are doing a prospective employer a favor.)

Please see attached resume; I look forward to hearing from you! Kind regards,

(This letter will ensure you will be ignored. Remember, the quality of your work will get your foot in the door. The brevity and sincerity of your request to be interviewed will get you the appointment you need.)

Graphic Design

What is graphic design? That question has vexed most practitioners who were compelled to answer when a parent asked, "What is it you do again?" Graphic design was once enigmatic—a specialized field that was visible and yet a mystery. Then the computer revolution of the late 1980s brought enlightenment. Apple Computer ran a TV commercial showing a pair of hands doing a pasteup. To paraphrase the voice-over: This is what a graphic designer does. With the Apple you no longer need a graphic designer. With one 30-second spot, the world was introduced to graphic design and told it was obsolete—anyone with a Macintosh could do it. That was the age of "desktop publishing," a moment in time when it seemed that graphic design was about to be devalued. But clear heads and machines prevailed. Instead of taking over the field, the Mac became its foremost tool. What's more, graphic designers became culturally significant as communicators, aestheticists, stylists, and even authors.

The world became aware that all those beautiful (and not-so-beautiful) books, book covers, posters, magazines, record covers, typefaces, signs, packages, exhibitions, trademarks, and information graphics were all components under the graphic design umbrella. Graphic design is not just about making pasteups and mechanicals or the equivalent on computer using InDesign; it is about conceptualizing, conceiving, imagining, constructing, producing, managing, and realizing an aesthetically determined functional piece of visual communication. Once it was primarily paper; now graphic design affects screens of all kinds. But the fundamental definition of graphic design as a way of organizing, "formatizing," and functionalizing word and image remains constant. Graphic designers all speak the same basic language (and use the same jargon), but graphic design is not an intuitive endeavor: Some designers are more adept at fine typography than others, who may be better skilled at sequential narratives or information management. It cannot be done without knowledge of the task, genre, or medium in question. Graphic design must be studied, learned, and continually practiced to achieve even basic proficiency. To go further, to transcend simple service and craft with inspiring work, graphic design must be totally embraced—body and soul.

This section offers a brief survey of some of the current design specialties and hybrids. Some of the viable opportunities discussed in the previous edition have disappeared or are now marginalized. Print work is increasingly being integrated with digital (online or handheld). The following interviews provide insight into and wisdom about the overall graphic design experience—how people became designers and how their careers evolved—with emphasis on each designer's unique specialties.

1 Inspirations and Motivations

The decision to become a graphic designer can hit you on the head like a wave on a beach or sneak into your consciousness like a fragrant aroma. Whatever the reason for joining the ranks, inspiration and motivation must be present. This is not just a job—graphic design is a passion. In these next interviews, designers reveal the various ways they were drawn into the vortex by inspirational yet magnetic forces.

Michael Bierut

On Being a Graphic Designer

After graduating in graphic design at the University of Cincinnati's College of Design, Architecture, Art and Planning, Michael Bierut worked at Vignelli Associates, ultimately as vice president of graphic design. "I had learned how to design in school, but I learned how to be a designer from Massimo and Lella," he says. In 1990, he joined Pentagram, where he designs across disciplines for a wide range of clients. His awards and distinctions are countless: president of the New York Chapter of the American Institute of Graphic Arts from 1988 to 1990; president emeritus of AIGA National; Senior Critic in Graphic Design at the Yale School of Art; coeditor of the five-volume series, Looking Closer: Critical Writings on Graphic; cofounder of the website Design Observer; author of *79 Short Essays on Design*; member of the Alliance Graphique Internationale; elected to the Art Directors Club Hall of Fame; awarded the AIGA Medal in 2006. Last but not least, he was winner in the Design Mind category of the 2008 Cooper-Hewitt National Design Awards.

When did you know you wanted to become a graphic designer, and how did you achieve that?

I did a lot of art classes in public school in suburban Cleveland where I grew up. I liked going downtown to the art museum, but I liked looking at the covers of 12-inch records even more. Finally, in the ninth grade someone recruited me to do a poster for the school play. I did something entirely by hand and turned it in on a Friday. By Monday morning it was all over the school. It was thrilling, seeing something I had drawn at home on my kitchen table, out there in the world, seen by everyone. It was also fun to work with the drama people, who were entertaining and dramatic, unlike the art people who were usual circle. Without knowing it then, I decided that Monday morning to be a graphic designer. This combination of entering other private worlds and interpreting for those worlds for a broader public, was what excited me then, and it still excites me now.

Did you have a clue you were doing graphic design?

At that point, I still couldn't figure out what the connection was between the

Saks Fifth Avenue LOOK
Shopping Bags
Saks Fifth Avenue
Designers: Michael Bierut,
Jesse Reed
Illustrator/photographer:
Pentagram
2013

famous artists who had paintings in the Cleveland Museum of Art and the less famous people who were credited on the covers for my favorite bands. Right around then, and pretty much by accident, I happened to find a book in my high school library called *Aim for a Future in Graphic Design/Commercial Art*. It was by a man named S. Neil Fujita, whom I would eventually learn had designed the Columbia Records logo and the famous cover of the 1972 novel, *The Godfather*, by Mario Puzo. It was filled with profiles of designers and art directors. All of them were doing exactly what I wanted to do, and it was then I found out that this aspiration had a name: graphic design. I went to our neighborhood public library and looked up "graphic design" in the card catalog. It turns out they

had a book by that name. For reasons I cannot fathom, they had a copy of [the] *Graphic Design Manual* by Armin Hoffman. I'm not sure anyone had ever taken out this book, which was the cornerstone document of design as it was then taught at the Kunstgewerbeschule ("school of arts and crafts") in Basel, Switzerland. I was enthralled. My parents asked me what I wanted for Christmas, and I told them I wanted the Hoffman book. Of course, there was no Amazon, so they called every bookstore in town before finally someone said they had it. It turns out this was the wrong book: *Graphic Design* by Milton Glaser, which had just been published. My parents thought this was close enough and bought it for me anyway.

I ended up going to the College of Design, Architecture and Art, at the University of Cincinnati, which coincidentally had several instructors who had studied under Hoffman in Switzerland. It was a great experience. Right before my senior year, I took a trip to New York and dropped off my portfolio at Vignelli Associates because someone I had interned with had gone to school with someone who was working there. I never expected Massimo Vignelli to look at my portfolio, but he did, and he liked it, and he offered me a job.

You worked for Massimo Vignelli for 10 years. What did you learn from that experience?

I started working for Massimo and Lella Vignelli the week after I graduated from college. It was an amazing experience. Everything there was at the highest level: not just the design work, but the clients, the everyday life in the studio. It's not enough to do great work. You have to get clients to hire you, and then you have to get them to accept your recommendations. This is hard to learn in school. And, to be honest, it was hard to learn from Massimo. Not that he wasn't a great teacher, but the way he worked with clients was so unique that it wouldn't really work for anyone other than him. I had to take what made sense for me and combine it with my own style. That's really what happens with every one of your mentors.

When you were invited to become a Pentagram partner, how did you know you were ready?

I worked at Vignelli Associates for a little more than 10 years, which was probably 3 years too long, to tell you the truth. I had gotten past the stage where I had a fantasy of having my own thing with

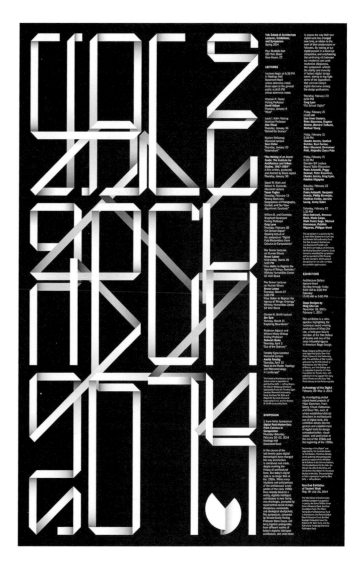

Yale School of Architecture
Spring 2014 Poster
Yale University School
of Architecture
Designers: Michael Bierut,
Jessica Svendsen
Illustrator/photographer:
Pentagram
2014

NYC Pedestrian
Wayfinding Sign
New York City
Department of Transportation
Designers:
Pentagram: Michael Bierut,
Tracey Cameron, and
Hamish Smyth; Jesse Reed,
icon designer; and Tamara
McKenna, project manager;
in partnership with PentaCityGroup
2013

my name on the door. I liked being around people, I liked the buzz of a bigger office, and working on my own had very little appeal. Massimo was very generous with me, always giving me credit for my work, allowing me to do a lot of extracurricular activities. As a result, I had begun to build a small reputation as an up-and-coming designer. So when Woody Pirtle asked me whether I would be interested in joining Pentagram as a partner, I was ready. Still, to go from a nurturing and very disciplined environment like Vignelli Associates to Pentagram was

a shock. At Pentagram, each partner is autonomous. No one tells you what to do. You sort of have to figure it out on your own. It took me a few years to start to find my own voice. It was my second job after graduation, and I've never had another one.

As a designer, what is your greatest strength?
I think I'm a good listener. I enter every project with an open mind and wait for someone or something to say that special, unpredictable thing that will lead me to a solution.

And, conversely, what is your weakness?

I have a short attention span and a low tolerance for ambiguity. As a result, I tend to rush to a solution and settle for the first thing I come up with. As a result, I'm always grateful when I'm forced to slow down and think again.

You are one of the most articulate designers in an increasingly literate field. How does this work as an advantage in your work life?

I think that designers tend to expect the rest of the world to be as visually sophisticated as they are, and they're disappointed when they aren't. Why is that? It's not like the whole world is born with four years of design training. So often there's a gulf, sometimes a vast one, between the designers and the people they work with, or collaborate with, or work for. I learned early on that conversation was the best way to bridge that gap. I listen carefully and then try to explain design in terms that will connect with the person I'm talking to, on whatever the level they're on. I am articulate, and I'm a good and enthusiastic salesman. But I learned early on that the sooner I stopped trying to sell the other person something, the sooner I'd learn something that might genuinely help me.

Is writing like designing?

Writing is like designing in that you need a structure, you need an idea, you need the technical skill to execute that idea, and you need to do it with some style that will give pleasure to the person who's going to read it. These same four elements exist, more or less, in every design project. In both cases, you're trying to communicate something, often to someone you've never met. And both disciplines are such fun ways to learn about the world.

How would you define a good client?

A good client is smart enough to know what he or she thinks about my work, and brave enough to tell me. (My least favorite reaction is something noncommittal like "Hmm . . . you've given us all a lot to think about!" I have been really lucky to have many clients who have been smarter than me. I have never missed an opportunity to learn from them. The very best are inspiring and are really just as responsible for my success as I am.

How would you define a designer who is well suited for Pentagram?

Each partner here is responsible for hiring the designers who will work on his or her own team, so there's no one answer to this. Some of us hire almost entirely on portfolio and craft skills. Others look for designers who can work with clients and take on project management roles. So the designers are different. Because we work in an open-plan office—no one has offices, not even the partners—everyone has to get along and work well with others. Because the teams are small, we all tend to work quickly and look for people who can do a lot of different things. This is not a place for those who want to close their office door and work quietly on one thing all day.

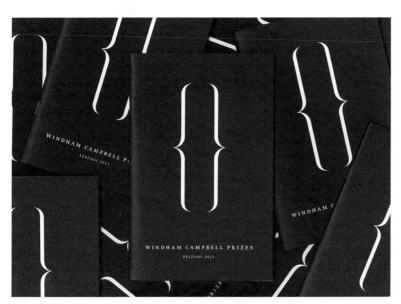

Windham-Campbell Prizes Program
Yale University, The Donald Windham-Sandy Campbell Literature Prizes
Designers: Michael Bierut, Jessica Svendsen
Illustrator/photographer
Pentagram
2013

What do you look for in an assistant or associate designer, given the current requirements?

I look for people who love typography, who love to read, who have a good sense of humor, and who just plain love graphic design as much as I do.

What job that you've recently completed would you say is the most satisfying and challenging?

Last year we did a series of projects for the New York City Department of Transportation that included a city-wide pedestrian wayfinding system, maps for the city's new bike share program, and redesigning New York's parking signs. All of these are being rolled out now, and I have to say that every time I see a new one out on the street—and I usually just encounter one by accident, or someone on my team does and takes a picture—it's just a great surprise. This kind of work is really complicated. We were part of a much larger team of planners, cartographers, product designers, and engineers. Yet the results of the work are simple: every day, for instance, I see someone looking at one of those maps to find their way around town. Being responsible for something that is playing a role, a positive role, in people's lives is really satisfying. The fact that most people can't even imagine that they are looking at the final outcome of a tremendously complex design process makes the whole thing even more gratifying.

Graphic design is no longer just graphic design. How do you explain today's profession?

I know that people tend to have an expansive idea of what graphic

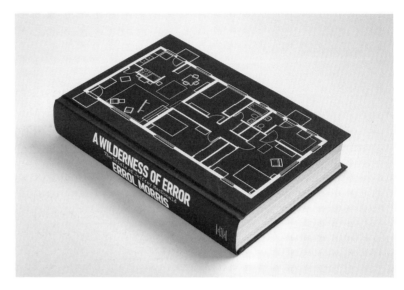

design is, but I tend to come back to a definition that isn't that different than what it would have been when I first picked up that copy of *Aim for a Future in Graphic Design*, 40 years ago: graphic designers combine words and pictures to convey a message. The way we combine them has changed, and the messages are always changing, but I still think the basic challenge is the same.

What's next for you?

I don't know, but I hope it will be a surprise.

A Wilderness of Error
by Errol Morris
The Penguin Press
Designers:
Michael Bierut, Yve Ludwig
Illustrator/photographer
Pentagram
2012

Cathedral of St. John the
Divine Signs
Cathedral of St. John the Divine
Designer:
Michael Bierut, Jesse Reed
Illustrator/photographer
Pentagram
October 2013

Stephen Doyle

On Being Selfish—in a Good Way

Truth
Illustrator: Stephen Doyle
Client: The *New York Times*,
Op-Ed
Art Director: Nicholas Blechman
2001

Stephen Doyle, proprietor of Doyle and Partners in New York, admits that he began studying graphic design because he got thrown out of his painting classes at Cooper Union and needed more credits to graduate. "But I liked it," he notes. "The idea of design as a storytelling medium was much more appealing than painting as a means of self-expression, especially since my version was not being tolerated by the guys deciding pass or fail." His first job was as a designer at *Esquire* magazine, under his teacher Milton Glaser. "I think he hired me because he confused me with another kid, but I loved reading articles and then translating them for the reading public by making layouts that were responsive to and expressive of the content." Thirty-five years later, Doyle is still telling stories, but now in more public ways and in a wider range of media.

You've had your own studio for close to three decades. What is the key distinction between then and now?
Having run a studio for 28 years, it is interesting to observe that even though our media and processes have changed exponentially, we are still working within a conceptual sensibility that is true to our starting point. Our work tries to hover in a zone of humanism and sparkle, never addressing vast audiences or demographics, but rather seeking to engage just one person at a time, with a wink or a gesture, or, if we're lucky, a little moment of wonder. Having a small studio allows us to be selective about the work we take on, and one of our mantras is to try to take on projects that only we can perfectly solve. We are less interested now in graphic design per se but chase the grail of engagement and pleasant surprise.

Are you in fact freer now to do the projects that most appeal to you, or do you have to keep the studio fed?
Another advantage of a small studio of 10 is that we get to consciously push away from work that might lie in our comfort zone. If we have a track record of breakthrough mass-market packaging, our instinct is to search out projects that need environmental graphics or to create a video for a conference. That's what makes it worthwhile—and scary to get up every morning. Frontiers!

Is the studio a creative expression of your sensibility or not?
Someone who I'm married to once commented that my way of practicing design was completely "selfish. But, um, selfish in a good way," she backtracked. Pressed, she clarified that I had a way of hoodwinking my clients into being "patrons"—people

Fresh Dialogue Poster
Designer: Stephen Doyle
Client: AIGA
2009

Teaching Grit (Opposite)
Designer: Stephen Doyle
Client: The *New York Times Magazine*
Art Director: Arem DuPlessis
Photographer: Stephen Wilkes
2011

who finance my explorations into art and unwittingly sponsor my personal fulfillment as part of the design process. Ultimately, this means that my interests and sensibilities infiltrate the studio and the projects we take on. Aromatherapy!

You do your own art—3-D objects,— often using books. How did this come about?

The sculptures that I make from books spang from a satire that I was making about the subject of "hypertexts." I was trying to illustrate the ridiculous notion that one message might lead to another (via hyperlink) regardless of sequence. However, this exploration of setting text lines free of the pages that held them jumped up and bit me with the bug to set lots of ideas free from their books and to explore sentence structure in a whole new light.

Is there a problem or not in retaining boundaries between Stephen Doyle designer and Stephen Doyle citizen?

As a designer, it's very hard to separate work from life, travel from research, real from Memorex. It's actually the blurring of the borders that keeps things interesting for me. When something as private as a sculpture can invade my professional work, it is thrilling. It's the curiosities and passions that fuel a creative life, so why wouldn't one try to allow those to flourish in one's design practice? When a paint color that my wife and I mix at home becomes a part of a color palette that others can buy, it is gratifying. My wife and I have turned our home life inside out so that others can share our taste and style and ideas, so public and private, art and design are all woven together. One rule, however, has proved helpful: Never talk about work . . . in the bedroom.

What is your creative management style around the studio?

My motto is never to ask if it's okay to do something. So, in the studio, the designers are encouraged to do everything they want to do. There is nothing off-limits, and there is no creative ceiling for creating work or experimenting. Not all experiments see the light of day. They have to work, hold up, and communicate. We do not have any special regard for reason, if abandoning it can lead to a solution that has lift. For us, levitation is the better part of design valor.

When hiring, and I presume you do the hiring, what do you look for?

When we look for a designer, we consider the usual qualifications: smart portfolio and good footwear. In a small studio environment, a personality match is really critical.

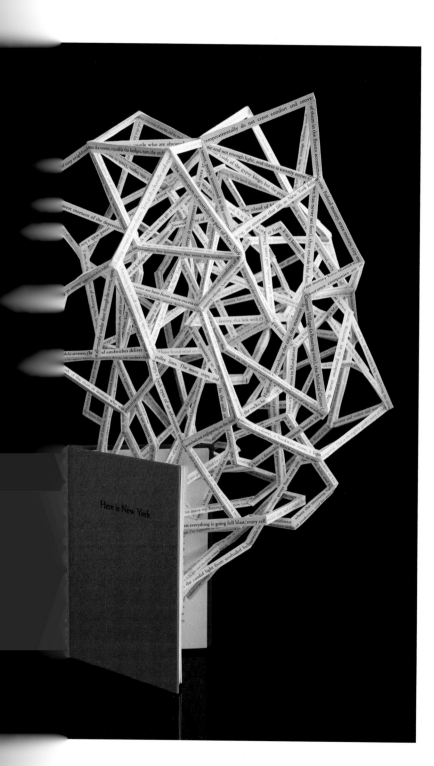

We like designers who read the paper and whose work is an invitation to get closer. We are not wowed by style but by thoughtfulness with an occasional spark of brilliance. We try to keep our team diverse, having some members who lean toward science, and some who lean toward art. I look over shoulders a lot, and shape a direction in tandem with a designer. I help them craft the details and sharpen their intuition.

Do you see the studio as expanding or remaining constant?
It is delightful to have a small studio —we are 10, and we have been about this size for over 25 years. It is a scale that allows designers to be thoroughly involved in their projects and the execution of them, but it allows for a diverse range of clients and wide exposure to the designing arts. Too, it allows our relationship with our clients to be intimate and earnest.

Here Is New York Hypertext
Designer: Stephen Doyle
Personal work
2012

Stefan Sagmeister

On Being Self-Motivated

Much has been written over the years about Stefan Sagmeister, the Austrian-born, New York–based graphic designer and international speaker. His promotional antics have earned him lots of attention, too. He worked for Tibor Kalman at M&Co., a conceptual studio, and then moved into advertising in Hong Kong, and currently, after having a small solo studio, he has a partnership with a former employee, Jessica Walsh, "because she was uncommonly talented." He is known for unconventional work that balances function and aesthetics—and for taking a sabbatical every seven years, leaving work to his colleagues so that he can pursue new ideas.

You began seven-year cycles interrupted by year-long sabbaticals. Aside from being a civilized way to do business, what has been your goal?
As with many big decisions in my life, there were several reasons: One was to fight routine and boredom, but there was a second one, more complex. I had the insight that I could come up with different kinds of projects when given a different time frame to spend on them. I also expected it would be joyful. What I did not expect was that these sabbaticals would change the trajectory of the studio, and I did not dare to imagine that they would be financially successful. But they were.

You've done some juicy promotions through the years, including baring yourself for the world to see. What motivates this? What do you hope the result to be?
I had opened the studio with a card

showing me naked. That card turned out to be highly functional. Not only did our then only client love it (he had put it up in his office with a note saying, "the only risk is to avoid risk") but it also attracted more clients who were likely of a more adventurous nature. The card that announced the partnership between Jessica Walsh and me was intended as a little joke on that opening card and turned out to have worked just as well: Everybody anywhere seems to know about that partnership (and that card).

As studios go, yours is very modest. In fact, you don't have a conference room for clients. What is your rationale?
I always wanted to keep our overhead small so we could luxuriate in the luxury of choosing our jobs on merit. This satisfied us more than luxurious offices.

The Happy Show
Creative Direction:
Stefan Sagmeister
Art Direction & Design:
Jessica Walsh
Design: Verena Michelitsch,
Jordan Amer, Simon Egli,
Martin Gnadt, Santiago
Carrasquilla, Esther Li

SVA Poster (Left)
Art Director: Stefan Sagmeister,
Jessica Walsh
Designer: Stefan Sagmeister,
Jessica Walsh, Santiago
Carrasquilla
Photographer: Henry Leutwyler
Creative Retoucher:
Erik Johansson

When I was visiting your studio, I saw your partner, Jessica Walsh, and six or so other workers. What do they do? And do they do their own work, or only your work?
When you visited, we were at our busiest; unusually, we had three interns working at the same time. Among the designers who work for us, usually every job is owned by an individual and everybody else chips in.

What qualities do you look for when you hire or chose an intern?
Good ideas well executed.

You are known for unpredictability. What is it that you haven't tried that you'd like to do?
I have found that it is not so helpful to talk about things I have not tried yet, as the act of talking about it removes some of my desire to actually do them.

Arnold Schwartzman

Still Designing after All These Years

Arnold Schwartzman is a graphic designer and an Oscar®-winning documentary filmmaker. As a young child during WWII, he survived the enemy bombing of his home in London; consequently, he was sent to the countryside and to the village school there. Because he was not able to catch up with the much older pupils in his class, his teacher gave him cards and foreign stamps to keep him busy. "It was a blessing in disguise," he notes, and "as a result, I grew up in a visual, nonliterary world." He ultimately enrolled at the local art school to learn to be a commercial artist. Schwartzman began his career in British network television, moving on to become an advertising art director, and later he joined the board of directors of Conran Design Group, London. In 1978, he was invited to Los Angeles by Saul Bass to become the design director for Saul Bass and Associates. Later, on the recommendation of Bass, he produced and directed the 1981 Oscar-winning documentary feature film, _Genocide._ Since then he has designed Oscar posters, programs, billboards, cinema trailers, and related collateral print for the annual Academy Awards; created two murals for the grand lobby of Cunard's Queen Elizabeth; and designed the UN Peace Bell Memorial for South Korea.

You've been practicing graphic design for almost six decades. How has it changed, and how has it remained the same?

Apart from the craft's ever-changing nomenclature, my thought process has not changed. I believe that the concept must come first, form later. My first job in 1959 was as a graphic designer for a British television station, where all programs where transmitted in black and white and went out live. Apart from my not too perfect hand-drawn lettering, the only other method available to me for producing text was the limited fonts of Letraset. This was before the introduction of rub-down type. Each letter had to be cut out from a sheet and laboriously transferred onto a cotton screen, then pressed down onto the artwork.

Do you actually consider yourself a graphic designer, or is there another rubric?

Yes, I consider myself to be first and

Peter and the Wolf
Illustrations for television
gala program, narrated
by Richard Attenborough
Art Director/Designer:
Arnold Schwartzman
1960

foremost a graphic designer, but other
add-ons include filmmaker, illustrator,
animator, photographer, author, and
also sometimes muralist and sculptor!

**Today, graphic design is no longer
static. You began making films a
while ago. How did you transition
from paper to film?**
My transition from paper to film was
quite seamless. I made my first film
shortly after graduating from art college, during my military service in the

Death by Choice
Art Director/Designer:
Arnold Schwartzman
Client: BBC
1960s

British Army in South Korea, where I purchased an 8-mm camera and projector from the U.S. Army PX Store. My film of postarmistice Korea is considered an historic document, and the footage is now housed in London's Imperial War Museum. I eventually moved from the local television station to Britain's premiere TV network. There I had the opportunity of working with an animation camera and was able to experiment with the rudiments of animation, which finally led to working in live action.

How do you remain fresh as a designer, after so many years?
Style seems to go out of fashion quickly; good ideas will never lose their appeal.

Would you say that yours is a style or an attitude?
I do very much envy designers that have a distinctive style. I don't know if one could immediately recognize a Schwartzman design. So I suppose it must be an attitude of thinking. I was amused to read recently that my work was considered to be surreal. I rather liked that! I love research, and many of my ideas and films look to the past. I don't seem to have the capacity to think visually into the future.

What one piece of wisdom would you impart to young designers?
The key word is to bring *passion* to everything you do.

RSG Logo
Logo for television program
Ready, Steady, Go!
Art Director/Designer:
Arnold Schwartzman
1963

Gail Anderson

The Joys of Print Design

A specialist in conceptual typography, Gail Anderson, a New York–based designer, is a partner at Anderson Newton Design. From 2002 through 2010, she was creative director of design at SpotCo, a New York City advertising agency that creates posters, advertisements, and commercials for Broadway and institutional theater. From 1987 to early 2002, she worked at *Rolling Stone* magazine, as designer, deputy art director, and finally as the magazine's senior art director. Anderson's accomplishments are many: she teaches at the School of Visual Arts, serves on the boards for The Citizens Stamp Advisory Committee and the Type Directors Club, and is the recipient of the 2008 Lifetime Achievement Medal from the American Institute of Graphic Arts; she is also coauthor, with Steven Heller, of *The Typographic Universe*, *New Modernist Type*, *New Ornamental Type*, and *New Vintage Type*. "Graphic design has changed in just about every way possible," she notes, "especially in terms of technology. In my last year at SVA, the design department began to tout its first computer class, to be taught on what were Apple CII's. I didn't sign up, assuming that computers in the workplace were many, many years off—and something that wouldn't really apply to graphic design, anyway." Now she teaches a class called Type in Motion, which combines computers and handwork.

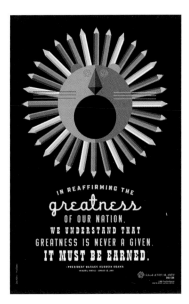

SVA Poster
Client: School of Visual Arts
Creative Director: Anthony Rhodes
Art Director: Michael Walsh
Designer: Gail Anderson
Illustrator: Terry Allen
2009

You've been involved with magazines, posters, and books. How has graphic design changed since you began?
The computer! Of course, good design is not all about how you execute it on your computer, but a young designer with a limited digital skill set will have far fewer opportunities than one who is well versed in contemporary software. And it's pretty key to have even a working knowledge of interactive basics. I strongly advise my students to add at least one motion or interactive class to their schedules. There's just no getting around it now, and the technological advances make me wish I were just starting out. Design is so much bigger and all-encompassing than it was for the class of 1984. It's kind of amazing.

How have you managed or challenged those changes?

I don't know that I've adapted as well as many of my peers. I still operate almost exclusively in the world of print design, though I am certainly more intrigued by the interactive realm than I was even a few years ago. And I teach a class that involves aftereffects, so motion is becoming more and more appealing. But I'd be lying if I said I was able to do more than art direct the way something moves. I'm still not hands-on, but I'm more than ever curious about the possibilities of design. I'm glad I continue to have a little of that fire in my belly.

You are also known for your typographical prowess, which might be described as "conceptual typography." Would you explain what you do with type?

I joke that I love to make type talk, but I guess that's really true. I'm lucky to have a decent memory for fonts, and I peruse the various font sites most weeks to see what's new. I'm open to almost anything, though there are times I'd be just as happy setting all of my type in Trade Gothic Bold Condensed.

Has your typographic language (or style) changed with the digital revolution?

In my *Rolling Stone* days, we'd sketch our designs and then work with a letterer to render the concepts on film. Often it was as simple as redrawing letters that were photostatted from books, and other times, it involved drawing type from scratch. Either way, it was a lot of work, time, and

SVA Poster
Client: School of Visual Arts
Art Director: Michael Walsh
Designer: Gail Anderson
2008

expense. Designers, including myself, are relatively self-sufficient now, and commissioned lettering has the possibility of being so much more elaborate. The digital revolution made the excess that I love readily available, but the abundance of excess is now causing me to pull back a little.

You work in movement as well as static. What is different about making typography for screen and page (other than the obvious)?
Type that's on screen is generally absorbed pretty quickly, and then it's time to move on. You have to turn up the volume a little to make it resonate or strip away a few layers to make it legible. It's a tricky balance. Typography for print has the opportunity to be much more subtle.

You used to hire designers. What do you look for in an intern or assistant?
I still hire the occasional designer, and certainly interns, but my focus has shifted to teaching aspiring designers. I look for sensitivity to font selection when I'm working with designers, flexibility, and a willingness to experiment with words. It's important for designers to be well read or at least tuned in to what's going on in the world outside of our little design bubble. I look for good communicators, whether the position is for that of a designer or an intern. An intern shouldn't be too set in his or her ways yet and should be an active contributor to the team. I am always willing to give an intern as much responsibility as he or she is willing to take on.

Peer Gynt
Client: SpotCo
Designer: Gail Anderson

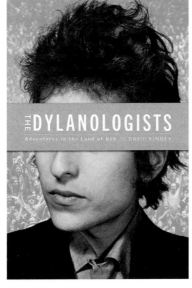

Mo' Meta Blues (left)
Client: Grand Central
Art Director: Claire Brown
Designers: Gail Anderson and Joe Newton
Illustrator: David Cowles

The Dylanologists (right)
Client: Simon & Schuster
Art Director: Jackie Seow
Designers: Gail Anderson and Joe Newton

2 Starting a Studio or Working for Someone Else

There are at least two options when building a design career: working for someone or working for oneself. The former requires getting hired by an existing studio or firm; the latter, and more complicated option, is to start your own business. Some designers take this leap immediately out of school; others acquire more experience through employment with businesses on which they might model their own.

Hipster Studio Names

Old school names are not always as effective as hip names. With the current rage in digital business names like Google, Twitter, Pintrest, Spotify, and the like, design firms are taking on names that sound like music groups. Among the quirkiest are Psy Op, Heads of State, Change Is Good, Razorfish, Original Champions of Design (see page 58), Lust (see page 234), and Simple Is Beautiful (see page 260). If you are appealing to a youth cultural or artistic clientele, a name like my favorite, World Domination Studio, may work. However, think carefully about how far out on a limb you want to go. But speaking of music groups, try to avoid The Beatles, as we believe it is a registered trademark.

Increasingly, the trend is for young designers to acquire a minimum of two to four years of experience working in an established studio or firm to learn the ropes and the nuances of running a studio. Depending on the quality of the job, that should be enough time to then branch out into a studio or partnership. Yet there are dozens of business scenarios (some of which are outlined in the interviews).

Starting as a freelancer, which does not involve hiring staff or maintaining office overhead, is probably the safest option. It allows you to determine whether or not a business is what you want to do early in your career. Often freelancing feeds other ambitions, as it provides the confidence necessary for engaging in a full-fledged operation.

Some designers cannot, how-ever, wait for what was once called an "apprenticeship" to end before jumping headlong into building a design business. Beware! But nonetheless, don't be timid. You are only foolhardy if you are ignorant of the responsibilities you'll have to assume. But if you are aware of how a business operates, then you will doubtless find a partner or associate who can help on many levels: finances, selling, promoting, and so on. A good advisor will guide you through and help you neutralize what might otherwise be a mine field.

The goal of a design business is to make great design while earning a respectable living. Designers do not become proprietors or partners because it is expected. So whether you work for yourself or work for others, the best advice is to do what will best advance the quality of your work and maximize the longevity of your career.

Lynda Decker

Mapping Out the Future

Lynda Decker is a New York City–based graphic designer who began her career at Lubalin Peckolick Associates, working at the foot of the great typographer Herb Lubalin. At the studio, she learned skills (never to be used again) such as setting type on a Photo-Typositor and drawing perfect hairline rules. She spent several years in the advertising industry at McCaffrey & McCall, Backer Spielvogel Bates, and Wells Rich Green, working with clients such as Mercedes-Benz, Falcon Jet, CBS, and IBM. Decker Design began in 1996 to combine the energy of the team-driven approach of an advertising agency with the craft-based environment of a small design firm. Decker Design currently creates branding and interactive and print solutions for a diverse client base that includes everything from academic institutions to the world's largest financial firms.

Centerline Capital Website
Creative Director: Lynda Decker
Design: Michael Aron, Susanne
Adrian, Bradley Cushing
Programming: Michael Aron
and Bradley Cushing

Why did you start your own design firm?

A friend said, "Lynda, stop complaining about your job. I'm tired of hearing this. Start you own business. I did it, you can do it; I will help you." And so, for the next few hours, we kept the restaurant open and mapped out what I would do, what type of clients I should go after, how much money I needed to get started, and then he made me pick a date to quit my job. We worked out detail after detail. I was terrified but exhilarated.

Was there a focus that you had in mind, or was it general at the outset?

I had worked in both advertising and graphic design before starting my firm. My clients were large corporations such as Chase Manhattan, IBM, and CBS. My friends encouraged me to start building clients based on the work I had done and also to speak with anyone I had worked with in the past. So I spoke to financial companies—they were assigning tons of work to designers in the late 1990s, and some of those assignments were really fun—there were magazines, lavish brochures, and insanely elaborate party invitations—this was the era of fancy paper, twigs used for binding, and lots of die cutting.

How would you describe the style or form your work takes?

My work has evolved over the years, and I've noticed that as I matured, it has become more simplified, especially in relation to typography. I'm sure it

Urban Archaeology Ad
Campaign
Creative Director: Lynda Decker
Design: Lynda Decker, Kevin
Lamb, Natalie Marshall
Photos: Ken Skalski

is a reaction to the complexity of life in the twenty-first century—I have a desire to strip away anything that is nonessential. I also have a strong interest in photography, which has an ability to bring humanity to subjects and reach people on an emotional level. Recently, I decided to return to graduate school to improve my writing and research skills. This, of course, is providing another level of influence on my work—I'm affecting content more. If I had to sum it up, my work has clarity; it is clean, simple, and uses a great deal of photography.

Do you inject personality into the design, or is it devoid of it?

I think everyone injects personality into his or her design work; as an interpretative form of expression, it is unavoidable. I would say my work reflects my clients' personalities, but in truth, the work is a result of a blend of my personality and theirs.

How much has the digital world entered what began as a print design business?

The digital world has completely changed my business as well as the design industry. Some of these changes are great, and others are painful. I began my career in an era of glue and razors, and I couldn't be happier to escape the drudgery of a pasteup. Thank God the days of having to change the leading of a book with a ruler and razor are over!

Technology has made so many forms of expression accessible—it's easy to experiment with photography—there's no cost of film and processing to hold you back. Video equipment and editing software are relatively affordable—you are only limited by your imagination. You can revise a website easily, publish a book using Lulu or some other service —digitally print a new card overnight. I can tweet a writer and tell him I thought he wrote a great article, and he can tweet a note of thanks back in minutes. We can do so much now that was never possible before.

What about the economics of a design business?

Fees are now much lower, and there is a greater level of competition for the available work—it's harder to sustain a business. This has created an environ-ment where designers often do not like to say the word *design* in the context of their work. "Graphic designer" has morphed into "brand strategist" or some other title that implies more importance. Few designers would now refer to their businesses as a "studio," which was a popular term 20 or 30 or 40 years ago. One will see the terms

design firm, agency, office, or design practice more often now. Design industry business consultants advise their clients to specialize in a market segment to differentiate themselves.

Do clients want more? Are their expectations reasonable?

There is an expectation from many clients that technology should make everything very inexpensive. Writers are now asked to contribute to blogs for free, stock photography can be almost free on certain websites, and I think you can buy a logo for $5.00 or less online. I have concerns that all of us who are in the creative class are being seriously devalued.

While technology has removed a portion of the labor from our work, we still have to solve problems and come up with ideas, and those ideas have a value, and designers, writers, and photographers should be fairly compensated. Technology fabricates; it facilitates, but it is not a substitute for ideation and creativity.

What today do you look for in hiring designers?

First, designers have to have a terrific portfolio of work. Second, they should have language skills—the ability to communicate with clients, research a subject, or write an articulate e-mail is important. I will not let anyone in our office use "Lorem ipsum" and treat text as just another element on the page. As a result, most of the designers I hire have the ability to write headlines and frame outlines to create a fully integrated design concept.

After talent, personality is a key to success—so we look for enthusiasm, people who are excited about work and are motivated to do their best. We look for a desire to learn, curiosity, and a sincere desire to contribute to the team. And of course they should be nice.

I place technical skills after personality—we can teach skills, but talent and drive are qualities that come from within a person. That said, every designer should be adept in all of the Adobe programs, and more and more we look for designers who can code as well as design.

Do you prefer to hire mature designers?

Diversity is the most important thing to achieve in an office with a team of designers. I've made tons of hiring mistakes over the years, so the following is my personal experience: When our office is all male, it becomes filled with too many jokes about bodily functions. When it is all female, it's too emotional. There are tons of tears. I'm really sorry to resort to stereotypes; this is maddening, but true. When the office is too young and inexperienced, mistakes happen and things can get chaotic quickly. The best team is one that is a mix of gender and age, and when there are people from other cultures. For the most part, the best of all worlds is when you have younger designers to bring tons of energy and new ways to do things, and mature designers to provide guidance and mentorship. When the boys and girls are equally mixed, they stay on good behavior—no weird jokes and no tears—the boys don't want to sound crass, and the girls don't want the guys to think they are weak. It's lovely. There should be a rule: no crying in graphic design.

New Jersey Resources
Creative Director: Lynda Decker
Design: Lynda Decker,
Carrie Leuci
Photography: John Madere

Fernando Music

From Boss to Employee

MTIV Process, Inspiration and Practice for the New Media Designer
Client: Hillman Curtis
Creative Director: Fran Gaitanaros

Fernando Music, former partner in Rooster, New York, is the managing director at a design company called Partners & Spade. His job is to oversee all aspects of specific client relationships. On any given project, he defines the scope with the client, writes and negotiates the estimates and briefs, builds and maintains the client relationship throughout the life of the project, and works internally to make sure they are delivering the best work possible. Music studied to become an architect, but after graduating he found the world of architecture was moving more slowly than he could bear. "What I quickly discovered was that architecture was a training that set me up for a lifetime of creative problem solving," he says.

Warby Parker Class Trip
Client: Warby Parker
Creative Directors:
Andy Spade, Anthony Sperduti
Photographer: Devon Jarvis

For 13 years you ran your own design firm, Rooster, first, why did you call it Rooster and what type of work did you do?

The Rooster Design Group was a studio I ran with a partner. One of our first challenges was to come up with a name that we could both feel ownership of. Calling the studio some mash-up of our monikers felt like a cop-out, not to mention old-fashioned. In a lucky twist of fate, we realized that we were both born in the Chinese year of the rooster. Rooster was a multidisciplinary design studio that worked on everything from identities to brochures and websites to package design. Over 13 years we had clients ranging in scale from Fortune 500 companies and upscale art galleries to start-ups and nonprofits.

What did you like about running your own business?

There is no question that the best thing about running any business is freedom.

What was the least enjoyable aspect of the work?

Although we said we were optimized for happiness, sometimes making tough business decisions involving staff and working with clients who aren't your cup of tea can make being the boss no fun at all.

How many employees did you have? And what did you look for in a designer?

Our office held steady at eight, although we took on freelance staff as projects required. Because we tried to work across disciplines as much as possible, I

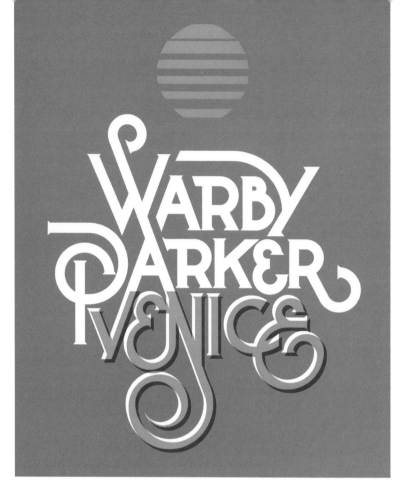

Warby Parker Venice
Client: Warby Parker
Creative Director: Anthony Sperduti
Art Director: Danny Demers

What kind of work are you doing at Partners & Spade, and how different is it from running your own firm?
As a studio, Partners & Spade does many things but excels at giving a voice to brands. Describing how a company is going to look and feel, communicate, and ultimately behave is a great place to start because it means you get to make the rules. At Rooster we weren't involved with as many start-ups or new businesses; as a result, we did less work at the earliest planning stages.

At Partners & Spade, my role is to provide leadership and, represent the company. In this way there are many similarities, but there is still enough learning every day to make it interesting.

What are the advantages of working for this firm?
Prior to Partners & Spade, the founders met and worked together in advertising. In addition to creating traditional advertising campaigns, they went on to build, operate, and sell the Kate and Jack Spade brands. This experience gives way to an understanding about brand building that few studios possess. As it turns out, Partners & Spade is really good at creating, nurturing, and growing brands, which is what we enjoy doing for clients. I remember very early on my father telling me that if you like what you do every day, it isn't work—and that is the secret to a happy life.

always appreciated a designer with these innate qualities: a good eye, great taste, curious intelligence, and what Danny Meyer calls the "excellence reflex." In his book, *Setting the Table*, he says: "The excellence reflex is a natural reaction to fix something that isn't right or to improve something that could be better." If a candidate has these qualities, he or she can learn to be a great designer.

Would you say that running a business was an added layer of stress or simply part of what you signed on for?
Running a business was a layer of stress I willingly signed on for. I won't say I knew how hard it was going to be, but on the flip side I also couldn't have imagined how gratifying it would be either.

In 2013 you closed your firm and joined Partners & Spade. First, what is Partners & Spade? And why did you go from boss to employee?
Partners & Spade is many things. It began as a way for its founders to work with the brands and individuals they most admired. Since inception, the company has evolved and grown to function as a design firm, creative consultancy, gallery and storefront, advertising agency, and brand incubator while avoiding becoming just one of those things.

Working with world-class brands on some of the most prestigious initiatives without the day-to-day responsibilities of running a business is something I really enjoy.

Allison Henry Aver

Working Holistically

Allison Henry Aver is the (now former) design director for Kate Spade Saturday, a new brand from kate spade new york. Aver went into graphic design because she sensed it was a field that "would allow me to partake in all my interests growing up—writing, history, books, art, fashion, TV—there were so many paths to choose from; how could I pick just one?" She began her relationship with kate spade as a freelancer filling in for the design director, who was on maternity leave. In this role, "I got to know many of the team members who were working on the possible launch of this new brand called Kate Spade Saturday." She left the freelance position to take a full-time job elsewhere but kept in touch with the creative director of Kate Spade Saturday, Theresa Canning Zast, who hired her as design director. "I was employee #7."

Kate Spade Saturday
Business Cards
Creative Director:
Theresa Canning Zast
Design Director:
Allison Henry Aver
Designer: Kristie Malivindi

You had worked at design firms. What do you feel was the greatest attribute giving you the edge in becoming a design director?
I had worked in a small design firm called Number Seventeen for many years under the creative direction of Bonnie Siegler and Emily Oberman. Working there taught me to work fast, generate lots of ideas quickly, be comfortable transitioning to new concepts or project on a dime, and most importantly, realize that whether the project was naming an apartment building or designing title cards for a TV show, the creative thinking was still the same.

The term "graphic designer" felt like a misnomer for those of us working there. We worked so holistically with all our clients. We didn't just affect the design, but we thought about the content, the copy, and the experience. This was also reflective of the MFA Design/Designer as Author + Entrepreneur program at SVA, where I was a student, and where as designers we were encouraged work also as the author of our work.

This ability—to understand that my role is much more than a graphic designer—that I need to think like a marketer, see like designer, and understand messaging like copywriter—is what I find thrilling and exciting and challenging about this role. I also realize that I would never be in this situation if I had only been taught to "make something look pretty" and not read the words. Making something look great is extremely fulfilling—but I believe being able to want to care and curate an entire experience is what has helped me get where I am.

Kate Spade Saturday
Window Shops
Creative Director: Theresa Canning Zast
Design Director: Allison Henry Aver
Designers: Nikelle Orellana,
Kristie Malivindi
Copywriter: Khira Jordan

Kate Spade Saturday Pencils
Creative Director: Theresa Canning Zast
Design Director: Allison Henry Aver
Designer: Allison Henry Aver

What do you do as design director of a fashion and style business?
As the design director for Kate Spade Saturday, I am responsible for directing all creative marketing work related to the brand—determining overall photography and brand direction related to the website, e-mails, campaigns, advertising, and social media as well as the voice and copy direction. I have a counterpart who is responsible for all product, and the two of us report in to the creative director.

How do you keep the design of Kate Spade Saturday fresh and on point with the brand's mission?
The brand's mission is to channel the spirit of Saturday seven days a week.

When you think about it, that's pretty open ended, and there's so much fun content that can be created around this concept. The graphic design aesthetic of Kate Spade Saturday is fairly basic and utilitarian. I knew going into this we'd need parameters that could support the trends of fashion, a known colorful aesthetic and seasonal imagery. It's the imagery and copy writing that gives us our personality. And we have a lot of it!! Conceptualizing new seasonal campaigns, working with new photographers, trying out new technology in social media or on the site, or collaborating with outside creative partners are ways we keep the brand feeling fresh every season.

What has been your most challenging project? And the most satisfying?
In the summer of 2013, we worked with eBay to create shoppable storefront windows. eBay had developed the technology to allow a customer to shop from a very large monitor placed against a window, buy product from the interface, and then have it delivered by bicycle messenger within the hour.

The technology was cool, but it had no heart. For us, the challenge was "Why would you do this?" and "How do you make it feel cute and fun for our customer?" It's not like anyone really needs a beach towel in an hour. At first it felt like the technology was overpowering the experience and would turn off the girl we were trying to target. We spent a lot of time role-playing out the user experience and pretending we were the customers. We tried to create scenarios in which we would buy a sunhat and absolutely have to have it in an hour. Well—if you suddenly decide to have a picnic in the park, you might. Or you might need a jacket for the cold movie theater. From this we created stories about the product to give them a reason to be there, and it was this that gave the project its charm and made it a unique experience for us.

How much responsibility do you and your staff have for the brand?
One of the perks of working on a new brand and a small team is that we get to work on literally everything for the brand—from the price tag design and every individual tweet to the campaign photography to how the models look on our website and to much larger brand initiatives with outside partners like eBay and jetBlue. In our setup, the right hand knows what the left hand is doing, and thus the messaging and design in our all channels are fairly tight.

When you hire for your department, what do you look for in a candidate?
A strong designer, I feel, should be able to create strong, thoughtful solutions for any client—regardless of personal style—and I try not to be swayed by an aesthetic but rather look for a strong typography foundation, a respect and understanding of copy, and someone who shows an interest in creative problem solving versus just loving tweaking typefaces (although we do that, too). I also look for a strong cultural fit when hiring. I need people who love what they are working on, to be cheerleaders for the product, and in many instances be the target consumer themselves. If they like and get the brand—it's so much easier to create and design for it. It makes it fun!

Kate Spade Saturday
Window Shop Billboard
Creative Director: Theresa
Canning Zast
Design Director: Allison Henry
Aver
Photographer: Thomas Schenk
Designer: Allison Henry Aver
Copywriter: Khira Jordan

Romain Rachlin

Creative Space

Romain Rachlin and Maxime Tétard, with Cyril Taieb and François Dubois, are the founding partners of a Paris design agency, Les Graphiquants, "a place where fun is taken seriously, and where creativity is the result of a rigorous work methodology." Their partnership is structured in such a way as to give them the freedom to develop all sorts of projects, some of them more personal than others. A case in point is "Floating," designed about four years ago. It's a poster that features a geometric pattern of folded origami. It has been bought by the Public Transportation Agency and displayed all over France, in practically every train and subway station, to fill empty advertising spaces. A "low-tech" poster, it has become a cult image—in contrast with the now ubiquitous and aggressively garish LED display panels.

Lyon Dance Biennale Poster
Designer: Romain Rachlin
Art Directors: Romain Rachlin
and Maxime Tétard
2012

Describe what you do.
Maxime and I are the "creatives"—Cyril is the account executive, while François is the IT expert. We like to think of our work as exploring the world of signs—signs that are graphic, abstract, poetic, explicit, typographic, black and white, and sometimes, though not too often, colorful. These signs are never gratuitous, but they are always imbued with style.

All four of you are members of the millennial generation, people who take the digital culture for granted. Yet, you work mostly in print. How do you explain your choice?
It is not exactly a "choice." It sort of just happened. One print-based project led to another. We all come out of the same school, the Arts Décoratifs,

where we have been nurtured with a love and respect of printed images and objects. It's part of our DNA.

That said, we are all technologically savvy. There is always a digital component to all our projects. It is usually a website. Nowadays, you cannot be a graphic designer and ignore this fascinating dimension of the visual culture.

How does the digital culture influence your graphic sensibility?
What do you mean by "digital"? If you mean the tools, they have practically no incidence in the way we conceptualize projects. Sure, they allow us to work faster and make communication with clients easier. However, the digital language is only one of the means of expression we use. We would rather play with physical objects than virtual ones.

Then there is "Floating." The poster wasn't commissioned as such; it was originally a paper sculpture, a personal project. The fact that it has become a cult image is a fluke. How do you explain its appeal?

We are not sure that it's a cult image! Only time will tell. There has been a lot of press about it, but is the public really enthralled by this "campaign"? We don't know. The extreme visibility of the posters is oddly compelling. Their message is clear: Advertising budgets are down; the economy is in trouble.

We do not consider the posters to be "low-tech." They are always displayed on brightly illuminated panels. Their design is deliberately geometric, as is most of our work. The patterns show small variations in the folded paper, to give the image a sensual dimension. For us, this "campaign" has been a defining moment, philosophically and aesthetically.

You often use data visualization as a communication tool in your work, as for example in the series of posters on filmmaking for the television station Canal+. Why this fascination with data visualization?

We design information systems the same way we design type. It has to do with our love of the language of "signs." The example of the Canal+ posters is not typical, in fact. In this particular instance, we were asked to illustrate someone else's concept. The result is highly narrative, whereas we usually create more conceptual graphic systems, as we did for the Familistère exhibition or for the annual report of the CNAP (Centre National des Arts Plastiques).

Floating
Metrobus
Concept: François Kenesi
Designer: Romain Rachlin
Art Directors: Romain Rachlin
and Maxime Tétard

Ballets de Lorraine Poster
(left)
Designer: Romain Rachlin
Art Directors: Romain Rachlin
and Maxime Tétard
2013

Paris Leather and Fur Trade
Show Poster (right)
Designer: Romain Rachlin
Art Directors: Romain Rachlin
and Maxime Tétard
2014

You often use minimalist typography for your posters, your signage systems, and your information panels—for the Pompidou Center in particular. Are you careful not to be "commercial"?

Yes, indeed, we favor a low-keyed communication style. We want it to be discreet, and we avoid at all costs marketing codes. We want the featured artist or artists to be presented in a neutral fashion. We feel that our job is to highlight the more subtle curatorial intentions. As a rule, we steer clear of obvious visual connotations as too easy to interpret—and too easy to forget. We favor slightly more esoteric forms of communication that are more memorable in the end.

You are designing, publishing, and selling examples of your personal work. Does this artistic production help establish and maintain the "creative" reputation of your design studio?

There is no commercial strategy behind our personal work!!!! It is the expression of an ongoing dialog between Maxime and myself. We make sure that we speak the same language. The fact that we have had various opportunities to show our "authorial" production in galleries is almost a fluke. But, ultimately, maintaining our positioning as a "creative team" depends on the kind of answers we propose to our clients.

Alexander Isley

Staying Independent

Alex Isley founded Alexander Isley Inc. in 1988. His studio creates identity, communication, and environmental design programs for a variety of companies and cause-related organizations. "I prefer to keep the size of our studio smaller, as I've found that's the best way to make collaboration efficient and our work nimble and focused," he says. His mission is to convince potential clients that a small firm with resourcefulness and vision can provide both strategic and design services. "Many times we're approached to work on a single initiative," Isley says, adding that what distinguishes his group is the way in which his work is strategically solid yet able to convey excitement, information, surprise, and delight—all at the same time. "This is what gets me going every day," he remarks.

A/X: Armani Exchange
Packaging
Client: Giorgio Armani
Advertising Agency: Weiss,
Whitten, Carroll, Stagliano
Design Firm: Alexander Isley Inc.
Art Director: Alexander Isley
Designers: Tim Convery,
Alexander Knowlton
1992

You were art director at *Spy* magazine. Why did you decide to open your own studio?
My first real design job was at M&Co., but I've wanted to run my own studio ever since I was young, and I started saving money to start my company back when I was in school. I like the idea of being responsible for and in charge of my own destiny, and running a studio makes this easier. This is not to say that running a studio is easy at all. My father headed up his own architectural firm, so the idea of having a design company seemed natural to me and was not an intimidating proposition. I saw firsthand that it required a vision, ambition,

and above all else the willingness to work very hard.

Why didn't you start right after completing your studies?
I first wanted to work in a "real" studio to get an idea of what that was about. Fortunately, for my first job out of Cooper Union, I was hired by Tibor Kalman at M&Co., where I worked as a designer for 2½ years. I learned a lot from Tibor, particularly how to present my ideas to clients and to encourage them to try unexpected things. I learned how to earn people's trust, which is the most important factor if you want your work to be embraced and implemented. It was a wonderful

Staten Island Ferry Terminal Signage
Client: City of New York
Architects: Schwartz Architects
Frederic Schwartz,
Douglas Romines
Design Firm: Alexander Isley Inc.
Creative Director:
Alexander Isley
Designer: Liesl Kaplan
1999

job, but I knew I had to move on. So I took a job at *Spy*, a humor magazine that was just starting up and needed an art director. They had a prototype in place, designed by Stephen Doyle. I'd never before designed a publication, so that was a challenge, but I believe if you are thoughtful and consider your audience, the content, and what you're trying to convey, you can design pretty much anything. Fortunately (that word again), the editors took a risk with me, and I designed *Spy* for 18 months or so. I loved it.

But you got the urge to be independent?

I was 26, single, with no big financial obligations, some savings, and good health. I figured I could make it for six months without crawling back to a real job with my tail between my legs— although, to be honest, I couldn't think of another place where I really wanted to work. I tried making a list of potential employers (I still have it), but after having Tibor Kalman, Kurt Andersen, and Graydon Carter as my first three bosses, I didn't think I'd be able to do any better. (It was so fun being young, nervy, and dumb.)

What has been and now is your goal for your studio?

My goals when starting out were: Be my own boss (meaning be in charge of my own destiny); design as wide a variety of

things as possible; do work I was proud of and be able to pay my bills.

These goals have not changed at all, but where in the beginning I juggled a lot of small projects for numerous different clients, I've gone on to make a real effort to focus on doing more comprehensive programs for fewer clients. A big part of this requires having the capability to provide up-front planning and strategic guidance: Brand positioning, establishing communication plans, and naming. So that's the biggest expansion of services that I've implemented over time.

So much of your work involves wit and humor. How does humor inform your output?

Humor is not something I try to wedge into an idea—it just has to happen— but I do think it helps engage people. I think that if you as a person have a sense of humor about yourself, it demonstrates self-confidence. I believe the same goes for companies and

organizations, and I try to make our work underscore this.

Are there jobs you will not take because you cannot inject wit into them?

The potential for creating humorous or witty work has never been a prerequisite for my taking on a client. I actually prefer the kinds of assignments that start out on the straighter side. I've always been a bit wary of doing work that is supposed to be humorous. Those can be tough to do: I don't want our work to be the guy in a clown suit saying, "OK, this is really funny," because what he says is never as funny as you hope. So I usually steer clear of the "funny" projects.

Typography is also a keystone for your work. Do you have a typographic "philosophy"?

A lot of our work is typographically based because I like to read, and words and letterforms interest me.

Goodwill Billboard
Client: Goodwill of Western and Northern CT
Advertising Agency: The Dave and Eddy Show
Design Firm: Alexander Isley Inc.
Art Director: Alexander Isley
Designer: Angela Chen
Writer: Dave Goldenberg
2012

Additionally, we do a lot of work for cause-related organizations that don't have the budgets for photography or illustration, so we often turn to type to help tell the story. I think it's an interesting challenge to make words serve as illustrations, and I enjoy making text expressive. This approach requires close collaboration between writers and designers. I write the text for many of our projects, and that makes it easier for us to get the content and visuals to work together.

How do you work? Do you still design or manage?

I wear a lot of hats. In addition to overseeing the business, I lead our positioning exercises and serve as the creative director. My name's on the door, and I enjoy (and feel a responsibility for) being involved in everything we create. I started out wanting to be a designer, not a suit, so I am very much immersed in the creation of all that we do. But by no means should that suggest it's all me: I have surrounded myself with trusted and talented collaborators, and I depend on them. I serve as more of a creative director/editor; when we start off each assignment, I develop the brief and indicate a few directions I'd like us to explore, but I ask that the project designers come up with a series of additional ideas as well. We then typically narrow down these approaches to a select few to refine and present to the client. Nothing makes me happier than when we are able to sell a client on an idea that didn't originate with me.

When you hire designers, what do you look for in their portfolios?

I don't just look at the work in the portfolio. I can often tell by the way a resume is written and laid out if someone is a good designer or not: Is it logical, succinct, and typographically well considered? Past that, I look for designers who are organized and thoughtful. When explaining their work, do they discuss why they chose to do something? Do I get the sense they'll play well with others? Can I put them in front of a client? Some young designers four months out of school have more poise than do veterans. I want to enjoy being around someone and for them to be dependable. You can teach design, but you can't teach organization.

After all these years, are you happy with the size and breadth of your studio, or do you foresee expansion or reduction?

We stay lean and mean. What this means is that I have to work my butt off. Fortunately, I love what I do and look forward to coming in to work every day, but I'd always kind of hoped that by the time I reached 50 this would all get a little easier, but that has not happened yet. Who am I kidding?

"Empty Sky"
New Jersey 9/11 Memorial
Inscription Program
Client: The State of New Jersey
Architects: Schwartz Architects
Frederic Schwartz, Jessica Jamroz
Design Firm: Alexander Isley Inc.
Creative Director: Alexander Isley
Designer: Hayley Capodilupo
2011

Agnieszka Gasparska

Small Is Sensible

Agnieszka Gasparska is the founder and "design captain" of a small New York City–based design firm called Kiss Me I'm Polish, which works on the web and in print designing identity systems, books, animations, information graphics, packaging, and websites. After several years of working full-time at an interactive agency, she started her own firm out of a desire to work across a broader range of disciplines and for a wider array of clients than what she was exposed to at her full-time job. "I was interested in all of the ways design thinking can be applied to as vast a range of projects as possible," she says, "and this is something that still very much drives our work today, 10 years later." Her clients are diverse, but she focuses on the arts, education, social activism, the media, and publishing.

Louise Bourgeois—
The Complete Prints & Books
Client: Museum of Modern Art
Art Director/Designer:
Agnieszka Gasparska,
Kiss Me I'm Polish LLC
Information Architect: Irwin
Chen, Redub LLC
2012

All photographs: © Louise Bourgeois Trust.
Portrait photograph: Peter Bellamy.

" I am a searcher... I always was
and I still am... searching
for the missing piece."

— Louise Bourgeois

This website, eventually numbering some **3500 images**, will document the complete prints and books of Louise Bourgeois (1911–2010), most of which are in the collection of The Museum of Modern Art. Designed to highlight the artist's creative process, the site emphasizes evolving print compositions and comparative relationships between prints, drawings and sculptures. Documentation will be added incrementally, three times a year.

This website has been generously supported by the Easton Foundation.

Many people who run studios do not do the design themselves. How do you work?

I definitely still spend time designing. Thankfully. It probably leads to much longer workdays than I would like but it's very important to me. I didn't start my own firm so I could spend all of my time managing only the business side of things so other people could do the fun stuff. Yes, there are certainly projects I don't get to design as much of as I would like, but there are only so many hours in the day, so there's that, too. I do my best and try and stay as involved as I can in the creative process—be it by actually getting my own hands dirty or by collaborating with my team—which is still design to me. I try and focus my time on those things that I'm best at and those that only I can do.

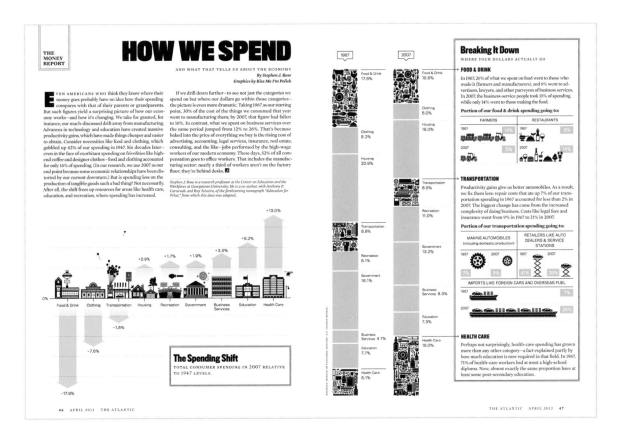

How many designers do you work with?

Kiss Me I'm Polish has three full-time people (including myself), two freelance designers, and one studio mate, in addition to an extended circle of other freelancers (i.e., illustrators, web developers, animators, sound designers) that come on board for specific projects as needed.

You do both print and digital work. What do you prefer?

I prefer both. Not only does it keep things more interesting to think across media boundaries, but, more and more of our projects include both print and digital solutions in one comprehensive outcome. There is genuine overlap between print and digital experiences, and the design process follows suit. We may work on a concept that will ultimately live both on paper and onscreen, so the formats are just part of the parameters. The approach and the story come first. How it's implemented will be dictated later, by a given point in time or a given application. As a multidisciplinary design studio, this is one of the things I love most about our work.

What do your clients want most?

Everything! It's funny, so many clients have no idea what they want. Or they do, but it winds up being that, while

How We Spend
Client: *The Atlantic Monthly Magazine*
Art Director/Designer: Agnieszka Gasparska, Kiss Me I'm Polish LLC
Designer: Mattias Mackler, Kiss Me I'm Polish LLC
2012

they thought they wanted A, all along, if you truly listen to what they are trying to do, they really want B.

Some of your work is information design. How did you become an information designer?

This isn't something I sat down one day and decided I would become. There was a point a few years ago when information graphics became a much bigger part of our visual culture and we naturally started seeing more and more of them come into play in our projects—whether as the focus of an assignment or simply as part of a larger suite of visual materials. Interestingly enough though, some of our most meaningful information graphic projects ultimately led to us doing much larger projects with those clients once the initial assignment was complete.

What do you look for in a designer?

Being such a tight-knit team, the designers we work with really need to have it all. A tall order, I know. But as a small studio, each of us really needs to be able to jump from discipline to discipline and from project to project pretty gracefully. On any given day, we each need to be ready to tackle a vast range of assignments from different angles and expertly navigate anything from a website design to an animation storyboard to a complex information graphic to a written article or pitch proposal. Verbal and written communication skills are a must. The ability to draw comes in really handy. As far as attention to detail goes, going back to fix something silly like a misspelled word or a mismatched color that should have been caught the first time

around can really waste a lot of time. Our clients have come to rely on our incredibly keen eye, so I try and make sure we all have a strong gene in that department.

TedCity2.0
Client: TED
Art Director: Agnieszka Gasparska, Kiss Me I'm Polish LLC
Designers: Rachel Matts, Min Jin Shin
2013

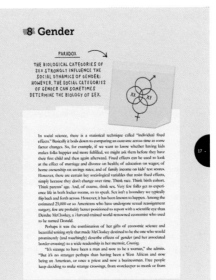

You May Ask Yourself:
An Introduction to Thinking
Like a Sociologist
Client: WW Norton
Art Director/Designer:
Agnieszka Gasparska,
Kiss Me I'm Polish LLC
Designer: Mattias Mackler,
Kiss Me I'm Polish LLC
Animator: Aaron Hughes
Sound Designer: Kevin Scott
2013

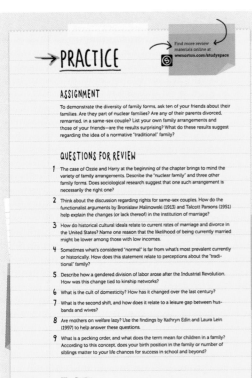

Bobby Martin and Jennifer Kinon

Championing Design

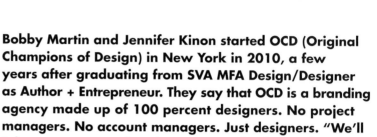

Bobby Martin and Jennifer Kinon started OCD (Original Champions of Design) in New York in 2010, a few years after graduating from SVA MFA Design/Designer as Author + Entrepreneur. They say that OCD is a branding agency made up of 100 percent designers. No project managers. No account managers. Just designers. "We'll take on any type of project: posters, books, packaging, exhibitions, videos, websites," Kinon says about finding a niche in refreshing high-value, long-established brands that have lost their edge. Start-ups are also great clients. When they launch a company or product, "we get to invent whole new visual vocabularies and thereby push the boundaries a bit." The duo decided to speak as one voice.

How did you two meet?
We've been working together forever. We were seated next to each other on the first day of grad school at SVA MFA Design/Designer as Author + Entrepreneur. We are extremely competitive. We pushed each other to work harder and longer and over time gained each other's trust through honest feedback.

What is the reason for the quirky name?
It's a little over the top, and we're a little over the top. We push our team, our students, and our clients to make bold and memorable design decisions. But really—to our core—we take championing design very seriously. Our name reflects who we are, what we do, and how we work: methodical, meticulous, relentless.

What areas are you complementary and others where you overlap in terms of your skills and aesthetics?
We're both designers, so it's all overlap. And we're both driven by our gut, so whoever shows up feeling most brave and ballsy really drives the work that day.

How do you break down the workload?
We still handle projects the same way we did in grad school. One person leads the charge, and the other offers honest feedback. We've found that even a brainstorm needs a single captain keeping the ship right. Ultimately, nothing goes out the door without both of us blessing it.

High Line Art
Agency: OCD | The Original
Champions of Design
Design: Jennifer Kinon, Bobby
C. Martin Jr., Michele Byrne,
Minjung Suh, Alex Boland

MC Kitchen
Agency: OCD | The Original
Champions of Design
Design: Jennifer Kinon,
Bobby C. Martin Jr., Jeff Close

Do you both sell? Do you both design? Do you both manage?

We both do it all. Happily, we share the design responsibilities with a great team. The work comes first; second is the other stuff.

What has been the most difficult and/or exciting challenge of your partnership?

Working together. It's tough to keep pushing, pushing, pushing, but it's also the best part of the job.

What has been the most exciting work you've done together?

Building the business. We've toned it down a bit, but during the first year of OCD, our mantra was "say no to nothing." We have no idea what we're doing, but—so far—we've been able to figure it out bit by bit.

What is the ratio of print to online or screen-based design?

Branding is media agnostic. It needs to work everywhere on everything, so we do it all without much thought to the silos. The big change is that a few years ago we were delivering brand guidelines. Now we are not just guidelining the work, but implementing it as well. That extra step allows us to fully flesh out every element of the visual language and drive the strategy home.

What do you look for when you hire designers?

10. Know why you want to work with us
 9. Know design history
 8. Ask (good) questions
 7. Have a vision for your future
 6. Present your work well
 5. Show us a passion project
 4. Be on time
 3. Over deliver
 2. Be nice
 1. Send a thank-you note

Studio Museum in Harlem
Agency: OCD | The Original
Champions of Design
Design: Jennifer Kinon, Bobby
C. Martin Jr., Justin Chen

WNBA
Agency: OCD | The Original
Champions of Design
Design: Jennifer Kinon,
Bobby C. Martin Jr.,
Thomas Porostocky, Alex
Boland and Joe Finocchiaro
Photography:
Jennifer Pottheiser

Antonio Alcalá

What a Dream Client Looks Like

Antonio Alcalá, a graphic designer and founder of Studio A, grew up in San Diego and moved East for college, majoring in history. In his senior year, he discovered graphic design and "fell in love," he says. He went to graduate school in design, followed by a year working for *Time-Life* Books. Eager to work on a wider range of projects, he left that job and opened Studio A, where he works primarily with museums. "Designing for clients whose mission is presenting the world's cultural heritage is emotionally rewarding," he adds. "In essence, I'm hired to work with material I'd otherwise pay to see." Alcalá also art directs stamps for the United States Postal Service. "It's incredibly satisfying to translate important American stories into tiny pictures that are printed by the millions and distributed throughout the country," he says.

Lines in Long Array
Client: Smithsonian,
National Portrait Gallery
Designer: Antonio Alcalá
2013

When and why did you found Studio A?
Studio A opened officially in 1988. My graduate school department chair always recommended students go into business for themselves. So I did. Opening my own shop allowed me to work on a greater variety of projects and devote extra attention to work that interested me.

How large is your studio and how big do you want it to be?
Currently, we are five designers. Running a smaller studio allows me to spend more time designing and less time in meetings and management. I'm interested in growing a bit larger as long as the quality of the work can remain high and I'm still actively engaged in the design work.

What or which of your clients do you enjoy the most from a creative standpoint?
My favorite clients are those who trust me and respect the design process. They're the ones who are confident I'll do research and provide solutions appropriate to their content. Also, when the proposed solutions are not typical, they still give their full support.

How much of the creative decisions and "making" are yours?
Most of the final creative decisions are mine. But the studio operates in a very collaborative manner. We're constantly asking for each other's opinion on projects as they are in process. I strongly believe the end results are almost always a result of everyone's input. That's why almost

Kaleidoscope Flowers stamps
(Above)
Client: United States
Postal Service
Art Director: Antonio Alcalá
Designer: Nicole and Petra
Kapitza
2013

Waves of Color stamps
(Right)
Client: United States
Postal Service
Art Director: Antonio Alcalá
Designer: Michael Dyer
2012

all our work is credited to Studio A and not specifically to me.

How much do you delegate to your staff?

Delegation depends on schedule and client. We do two magazines I barely see during production, and only when I'm invited. A few clients specifically want me to do the design, and those usually stay with me. Overall, a lot of work gets delegated, but then I review most of it before sending it to the client.

When looking for a designer, what do you want to see?

I'm interested in smart people who can think. Curiosity is good. It's essential that they have an appreciation or understanding of good typography.

I'm also interested in people who are interested in the kind of work we do.

You've art directed stamps for the U.S. Postal Service. How did that come about, and how does it function?

To be honest, I'm not exactly sure why I was tapped for the USPS work. But here's my best guess: Studio A does a lot of work with museums. One of our longtime clients is the Smithsonian's National Postal Museum. Word travels fast in Washington. On the strength of my work for the NPM and other clients in town, and a known interest in stamps, I was invited to join the Citizen's Stamp Advisory Committee. They're a group of people who meet quarterly to advise the postmaster

Modernism: A Chronology
1914–1939
Client: Corcoran Gallery of Art
Art Director: Antonio Alcalá
Designer: Corcoran College
of Art + Design Students,
Class of 2007
2007

general on what stamps the U.S. should issue and to review designs. After a year, I was offered a position as an art director for the stamp program. Now, along with three other art directors, I oversee the creation of the stamp designs for the USPS. The USPS gives me assignments (stamp subject) and production schedules. Sometimes I get to design the stamps myself. More often, I work with illustrators, photographers, or designers to help create the stamp.

Mark Pernice

From Band Member
to Design Leader

Mark Pernice is partner of Young Professionals, a creative studio based in the Pencil Factory, Brooklyn. A New York native and School of Visual Arts alumnus, he spent part of 2008 working under Stefan Sagmeister and Paula Scher in 2010. Pernice transitioned from early work in movie poster design to designing for a variety of clients and industries, as an art director, designer, and illustrator. Clients include, The *New York Times*, Sony, Anthropologie, Urban Green Council, Virgin Mobile, Esquire, Universal Music Group, and The Lincoln Center for the Performing Arts. In 2010, Pernice's Photo Booth Mask project gained viral attention with over 1.5 million image hits in the project's first three months. "What began as an exercise to teach a few relatives how to use their iMac's Photo Booth for fun," he says, "ended in a project that Fast Company called "delightfully horrible" and Gizmodo called "almost divine grotesqueness," garnering press in Wired, The Huffington Post, DesignBoom, Buzzfeed, and It's Nice That—to name a few.

EBIE Awards
Client: Urban Green Council
Creative Direction: Mark Pernice
Art Direction: Zhang Qingyun
Design: Mark Pernice,
Zhang Qingyun, Wing Chui,
Stephanie Miller
Animation: Stephanie Miller
Award Production Direction:
Vim & Vigor Inc.
Award Fabrication: Dave Marin
2012

What prompted you to start your own studio and to join forces with your studio partner?

I went to art school but for a different major entirely. SVA had a program called Computer Art. Even then it was a little nebulous, and I just floated around knowing I didn't really want to be a 3-D animator, which was then the unspoken focus of the program. During those years and soon after graduation, I was playing music and looked to that as a professional trajectory. I started designing things for our band and friends' bands and thought I could hack it as a graphic designer. I landed a job designing movie posters

for mostly indie films to pay the rent while waiting for the big rock star break. Like most young volatile bands, we didn't last long enough to see that happen, and the music industry went into a spiral, so I decided I'd stick with design (and later illustration).

Was it an easy transition?

As much as my first design job was a stepping stone, it was also death trap: bad ethics, bad bosses, bad design, bad vibes, bad everything. I guess it had me believing every job was going to be like that. I now know I was wrong from the very short time spent with Sagmeister and at Pentagram, but it pushed

29 Broadway Installation
Client: Zachary Smith
Art Direction: Mark Pernice/
Zhang Qingyun
Design: Mark Pernice, Zhang
Qingyun, Kathleen Fitzgerald
2013

me to build something myself. I've been freelancing for a long time, one man working in his symbolic underwear and slippers and for illustration that's endeared, but I realized that in design, companies want to work with companies. I was losing bigger projects because of this, even with scalable resources. At the same time, I was getting a little strung out and lonely trying to drive the ship myself. Partnering and starting a legitimate studio was the next natural step.

How did you find your partner?
Zhang had interned for me, and we just worked really well together. I would occasionally talk to a few designer friends about joining forces, but it always seemed like I was trying to convince them of something they didn't really want to do. I was a bit hesitant to approach Zhang at first because he was still pretty green in the professional world, so we kept in touch while he went out and cut his teeth at other

firms while we came up with a plan. Now here we are.

Do you approach your Web work differently than your print?
We try to have the same mind set creatively. If you would be proud enough of the site to put it on the coffee table as you would a book, that's the approach we like. However, there are different things to keep in mind when dealing with the differences of digital user experiences and tangible user experiences. Just a few years ago, there were many more limitations todesigning for the Web. The Internet wasn't originally designed to be designed. It never really came out of beta until recently. It's a way more freeing medium now to work in.

Which medium or platform do you prefer?
These days you need to be a studio capable of combining different mediums and platforms. If I did five

corporate identities consecutively, I'd prefer to do a poster for a museum or a book, or a music video, or some weird advertising next. Luckily, we always have different things going on as well as personal projects, so it's a non-issue. Nobody says they want to do one thing over and over forever—not even the things they like—and today anything that's a form of design or visual communication is fair game.

When you hire assistants or engage an intern, what do you look for?
Sometimes it's their work and ideas I'm drawn to. I can't say good work because it might be great, just not a good fit for our studio. Sometimes it's a mix of personality, ambition, professionalism, and skill in areas we're not skilled in. Sometimes it's just a feeling. One thing to note, I'm not a neat freak, but I like to keep the place as tidy as I can. If you're a mess, it's not going to work out.

The Deathbringers
Author/Artist: Jason Blasso
Art Direction: Mark Pernice
Design: Mark Pernice
Animation: Stephanie Miller
2013

Tamara Gildengers Connolly

Balancing Studio and Home

Tamara Gildengers Connolly is the founder and principal art, creative, and business director for We Are How, a full-service design studio providing branding, Web and interactive, print, and motion graphics services to our clients. After getting a BFA from RISD, she worked for a small design firm based in Boston that focused on print and identity. From there, she took a short foray into freelancing "just to try something new and not feel rushed into making a decision about where I would work next," she says. She fostered relationships with clients that led to ongoing work and decided to continue working independently because "I really liked that I felt so much ownership over what I was doing and how I was doing it. Over time, my freelance work turned into a full-fledged individual business."

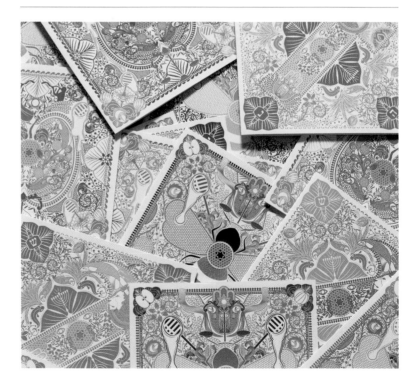

KLI Holiday Cards
Design: We Are How

Bitter and Esters Bottles
Design: We Are How

What prompted you to start your studio on such a small scale?

I knew I would gain valuable perspective from shifting between the various roles needed to make a business work, rather than focusing on one specific role within a larger organization. There also was, and continues to be, great pride in knowing that this is "the house that I built."

You do almost everything on your own, with one assistant. How difficult is it to find clients when you are so involved?

In our case, getting clients has almost always been through referrals. We concentrate on doing good work and being great to work with. We have steady clients whom we currently work with, some of whom I initially started working with years ago as a freelancer. When people from these organizations moved into new positions at other organizations, they continued to recommend us. Additionally, clients showcasing the projects and goals we helped them complete to others in their fields or professional networks have also brought us new clients and types of work; it's been a slow, steady process of organic growth.

Merrimack College Collateral
Design: We Are How

Do you fear getting big enough where you yourself do not design?
Yes, and I'm quite wary of that possibility becoming a reality. The way the business has been growing, if we don't get bigger, then this becomes more of a possibility to some extent.

You have your studio in your home. What are the pros and cons of that?
The pros and cons have shifted over time, as the particulars of my professional and personal lives have changed. Years ago, when I was first starting out as a freelancer, the challenges were around keeping a regular schedule and not getting sucked into work 24/7— my personality is more inclined to get absorbed by work then distracted by personal space. I've since learned to manage these expectations and my

time much more effectively; these days it's an asset that work is easily accessible to me and that it doesn't run my life.

What type of clients and jobs do you want to take on?
I love being a multidisciplinary studio with an extremely varied range of clients (size, industry, design needs, etc.)–this is certainly something I want to preserve as we grow. I care more about being able to foster good relationships with our clients than with what sector they are in.

Is what you are doing, so far, a successful business model?
I believe so, because thus far we're on the positive trajectory of growth we'd hoped for. Although I'd been freelancing

for years, the business as it is now is still in its nascency. You often hear about the first four to five years of a business being the "survival years," and to date, we are on the right track.

What do you look for or what do you want in someone you hire?
They need to honor thoughtful design and have an understanding of cultural relevance. In addition to that, they should also honor that life is about more than just producing, and work is much more effective and enjoyable when we are pleasurable to collaborate with, well organized, and clear in our goals, attentive to details, and mindful in our follow-through. We look for effective and empathetic communicators who can gauge how to involve team members such that everyone's resources are being used in the best way; a talented polymath, passionate about everything they do, who have a robust appetite for learning how to do things they don't know how to at present. It's also crucial that they have a healthy relationship with their own ego and receiving feedback—we are a team after all.

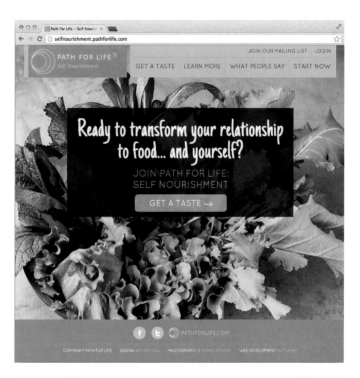

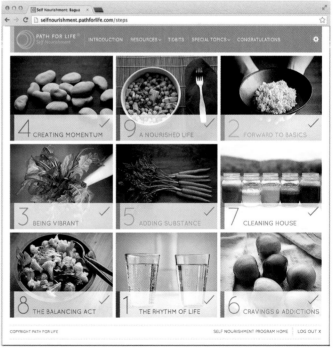

Path for Life Website
Designer: We Are How
Photography: Torkil Stavdal
Web Development: Yottaram

Araba Simpson

One Person, All Alone

Araba Simpson, a graphic designer and principal of her own studio, is a native of Ghana, West Africa, who lived in various countries until finally settling in New York. Simpson describes her convoluted path to design as a series of serendipitous encounters with "brilliant people, at just the right junctures in my life—believe it or not, I was planning to be a bio research scientist when I grew up." Prior to starting her own business, she was a student in the SVA MFA Design/Designer as Author + Entrepreneur program through which she obtained positions at The *New York Times*, Jazz at Lincoln Center, The Metropolitan Opera, and Johnson & Johnson's Global Strategic Design Office.

You are a one-person shop. What does that mean exactly?

I do it all: design, billing, new client development. I don't have a staff, but I do engage freelancers for specific skills I may need for a particular project.

Do you hire yourself out to different design firms, or do you locate clients on your own?

I try to work with my own clients from my home office. However, depending on the client, or the magnitude and duration of the project, I am opening to working for/at different design firms. On-site client projects are a bit tricky because they require a great deal of time management in order to make sure my other clients aren't neglected. Most of my clients come by recommendation, particularly through my good friends at Original Champions of Design and RED, and from former clients.

With only you doing everything, how do you get everything done?

I've been working on my own for a little over three years now, and in that time I have started to figure out systems. For example, I do billing and any sort of business-related tasks on Thursdays, I try not to commit to Monday design deliverables, and I do my very best to stagger projects. Staggering projects hardly ever works because projects tend to come in waves.

What is your biggest strength as a designer?

To be able to truly listen and understand my client's needs when I get into a project—and my ability to develop pretty good relationships with them.

And your weakness?

Sob stories are my weakness, and so many people have emergency design

Aesyna Lampshades (above)
Designer and Photographer:
Araba Simpson

sob stories that generally end with. . .
"and we don't have any money. . . ."

**How do you balance strength and
weakness in your practice?**
It's taken me a while, but I've started to
learn to sidestep the sob stories by explaining the value of design. If the sob-story
project is something that really piques
my interest, and if I can afford the time
to do it pro bono, I will take it on.

Who are your favorite clients, and why?
The clients who let me have fun and trust
my judgment are my favorites. Those
clients make my job so much easier—
those are the instances when I am working WITH someone rather than for them.

**Is there anything about the business
of design that you still need to know?**
There is so much more I need to know,
I am literally learning by doing.

Jazz at Lincoln Center Posters
Designer: Araba Simpson

Matt Luckhurst
Designing for Design Firms

Matt Luckhurst is a designer and illustrator from Vancouver, BC, currently working at Airbnb in San Francisco. He says he landed in design school a bit by accident. "I had intended to get a degree in Commerce at the University of Calgary but found the experience excruciating and managed only two years before dropping out." After traveling around Europe, working as a telemarketer, pizza delivery boy, and ice track scraper, among other things, he went back to school and attended the Alberta College of Art and Design in Calgary in order to major in painting. "Luckily, I took a design class in my first semester there," he recalls. That is where he was introduced to the idea of design, and he says, "I fell in love with its history, effect on the world, and the creativity it allowed for in a career." He ultimately graduated from the MFA Design/Designer as Author + Entrepreneur program. He is also the author of a children's book, *Paul Bunyan and Babe the Blue Ox: The Great Pancake Adventure*, published in 2012 by Abrams Books for Young readers.

Paul Bunyan and Babe the Blue Ox: The Great Pancake Adventure"
Editor: Howard Reeves
Art Director: Chad Beckerman
Author and Illustrator: Matt Luckhurst

Starting out you were hired at Collins, a design and business strategy firm. What was the adjustment for you? What new did you have to know?

There were a lot of surprises for me when I entered the workforce. One of the biggest was learning to articulate what I did, not just for a creative crowd, but also for those who are unaware or uninterested in the design process. I say quite often to young designers that it is important to have a point of view in your work. I think this helps you move forward in your professional life. If you're lucky, you'll have a great creative director to help guide you and inform your language, but you have to be prepared to fight for your work to progress and stand out. Quite often there are more support staff than "makers" in these firms, and to make things that matter, you'll need to articulate what you're passionate about doing. As my career continues, I have to focus more and more on strategy, particularly if I want to have creative influence.

What do you do now at Airbnb that is different from you last job? How have you evolved?

I never thought I would enter the in-house world of design, but Airbnb seemed like a chance to influence a very unique brand in a big way. I've been lucky to land at a disruptive company that does not lack for creativity and innovation. There is simplicity in working for an ad or design firm. Everyone is united around doing creative work for clients, and the employees speak the same or similar languages. In-house, people are from a multitude of backgrounds, and design is just one function of the company. You're exposed to working with dozens of different teams to find solutions, while also making sure design is helping inform the company's trajectory. I think there are huge benefits to being on both sides of the table, and learning how the entire process works is invaluable.

How do you work with clients? Is this collaboration, or do you hold your work close to the chest?

Lots of collaboration. You have to listen to what people want. Even if you disagree, they are the clients and it's up to you to lead them to an effective solution, not force it on them. I find the easiest way to do this is to keep an open dialogue and collaborate as much as possible. Part of that is defining an effective process early on. Make sure you have clearly outlined dates and expectations before you start working and, when possible, present and get buy-in on a strategy before you begin designing. This gives you and your client language to speak about and critique the work.

You went to graduate school. Was this necessary to reach your goals?

At the time I debated the value of it. I'd

Hackathon 2
Ogilvy & Mather
New York
January 23

Hackathon Poster
Design: Matt Lackhurst

advertising
women
of new york

Airbnb Hello LA (top)
Creative Director:
Andrew Schapiro
Design: Matt Luckhurst

Advertising Women of
New York Logo (above)
Creative Director: Brian Collins
Design: Matt Luckhurst

already done two years in commerce, plus four years in undergrad design, and here I was—26 years old. I felt like it was time to get a job. Also, I'm not the kind of person who "misses school"; it's fun, but so is having a job. Anyhow, when I was accepted, I was torn, but I did it and am very grateful for the opportunity. I'm not sure it's for everyone, but it gave me time to fulfill my potential and set me off on a far more interesting path for the rest of my career.

What did you learn on the job versus in the classroom?
The classroom allowed me to find an aesthetic approach I enjoyed and gave me a background and understanding of what design is. The classroom exposed me to a lot of ideas and concepts. The job has allowed me to put those concepts into action within a more defined structure. Work as a designer is hard. You have to keep developing and sharpening your creative skills while becoming a better strategist, leader, and businessperson. Learning to manage people and relationships is something that takes time out of creative work, and finding that balance is tricky. The classroom is a place that allows students to focus purely on the creative process, free from those distractions.

Mary
Design: Matt Luckhurst

What are the criteria for hiring at Airbnb? Do you see yourself in your hires?

I don't have a set criteria, but there are certain aspects of designers that excite me. I look for people with a strong work ethic and who have made surprising work, or people who give a shit and are weird. There are a lot of good designers in the world, but good design can be exceptionally boring. I'd rather take a chance on someone with a unique idea than someone that checks all the boxes. I look for corollaries in terms of work ethic and enthusiasm, and I do find people with an illustration background are more apt to experiment and get messy. Really, I look for people that intimidate me, who are younger, more interesting, and more talented than myself. There is a surprisingly large number of them.

3 Partners on Partnering

Ask any graphic designer and he or she will sing the praises of collaboration. In an interconnected, cross-platform creative profession, it is impossible to be a lone genius anymore. Granted, the genius will lead and others will follow, but working and playing well with others is more essential because the vast number of platforms and outlets require multiple expertises—more than one person can embody at the highest level. This may account for the growth of design studios and firms with two or more partners. It certainly is the reason for single-person studios to bring in a range of people to handle anything from conception to manufacture, from brainstorming to technologizing.

Hjalti Karlsson and Jan Wilker

Not a Lot of Verbalizing

Icelander Hjalti Karlsson and German-born Jan Wilker started Karlssonwilker in 2000. They met at Stefan Sagmeister's office in 1999 when both worked there. When Stefan announced his first sabbatical, it meant that they would need to look for something else to do. It was a natural progression to start their own studio. Today, their specialties are identity and branding, environmental and experiential design, digital animation, graphics, and print. Over the years, Karlssonwilker grew from a studio of two to a studio of four full-time employees plus two interns. "We started with a heavy tilt toward print design," Wilker says.

How do you practice design as a partnership? Do you collaborate or work individually?
The way we work seems to be a loose system of checks and balances—nothing is mandatory or standardized, but [is] based on trust and respect of the other's opinion and point of view. It seems like an unquantifiable mix of solo and joint thinking, where we both work individually and ask for feedback when tweaking something. We sit together, discuss together, and think together. We're always direct and frank with each other. Overall, it helps that egos are very small in our studio.

What are the differences in your method, manner, and aesthetics—if any?
This was observed by Megan Elevado, our director of creative operations: "When Hjalti is working, he seems to be in an invisible cocoon and shut off from everyone, while Jan is focused on work, but not completely zoned out to everything else. Both are pretty quiet and not effusive when speaking about their own work. There is a lot of quiet thinking—sometimes this thinking even reads (in terms of body language) as computing. There's not a lot of verbalizing."

Karlssonwilker has an overall attitude, if not a style, full of wit and irony (like your Doglamp). How would you define your approach?
We just recently banished irony from our work here in the studio. So far it's working fine. It's difficult to write about it, so it would be best to look at our work and see for yourself.

Your work is highly conceptual; when you hire designers, is it for their typography or their conceptual acuity?
Solid typography and overall craft is a basic prerequisite. The same goes for

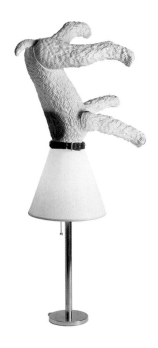

Dog Lamp
Client: In-House
2001–2011

flexibility in thinking. What we look for in designers (and that very rarely happens, since we're a very small studio and people tend to stay with us for quite some time) is personality and character—if we can see ourselves spending most of our waking hours in the same room with them.

How has your practice and graphic design changed since you began the business?

We still are in the same space we started 13 years ago, on 6th avenue and 14th street. The layout in the studio hasn't changed. Some furniture was replaced; the computers as well. The big changes happened and happen all inside. From a two-person operation with naive spirits and lots of energy, we became by way of lots of self-induced stress, mistakes, and sleepless nights [what] we are right now: a small studio of six people who try to enjoy every single day. And we stopped working on weekends. The design changed in a way that we don't see the client as an enemy, but as an important ally and collaborator through-out the whole process. We fight less with the clients.

Sculpture 3
Client: Wolf-Gordon
2013

Signage, Wayfinding, and
Identity for MoMI, Museum
of the Moving Image, Queens,
New York
Client: Museum of the Moving
Image
2011

Time Magazine 12-Page
Feature
2008

Stuart Rogers and Sam Eckersley

Sharing Responsibilities

RED stands for Rogers Eckersley Design—Stuart Rogers and Sam Eckerlsey—a pair of former classmates at the SVA MFA Design/Designer as Author + Entrepreneur program, who founded their studio upon graduation. Their studio focuses on brand identity, campaign development, and special events, but their partnership is based on trust and confidence. Focusing on print, they've taken on such clients as Abrams, Apollo Theater, and Playwrights Horizon but have also worked for the NFL, Chase, and ESPN.

What is the best thing about having a design partnership?
The best thing about it is that you have someone you trust to consult with about every aspect of the business. It gives you confidence. It doesn't hurt that you can divide up the responsibilities of running the company or that you can go on vacation assured that business will run smoothly. It also means twice the business development since we are both out there connecting with people.

What is the not-so-good-thing about having a design partnership?
We're pretty similar! Our names start with S, we have the same design approach, the same aesthetic. Occasionally, we show up at the office in the same shirt. Clients like that when they hire us, they're getting two for the price of one, but from a business perspective, we can end up with too much overlap sometimes. It can get muddled. A more efficient partnership might include someone with business training, or at least someone who

had strong interest in taking on the business-side responsibilities.

How do you split up the business responsibilities and the creative perks?
We have help with bookkeeping and accounting, but we divvy the other administrative roles pretty evenly. This happened organically over time, and these tasks have pretty much stuck. On the creative side, we have different interests. Sam leads the art direction of the staff. Stuart is less involved there but occasionally feels the need to get into the trenches and make something. We create opportunities for each other to do the work we like.

What percentage of the jobs you take on are accepted to keep the studio running?
50 percent.

Who are the clients that provide you with satisfaction but also challenges and why?
The dream clients are the ones who offer three things: creative promise,

Apollo Spring Benefit (opposite)
Client: Apollo Theater
Creative Direction: Stuart Rogers and Sam Eckersley
Design: Jane Huschka and Joe Brown

an adequate budget, and expertise in working with designers. We probably won't work with anyone who offers just one of these things, but many of our clients offer two. For instance, we have a wonderfully experienced client with money to spend, but the work is not superchallenging. We also have a client that is great to work with and offers the potential for projects we can shout about, but the client has tiny budgets. These are the challenges.

Are you equally busy with print and digital?

We're focused primarily on creating brand identities for events. When we're involved with the execution, there is a wide range of forms it could take—printed collateral, digital executions, signage, merchandise, stage backdrops, beer taps (yes). Most of what we make lives in analog form, but we are increasingly looking for opportunities to use video and other digital executions to make richer experiences.

When you hire designers, what do you look for?
We look for talent, hunger, confidence, consistent optimism, and attention to detail. A sense of humor is nice. Lots of new music is also a definite bonus.

How does an employee grow within your framework?
We expect our designers to juggle project management, production, and design. Our designers learn about how to schedule a project, how to keep things on track, how to communicate with clients and printers, how to set up files, and, of course, their design abilities grow since they work with us directly.

Stat Bats
Design: Stuart Rogers
and Sam Eckersley

Canyon of Heroes,
Street-level Exhibit
Client: Alliance for Downtown
New York
Creative Direction: Stuart Rogers
and Sam Eckersley
Design: Chris Ritchie

Justin Colt and Jose Fresneda

How Partners Become Partners

Justin Colt and Jose Fresneda are principals of The Collected Works, a New York–based design studio rooted in music, art, and culture. Fresneda from Bogotá, Colombia, and Colt, from central Pennsylvania, recently graduated from the MFA Design/Designer as Author + Entrepreneur program from the School of Visual Arts. Fresneda also has a bachelor's degree in industrial design from a program deeply rooted in design thinking. Colt graduated from Penn State University. Fresneda says that his work "has always been a reflection of my current interests and has provided me with the opportunity of meeting and collaborating with people in very different fields, most of them way more talented that I'll ever be." Colt used to work as a designer for Converse in Boston, Massachusetts, and also formally interned and later worked for Milton Glaser. They began their partnership immediately following graduation.

SteEvil Magazine—
Digital Publication!
Design: The Collected Works
Photo Courtesy: Joshua Harker

What caused the two of you to form your partnership?
Jose: We have very similar interests and we always understood how to push each other's individual work to new places. That and the fact that we are probably the only people who get each other's sense of humor.

Justin: In grad school, Jose and I would frequently take on and moonlight freelance projects that came our way. While independently working for clients, we would often share what we were designing with each other for input. The benefits of having someone removed from the project provide fresh feedback were extremely helpful–yielding much better work from both

of us. After helping each other on a few projects, we started taking on work as a partnership from the onset. It was also beneficial to tell clients we had another team member that would be on board for the projects. Instead of being an independent freelancer, we were a team—and that gave clients an assurance that we were capable of handling what they were entrusting us with.

What did you discuss regarding how the business would be set up?
Justin: Before officially forming the studio, we had a long chat about the management and legal aspects of the business. While we had the same mind-set for the studio goals and general ethos, we hadn't really discussed

Elsa y Elmar—
Album Packaging
Design and Photography:
The Collected Works
Model: Elsa Carvajal

some issues that might come up down the road. Must all studio decisions be unanimous? Does whoever finds the client get more money? What happens to the studio if one of us decides to leave, or who gets the mutual studio assets if it's dissolved? How much are we going to pay ourselves? Talking very openly about all of these business aspects, finances, and any future problems is an approach we now bring to all our client work as well. It's easy, but naive, to assume that everyone is on the same page for the scope of a project—especially when things need to change or go wrong later.

Who does what in the partnership?
Jose: We both do a bit of everything. It's more a case of figuring out who is cooking dinner and who's in charge of cleaning up the dishes.

Justin: Most jobs are split up pretty naturally when they come in. We have the same vision for where a project should go but often have different approaches, which leads us both to develop different directions to present to the client. It's not competitive, as we're very much helping each other along the way, and often a preferred direction emerges as we work. Having different angles on a problem is what

American Odysseys—
Book Cover and Collateral (Above)
Design: The Collected Works
Client: The Vilcek Foundation

Made Here—
Start-up Web Platform/Branding
Design: The Collected Works

we knew to be so helpful by getting
feedback from each other in the beginning. It's more challenging but makes
the work stronger, and [it] is almost
always appreciated by the client to
have a few options.

**You both met in graduate school.
Describe "partnership" at first sight?**
Jose: I remember as soon as I got the

e-mail saying that I got into grad school I started looking at my classmates' portfolios. Justin's was one of those that just made me nervous because of how good it was. After the initial shock, and realizing that we had many interests in common, it wasn't hard to start thinking of developing projects together.

What have been some of the bumps in your professional road?

Justin: It's really difficult to start a business. It's even more difficult when you have very little funds to get started. Before leaving our full-time design jobs and completely committing to The Collected Works, we had to pool our money from our client work for about a year. Funds were tight, and we had to be as resourceful as possible. We worked out an agreement to rent a couple of desks part-time in a studio, in exchange for doing design work for the owner. After this, we worked from various coffee shops, libraries, and public locations around the city. It's hard to work like this, though; working from just a laptop with choppy Internet isn't sustainable or very efficient.

We were hungry for paying work but didn't want to amass clients and projects that we didn't believe in or wanted to work with. After all, the studio was our opportunity to work with people we respected and be a part of the projects we wanted to work on. Our clients are a representation of us and would lead to the clients we will have in the future. We had to build a solid foundation of good work for smart clients—which is the work everyone hopes for—but that often means those projects don't pay too well.

At this stage, are each of you doing other work, freelance or part-time?

Jose: I just finished a six-month apprenticeship period with a small studio in Brooklyn called Dark Igloo. They have been very supportive of what Justin and I have been doing, considering that they started at about the same age. It's been an amazing learning experience in terms of seeing how they manage their business, how they treat the people who work with them, and how to keep the overhead low.

Justin: Nope, all of our time and energy is dedicated to the studio. Before, when we had part-time design jobs with other studios, any freelance work that came to either one of us was shared through the studio. If we were in it, we were in it together—we weren't going to pick and choose which work we handled independently and which work would be shared. All funds are consolidated into the studio account, from which we pay ourselves, [pay] our overhead, and save for the future.

What is the work you are most pleased with now?

Jose: I really like a recent project that we completed for a musician friend in Boston. It was a great opportunity to do not only the design but also art direction and photography for the piece. I enjoyed being part of the process since the beginning, and even if we had to get crafty to overcome a tiny budget, it pushed the final result beyond the client's or even our own expectations.

Justin: It's hard to pick a favorite, but there are definitely some top projects. Working with the School of Visual Arts is always good work. In addition to us having such an appreciation for the school, without fail everyone we've worked with has been a great client. We've done the collateral and promotion for three of the graduate programs, including Web, branding, print, and poster design. Other notable work has been from larger companies like *The New York Times* and Converse to smaller start-ups and musicians. One of the biggest advantages of being a small studio is that we don't have to only take on large businesses with massive budgets. We can also help people we believe in, which is what this was all about.

Greg D'Onofrio and Patricia Belen

Two Partners, One Passion

Kind Company is a small, independent Web and print design office in New York City, composed of two principals: Greg D'Onofrio and Patricia Belen. They handle a variety of projects (from a single logo to identity systems, printed collateral, and websites) for small to medium-size businesses, including art galleries, artists, restaurants, architects, authors, bookstores, and archives. They are also writers and the founders of Display (thisisdisplay.org), a platform devoted to research, writings, and discoveries in graphic design history. Before they became partners in business, "we were partners in life—it always felt like a natural fit and our mutual interests, trust, and respect for one another have made it feel effortless and uncomplicated," says D'Onofrio, who speaks below.

Do you both have similar or complementary skills and talents, or do you each come with different assets?
Both. However, after 10 years in business, we've learned to collaborate on virtually all aspects of running a design studio and making available a variety of skill sets, opinions, and ideas for each scenario. For us, the best results in design are often found via a collaborative process—this means sharing most tasks, including design, client meetings, business development, writing/researching, answering the phone, making coffee, and so on. There is hardly a task one of us does independently, without the other partner's guidance.

How would you describe your method or style of working?
We don't subscribe to one specific method of working. In general, our approach has always been centered around the belief that successful graphic design should be simple, smart, and usable. For us, that's always been a balance of function and aesthetics—communicating information honestly and effectively to solve our client's business goals. If a project is worth doing, it's worth doing well. Not all projects are glamorous, yet they all deserve the same amount of dedication.

In addition to being a design studio, you also produce websites on design history. How did this come about?
Alongside client work, we engage in self-initiated graphic design history projects. We're self-taught, and, unfortunately, we never had an opportunity to study graphic design history. Developing these "types" of projects as vehicles for modern, mid-twentieth-

GoodStory Films (logo)
Designers: Kind Company

Graphic Modern
USA, Italy, and Switzerland
1934–66 (exhibition)
Designers: Kind Company.

Tetra Images
(proposed logo)
Designers: Kind Co.

century graphic design history, pioneers, and artifacts is both educational and inspirational.

Is the Alvin Lustig (alvinlustig.org) site, a work of love?
Absolutely. We were never required to do it, and it would not have been possible without published articles and Elaine Lustig Cohen's generous support. When we set out to do the project in 2006, Alvin Lustig was still a little known, yet hugely important design pioneer who needed to be introduced (or reintroduced) to a growing online audience. We've always been fascinated by his work,

and we figured the best way to educate ourselves (and others) was to develop a website cataloging his work.

You also have your own digital "bookstore." What was the motivation for this? And what has been the result?
Our noncommercial projects take lots of time and dedication, and we often look for ways to help "fund" the projects. Our Display bookstore (thisisdisplay.org/bookstore) does exactly this, by offering an important selection of original and hard-to-find graphic design books, periodicals, and ephemera for sale. In addition to

the graphic design "classics," it also means the work of lesser-known designers or the lesser-known work of well-known design pioneers. As collectors, we have an affinity for print, and we see books as valuable tools to design practice, education, and research. The bookstore encourages this and connects us with others around the world with similar interests and passions.

There is also an exhibition component to what you do? Do you aspire to become curators?
As aspiring curators, we're encouraged to show and tell others a distinct point of view about midcentury graphic design, typography, and beyond—from the rational to the experimental to the playful. One of the primary responsibilities of owning our collection is conducting research about the items we acquire and finding out how they can far exceed their role as inspirational "eye candy." It's not enough to own the object—it's also about what the object can teach us. Ultimately, we hope to continue this through writing, curating, and perhaps publishing.

Do you feel it necessary to be diversified in today's marketplace?
It depends. For us, diversification is both a blessing and a curse. On the one hand, it offers the possibility of more work and/or clients. Yet, with two people and more work than we can handle, there's little time to specialize. Over the years, we've learned to not spread ourselves too thin and stick to the few things we do best.

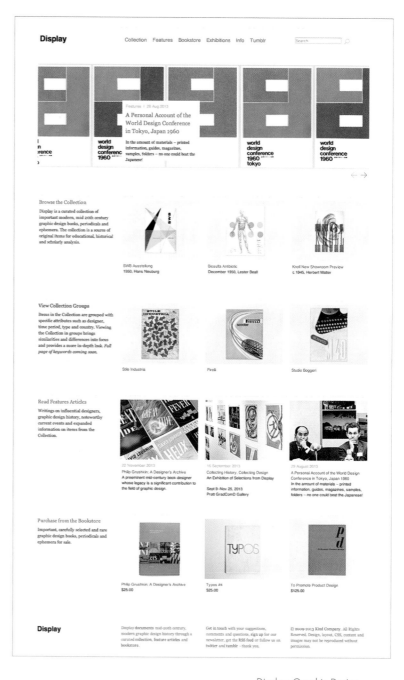

Display, Graphic Design Collection (website, thisisdisplay.org)
Designers: Kind Company.

Scott Buschkuhl

At Present We Are Three

Scott Buschkuhl is the founder and creative director of Hinterland in New York. Prior to establishing the studio, he worked as a designer at the New York office of Pentagram. Hinterland, founded in 2007, is a multidisciplinary design studio that creates brands and identities for print, digital, and environments; publication designs, including books and magazines; illustrations, both conceptual and information based; and more. "Our work is guided by the belief that the best design is often the result of a close collaboration with our clients," he says. The name Hinterland has multiple meanings—it describes an area that surrounds an urban center or the backcountry (his first office was in a far-off section of Brooklyn that pretty much felt undiscovered when he moved in). Second, it speaks to a depth and breadth of knowledge, specifically cultural, artistic, academic, and scientific.

The Nantucket Project
Creative Director:
Scott Buschkuhl
Designers: Scott Buschkuhl,
Michael Mercer-Brown,
Regina Puno

Where did you gather the experience and confidence to start a studio?
The idea of opening a studio came from a mix of ego and naiveté. I felt comfortable with my design skills and handling of client relationships but had no idea what it really meant to run a small business. Through a lot of hard work, some trial and error, and the good fortune of having repeat clients, I find myself here today.

How many are you, and what does each member do?
At present we are three, but we often hire freelancers to adapt to projects of any scale. We build out a team accordingly from a variety of collaborators, including developers, copywriters, photographers, and so

on. I am the principal of the studio, and I handle the creative direction and project management, but, honestly, we collaborate on everything as a team. Once we have been retained by a client on a new project, everyone here begins with his or her own research and then design development happens together. No idea is a bad idea.

Do you have a special business model?
We do not have a specific business model per se, but we do prefer to stay small and agile. Our flexible structure provides the opportunity to take on projects of any scope and scale. Being a multidisciplinary office of this size, it is necessary to be flexible in our approach to problem solving and

team building. We also work in a very collaborative manner with our clients through every step of the process, making sure that the final result effectively communicates the goals of their organization.

You are multidisciplinary. Is this a necessity for young studios these days?

It isn't necessary to be multidisciplinary these days, as there are many studios that are extremely successful through their specialization, but we really enjoy the idea that on Monday we can be designing an identity, Wednesday an art catalogue, and by the week's end, an illustration.

You work in a range of media and platforms. What do you prefer—print, digital, or textile?

Print is how we got started and a big focus of what we do, but there is no denying that the screen and the physical space are equally important. At the end of the day, our goal is to solve problems and create memorable experiences for the client and the end user.

Do you have a studio style?

Hinterland doesn't have a specific house style. We look for the appropriate response to each and every project, but we naturally bring our own personal experiences along when designing. We are constantly drawing inspiration from film, art, fashion, music, and trends in different cultures and countries that we visit. These experiences continually inform our approach.

MediaLink
Creative Director:
Scott Buschkuhl
Designers: Scott Buschkuhl,
Michael Mercer-Brown,
Regina Puno

When hiring, what do you look for?
We look for talent first and foremost, but the right candidate must also be enthusiastic, have a different perspective; a love of food, art, and film; a desire to contribute; and a passion to learn; and above all be normal. It's hard to describe being normal, but [it] goes a long way.

Wang Xingwei
Creative Director:
Scott Buschkuhl
Designers: Scott Buschkuhl,
Michael Mercer-Brown,
Zipeng Zhu

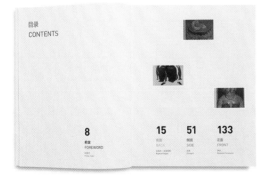

Design Genres

Editorial design is not the same as advertising; advertising is not the same as book design. Each has a unique focus and target. In most cases, the tools are similar but the methodologies are not. Many graphic designers perform a broad range of tasks, switching media as clients and jobs demand. A designer cannot always afford to specialize because the volume of work in a specialty may not warrant it or competition may be too intense. Therefore, it is prudent at the outset of a career to learn about and practice all the disciplines that strike your interest and fancy as well as those that are growth areas for employment. Although it is not necessary to be expert in everything, it is useful to be fluent in as many forms as possible, at least while you are looking for your favorite genre.

4 Letters and Type

The *lingua franca*, or common language, of graphic design is type. You can call yourself a designer only when you understand the rules of type and how to break them. Not long ago, type design was almost an airtight profession. Only the very skilled and highly motivated were allowed entry. One reason was the intense amount of time that it took to design a typeface in its various weights and point sizes. Breaking into this realm of design required years of apprenticeship.

Today, the computer has changed all that—some argue for good, others for ill. Type design software has increased the capability of serious type designers to create many more custom and proprietary typefaces and has made it possible for neophyte and fly-by-night designers to develop personalized type. Somewhere between these two extremes, graphic designers who are interested in or passionate about typefaces have entered the field, either developing the occasional face, which they then sell or license to a digital type foundry, or establishing their own digital type foundries. The computer has broken down the barriers. The technology is available for neophytes to experiment at designing typefaces on the desktop and then testing their applications in real documents. Never before in the history of type design and type

founding has this been so technically and financially accessible. Lettering is another indispensable component of graphic design. Lettering is the design of one-of-a-kind, often limited-use typographic or calligraphic compositions. The letterer is not necessarily a type designer, and vice versa, but the skills of one are certainly useful to the other. Letterers are most often used to develop signs, logos, book titles, package labels, and other custom items. Lettering classes are common in most art and design schools and are the only efficient way to learn the methods of the craft. Although much lettering begins as hand-drawing, the computer is used as a tool for detailing and finalizing work.

Type design is an extremely time-intensive field; the designer may work for many months on a single family, style, or even weight. Type designers who create custom faces for publish-

ing, corporate, or institutional clients also spend a large amount of time in revisions. The letterer works on a specific project, usually for a fixed period of time. This is not to imply that one field is more satisfying than the other, but if type and lettering are desired specialties, it is important to evaluate the investment required for each of these.

You don't have to design type or draw letters, however, to be a good typographer. All designers must be fluent in the language of type and letters, and that fluency governs how well or not their typographic composition will be. A designer has to love type and all its nuances.

Marian Bantjes

Lettering as Art and Business

Marian Bantjes is a Canadian designer, artist, illustrator, typographer, and writer. She is best known for her intricately ornate hand and computer lettering that began to emerge while she ran a design studio called Digitopolis in 1996. How she developed such a skill and talent is a bit of a mystery. "There's nothing in my life or the life of my family that was in the least bit baroque or patterned or ornamented," she says about her design aesthetic, which used to be clean, simple, unimaginative. Her book training was "bookish." The only source of influence she can find to explain her dense and exuberant lettering style is her travel to exotic countries in her twenties—and the many photographs she has taken in India, Thailand, Italy, Spain, Bali, and Africa "that are the possible seeds of my interest in intense decoration."

The Children's Hospital
Artwork and Design: Marian Bantjes
Client: Granta Publications
Art Director: Michael Salu
2012

The level of intricacy in everything you do is mind-numbing. You must be wired. Does the planning of your pieces come naturally or through struggle?
It comes very naturally. Ideas form in my head quite quickly, and while I've certainly had my share of false starts, the process is relatively simple for me provided I'm working under my own steam and/or have the full support of a client.

What determines for you where and in what style you will take a particular work? Is it the more detailed, the better?
It's really due to whim and what I'm interested in exploring or experimenting with at that time. I don't think that more detailed is better. Usually it's

whatever is challenging to me, whether that be the materials, or the structure, or figuring out some kind of system to work within. I'm particularly fond of systems—coming up, I'm interested in using new techniques.

Does the word *simplicity* have any place in your life?
Yes, absolutely. I'm very fond of Modernism, and I try very hard to pare down the number of things I have in my house and my life. I abhor tchotchkes, and I don't allow myself to collect, because I know where it leads. My ideal house would be a Modernist box; I can't think with clutter, and while I'm not currently living in my ideal environment, I'm slowly working toward it . . . it's all very strange.

In the scheme of contemporary design, do you see yourself as part of a movement, or are you an iconoclast?

A little of both. I'm certainly part of the ornamental movement that swept across the design scene in the past 10 years, but I'm one of the few who (a) practiced it with rigor and a true sense of form and attention to detail as opposed to pastiche, and (b) who took it into more interesting realms than the usual pretty decoration. In that I am still exploring the form and trying new things and constantly moving through "style," I think I'm some-what of an iconoclast. I'm prideful that I'm hard to pin down, while at the same time recognizing that this makes it very difficult for clients to choose me because they're never sure what they're going to get. Having said that, my best work has always been for those who trusted me to do something new.

What makes you the most happy about your practice?

Feeling understood. That is not to say I always am—in fact I think I'm often misunderstood, but in those times when people get what I'm trying to do, or experience something exactly the way I wanted them to experience it, that is incredibly gratifying.

The National (The Wiltern)
Poster
Artwork and Design:
Marian Bantjes
2010

G2 Cover: Puzzle
Special (This Page)
Artwork: Marian Bantjes
Client: G2 (The Guardian)
Art Director: Richard Turley
2007

Andy Cruz and Rich Roat

There's a Type Designer in the House

Andy Cruz and Rich Roat founded Brand Design Co., Inc., in March of 1993 and House Industries shortly thereafter. Their first idea was to make a living by doing good work for graphic design clients, but they soon found that the world and their ambitions were much more complex than that simple notion. Twenty years later, though, the goal is still the same, even if the scale, people, and process have changed. House Industries is a highly respected type foundry and entrepreneurial design producer. Their fonts are derived from popular cultural references, and they have the rights to the historic Photo-Lettering collection of the 1960s. Now they say that their mission is "Doing Good Work With Good People" wherever those people might be—licensees, licensors, clients, or collaborators. (Rich Roat is answering my questions for House.)

Was it the digital revolution that prompted you to start a type foundry?
No, that really had already gone down by the time we got in the game. We were just looking for an alternate revenue stream and started assembling some simple lettering styles cooked up by Andy Cruz and our original partner, Allen Mercer.

How many designers/workers are there at House, and how do you break down the work?
We have two people working full-time on type, but that doesn't mean they are drawing type all of the time. Ken Barber is an amazing type designer, but much of his time is spent creating lettering treatments for various projects and directing contract type designers.

We have three or four contractors working on the Photo-Lettering collection at any given time plus two or three contractors who are helping us expand the House Industries collection.

Did you have a long-term business plan, or was this seat-of-the-pants?
I don't think you can call it seat-of-the-pants because we are a fully functioning company in the traditional sense with decent salaries, retirement plans, and really good health benefits. However, we've always found that a long-term business plan is an impediment to the creative process because it would require us to set arbitrary deadlines and revenue goals. Our best work is finished when it's finished and doesn't have a price tag attached.

Cast Iron Ampersand
Photography by
Carlos Alejandro
Design by House Industries

House Industries Catalog
Photography by
Carlos Alejandro
Design by House Industries

Why the name House Industries?
That's an easy one. We were getting some good press for our new company, Brand Design Co., Inc., and didn't want the new font venture to reflect badly on us when it failed. The name came from a clip art logo sheet we found in our swipe file that had a house next to a factory, so we called the company House Industries.

What did you do to distinguish House Industries from other digital foundries?
I don't think we ever considered ourselves a "digital foundry" because there are so many other facets to our business. We would rather look at the House Industries and Photo-Lettering type collections as perpetual projects that we design for and around.

You have an interesting balance of type, type-related ancillaries, and products in your "store." How do you decide on what products to create?
Most of our product development is based on visual dynamics, which is a fancy way of saying that if something looks really cool, we try to produce it. The products are also a way for us to take a macro view of typographic elements as illustrative assets instead of components in a system of glyphs.

House, in fact, houses some important collections of letters and fonts, like the Photo-Lettering collection. What made you purchase vintage typefaces for retail use?
We never looked at Photo-Lettering as "vintage." The collection and the lessons we've learned from it are visually

relevant in any era. We use pieces of that collection every day in our design work, so it's been an amazing aesthetic investment.

When type designers approach you with their designs, what determines what you will take on to be published or distributed by House?
We work with an amazing group of type designers, but we do not normally take on submissions from outside the company. Most of the ideas and concepts are generated by us, and then we try to find the best person for the project.

When hiring for House, what do you need and whom do you look for?
Someone who has worked for us as an intern for at least six months. We're still not sure what we're looking for, but if they've stuck with us for that long, they're probably worth hiring.

Big and Tall Blocks and Box
Photography by Carlos Alejandro
Design by House Industries

Alphabet
Factory Blocks
Photography by
Carlos Alejandro
Design by House
Industries

Heath Neutraface
Tiles and Packaging
Photography by
Carlos Alejandro
Design by House
Industries

Wooden Koi
Photography by
Carlos Alejandro
Design by House
Industries

Pierre di Scuillo

Typography That Speaks Up

Pierre di Scuillo is a French graphic designer and typographer whose wayfinding signage systems are both original and visually arresting. His fanzine _Who Resists? (Qui? Résiste)_, published sporadically since 1983, is an experimental publication in which he writes as well as draws his distinctive letterforms and alphabets. His work—printed, painted, molded, carved, or chiseled—is often seen in public spaces in the form of typographical sculptures, designs for facades, banners, posters, and temporary or permanent installations. "It all began for me back when I had a Mac 128—one of the firsts," he recalls. "It had a fabulous little piece of software called Fontastic with which I could create my own typefaces, much nicer ones than the ghastly typefaces proposed by the computer."

How did you become a typographer?
In 1985, for the fifth issue of _Qui? Résiste,_ an underground magazine I published sporadically at the time, I began to design strange letterforms. I have always loved to pun and play with the sound of words (when I was young, I studied music). My odd-looking letterforms were an attempt to make my headlines heard as well as seen. Ever since, I have been obsessed with typography as musical notation—with letters as representations of sounds.

By 1988, thanks to scalable vector graphics now available, I was ready to design entire alphabets, which I did for the eighth issue of my magazine. I then realized that type design was at the crossroad of many of my passions: the music of words, the relationship between form and content, poetry, abstract signs, and playful mischiefs. Finally, in 1995, I hit my stride as a type designer when I was able to create a family of typefaces for the traditional Tuareg language, for the nomadic inhabitants of the Sahara. The experience taught me to look at letterforms critically.

Your typefaces are not commercialized. Do you create them for specific projects, and then, occasionally, you tweak them and use them again?
In my notebook, I design typefaces constantly, as I would practice the piano or do vocal exercises. I like to rearrange the letters of a word to produce new words. It is basically a musical exercise, one used by Bach in the playful contrapuntal composition of his fugues. Our alphabet is based on

Outdoors installation,
Royaumont, France (opposite)
Designer: Pierre di Sciullo
2012

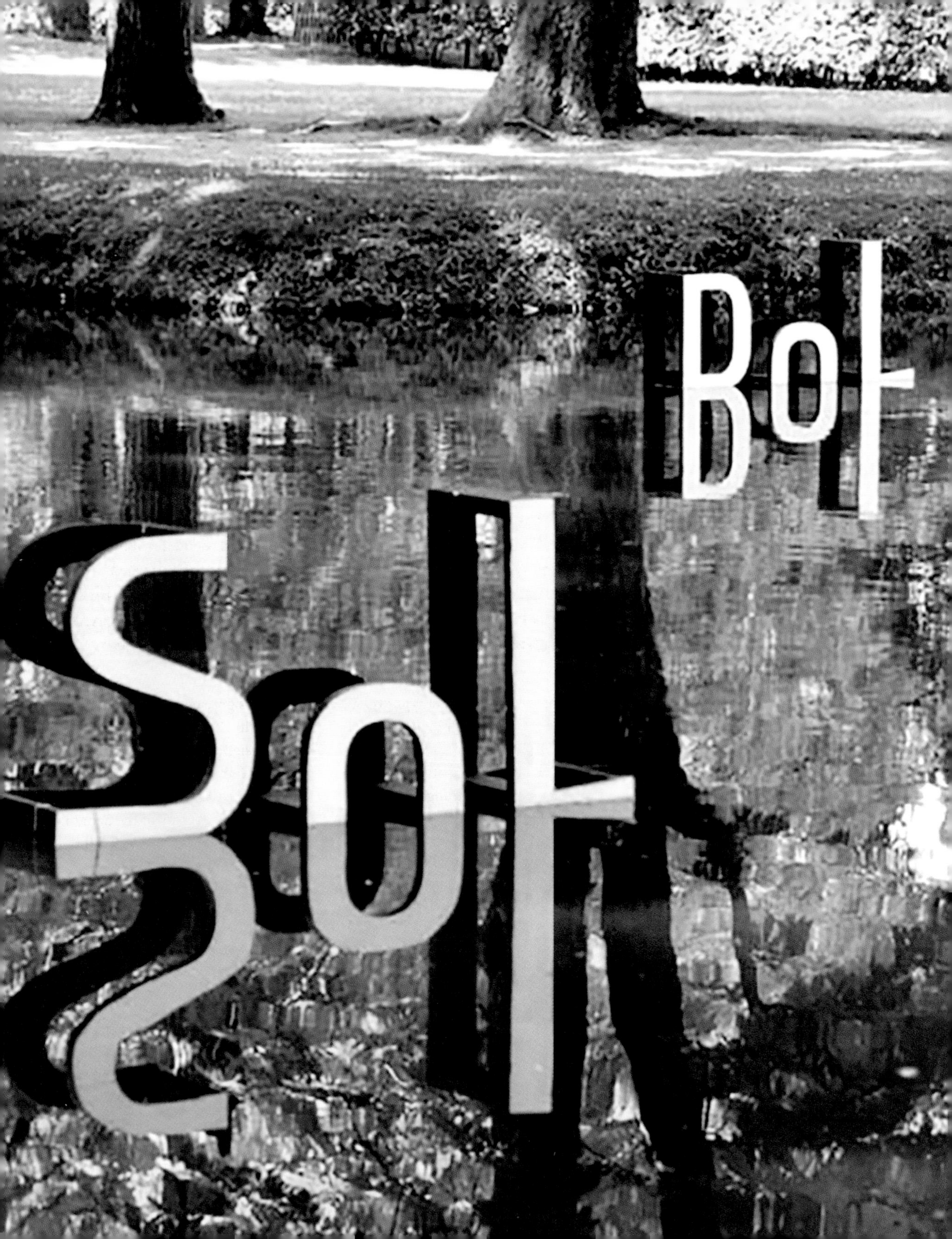
Bol
Sol

Signage for a Movie Theater,
Forum des images, Paris
Designer: Pierre di Sciullo
2008

sounds, so highlighting the oral quality of the letterforms with anagrams is both fun and tempting.

But I only develop full alphabets for specific jobs, as part of the problem-solving process. From time to time (in the last 25 years!), I think about perfecting some of my typefaces in order to commercialize them, but I procrastinate. The amount of work required to finalize a typeface is enormous, and I prefer to work on new projects rather than reassess old ones.

Was it difficult to "sell" your anagrammatic signposts to the city of Brest?

It was easy because the assignment was to make an "artistic" statement. My work was part of an initiative to create,

along the new tram route, a series of playful installations. It is not unusual in France for towns to ask artists to contribute to urban planning. Once I was in (I won a competition), the city officials trusted me. I had a good track record regarding urban signage—it wasn't my first "playful" project. But I have to confess that I had a lot of fun shuffling around the letters of the word *Recouvrance* to create serendipitous and surrealist wordplays.

Some of your alphabets mimic vocal intonations. How do you do that?

Practically, you cannot combine a traditional phonetic alphabet with correct spelling, but you can use intuitive graphic notations, such as the thickness or the relative height of letters, to indicate tone of voice and pitch. My goal is often to delight the eye and stimulate the voice.

How do you explain the effectiveness of your odd-looking letterforms and pictograms for wayfinding projects?
My work is not decorative—it is informative and serves a purpose. What could be more satisfying for a designer like me than to be able to combine functionality, fun and form?

In the press, you are described as an "artist." At the same time, your clients expect you to deliver rational and readable design solutions.

In France, is it possible to have credibility as both an artist and a designer?
You would have to talk to my clients to get this answer. Let's say that I am a "creative type" working in the field of graphic design. My clients come to me when they want something different or when they have a hybrid project that's hard to describe. I never boast about my work as being "poetic"—that would be counterproductive. Poetry, like true elegance, comes and goes as it pleases, slipping away when you call it. I prefer to focus on the way I work: I collaborate with architects, with city officials, with urban planners. What I love about my work is not so much the result but the challenges along the way. I am particularly aware of how difficult it is to stay creative in the face of administrative hurdles and political pressures. I meet incredibly smart peo-ple—people involved with public work and cultural programs—and that is what's most stimulating. I am learning all the time. What a treat!

Anagrams of "Recouvrance," Signage for a Tram Route, Brest, France
Designer: Pierre di Sciullo
2013

Signage, The Briqueterie Dance Center, Vitry, France
Designer: Pierre di Sciullo
2013

Ross MacDonald

An Illustrator's Passion for Type

Walpurgisnacht
Client: Steven Smith
Designer: Ross MacDonald
Director: Steven Smith
Illustrator: Ross MacDonald
2010

Ross MacDonald describes himself this way: "I do illustration for books and magazines, I write and illustrate children's books, I design—mostly book covers—and I design and make props for movies. The props are mainly graphic props—documents, books, magazines, maps, and so on" He also is proprietor of Brightwork Press in Newtown, Connecticut, where he prints ephemera on a few antique letterpresses with vintage wood and metal type. He may emphasize his illustration work, but he is typographically fluent and design savvy. He also knows the past and present of art and design and how to make them work together.

You've worked as an illustrator. How has the digital media affected your work in the past decade?

Initially, there was a lot of fear that digital media would supplant traditional media. I haven't seen that happening so far, but the day's not over yet. It just seems to have added a lot of additional outlets. Some of the magazines and book publishers I work for now have very active websites that publish new material, so I'm doing separate work for the print and digital publications.

How would you describe your illustration style?

I work in traditional media—watercolor and ink and pencil crayon—and I draw most of my inspiration from illustration styles of the late nineteenth and early twentieth centuries. Sometimes I will work directly in the style of an old comic book or a Dick and Jane reader, using that style as part of the concept of the piece.

You've also created "vintage" film props, often relying on letters. Did this just fall into your lap?

I had done a little television work off and on for years, but in 1993 I was hired to work on a movie called *Baby's Day Out*, produced by John Hughes. They were looking for someone to create a faux 1930s children's book and had seen my work in that style in magazines. The book was a major plot point in the movie and integral to a lot of scenes, so I worked on set in Chicago for six months and met a lot of people. Some of those people hired me or recommended me when they went on to work on other movies, and it kind of snowballed from there.

Tree
Client: Northern Credit Union
Art Director: Michael Bryden
Illustrator: Ross MacDonald
2013

Having It All
Client: *The Atlantic*
Art Director: Eliza Glass
Illustrator: Ross MacDonald
2013

You are an antique type maven. How did this come about? And how do you maintain it?

I actually started life as a printer, in my teens. In 1974 I worked at a place in Toronto called Coach House Press for a year, and setting type and printing on the Vandercook was one of my duties, in addition to offset printing. I moved on to doing illustration and writing and left printing behind for a while. In the mid-1990s, I was living in New York and started getting the letterpress bug again. I got a Poco proof press and a few fonts of type, and then something snapped and in a couple of years I had amassed a bunch of wood type and presses. In 1996 my wife and I moved out to Connecticut, where I have a small barn/studio, and I was able to expand the letterpress opera-tion. At one time I had four presses. Now I have two, and hundreds of fonts of wood and metal type.

You are proprietor of the Brightwork Press. What do you do at the press?

It's a one-man shop. Occasionally, I have interns here who help a bit, but I do most of the setting and printing myself. I don't take on much printing work for other people—a few things for friends here and there. I mostly print things I design myself. Often it's paper props—cards, letterheads, tags, posters—that kind of thing.

Your typography is based on the old types you've collected. Why should designers be fluent in the antique?

Understanding why typefaces look like they do, and where they came from, can have a huge effect on a designer's work. I always say that digging into the history of design will take you places you will never find on your own.

How would young designers become knowledgeable about metal, wood, and letterpress printing?

There are lots of great books, for starters. There are also a lot of good websites. You can spend hours watch-ing videos of type and presses and typecasting machines on YouTube. Hands-on experience is the best way to learn. There are places like the Arm in Brooklyn and the Center for Book Arts in New York where you can get your hands on type and presses. Taking classes on typesetting and printing is a lot of fun and will give you the kind of understanding that you can't get from books.

What is the greatest benefit for you?

The main benefit is that I find it hugely interesting and a lot of fun. One of the other benefits has been the ability to produce historically accurate period props.

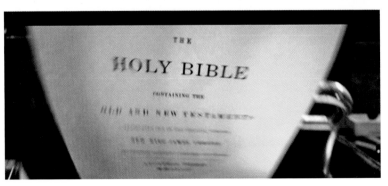

The Book of Eli
Client: Alcon Entertainment/
Warner Brothers
Designer: Ross MacDonald
Leadman: Tommy Samona
2010

Boardwalk Empire
Client: *Boardwalk Empire*, HBO
Designer: Ross MacDonald
Propmaster: Vinny Mazzarella
Illustrator: Ross MacDonald
2013

Roberto de Vicq
de Cumptich

For the Love of Type

Roberto de Vicq de Cumptich was born in Rio de Janeiro, Brazil, and moved to New York to pursue an MFA at Pratt Institute in the early 1980s. He has worked primarily with publishing houses in New York, first with Condé Nast Magazines, then as creative director for Broadway Books and later HarperCollins. In 2007 he left HarperCollins to start his own design firm—de Vicq design. "The great part of my clients are still in publishing," he says, "but slowly I am branching out in other areas like restaurant design and branding." His main interest is the expressive use of typography, which comes through in his book jackets and covers. "I fell in love with the work and the process," he adds; "book jackets are a blend of editorial and product design. Each book is different; each has its own story."

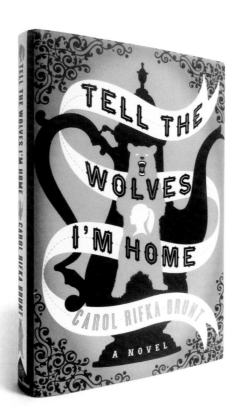

...Wolves I'm Home
...er: Roberto de Vicq
...ptich
...ctor: Tom Stvan
...Random House

Me Before You
Designer: Roberto de Vicq
de Cumptich
Art Director: Roseanne Serra
Client: Penguin

How would you describe your typographic approach?

For me, type is the best indicator of the zeitgeist. Type is an imperfect version of ideal forms where you try to peg your concepts. Type is like silly putty: endless possibilities and lovely to play with.

You were typographically designing book jackets for ages. How did you begin in this specialized genre?

It was a series of trial-and-error situations. I began my career designing corporate work, but perhaps being at the bottom of the ladder and the kind of clients I had, it was dreary. I then

...azines but discovered that unless you were the art director, the fonts and images were already chosen; you have very few liberties. I was ready to move to Paris, but while polishing my French at Alliance Française, a fellow student, who was going on maternity leave, asked me if I could fill in for her at Pantheon Books.

When it was time to branch out into other client areas, how did you go about it?

I asked friends to send me any work that was not in publishing and made some cold calls myself. My first major restaurant, My Thai, was for a family friend in Brazil. In lieu of a design fee,

she kindly allowed me full creative control and a healthy budget. I saw endless possibilities in this market and the opportunity to branch out from book jacket design.

You do food, restaurants, publications, and logos. What is the most satisfying?
Good work and good clients are the most gratifying should be the answer, but I have to say I enjoy restaurant design. They are special spaces where the purpose is the enjoyment of the experience. Translating this into every-

Le Diplomate
Designer: Roberto de Vicq de Cumptich
Creative Director: Randi Sirkin
Client: Starr Restaurants

thing from large signage to business cards is challenging yet fun.

What do you look for in a client?
Normally, I look for Catherine the Great: the enlightened tyrant. Someone with taste and ideas that I can grow with—even if we disagree.

What do you look for in an employee?
Curiosity, flexibility, and an ability to critique one's own work: the basic predispositions for a good graphic designer. I am also lazy, so I badger my wife to help me.

What is the most important bit of knowledge a designer should have?
There are always several different solutions for any problem, but only one at a time.

How many typefaces can you love?

Letterforms are like people: It takes time to get to know them. If you lived to be 100, you might befriend two or three font families—maximum. Some of the best graphic designers have become up close and personal with only two typefaces.

In contrast, some of the more really dreadful designs stem from the notion that the choice of a typeface must reflect the personality of the client. Sappy-looking cursives are used to enforce stereotypes about femininity. Antique typefaces are recruited to evoke old-world flavor. Sturdy slab serifs are reserved for situations that require you come into a room, shut the door, and pound your fists on the table.

Picking typefaces as you would an outfit for a costume party is a recipe for trite blandness. Instead, look forward to your life as a graphic designer as the opportunity to develop a meaningful relationship with a very small coterie of intimate friends: Franklin Gothic Condensed (you'll love the lower case "g"), Garamond Regular (but not the italic), or Interstate, so snazzy with its short and slanted terminals. On the other hand, you may never ever want to have anything to do with Aldus or Cooper Black. It's alright. Typefaces are personal. So personal, in fact, that you will end up only liking your favorite fonts in some sizes, but not others.

You'll be a bully when it comes to letter spacing, as you should. And colors! Not green, please! That's for pool tables, not typefaces. Then, one day, on a road in rural England, you'll come across a highway sign set in lowercase Transport Medium: white letters on a green background. You'll stop the car, put it in reverse, and back up on the shoulder, just to take a picture.

Transport Medium, by Jock Kinnear and Margaret Calvert. You'll be smitten.

Willem Sandberg was partial to Bodoni Stencil—drawn by hand—but he also had a soft spot for Clarendon.

Massimo and Leila Vignelli only had eyes for Helvetica and called upon Boboni just as an occasional sidekick.

Whenever in doubt, Paul Rand reached for Futura.

Jan Tschichold was a fan of Akzidenz-Grotesk and Haettenschweiler (only later in life did he desert them for Sabon).

Fabien Baron built his stellar career as an editorial art director solely on Didot.

5 Making Logos and Marks

The logo or trademark is the cornerstone of graphic identity (not to be confused with "branding," which is the entire process of creating an identity). The logo is the mark that reduces all business attributes into a recognizable sign. The reason for developing a particular mark is often based on research into a company's mission and the synthesis of its ideals into a symbol or brand. The mark itself might be so abstract that no obvious connection can be made, but, simply, the imposed relationship between it and the company imbues it with meaning.

The logo is usually the most charged design element of a company, sometimes inviolate, other times mutable, depending on the client's faith in the mark's symbolic power. A logo must appeal to the client (and the public) on cognitive and emotional levels; it is not simply a graphic device to denote one business from another, but, like a national flag, a charged symbol of corporate philosophy.

Much has been written about the philosophy and psychology of logos and marks. Marks have value when associated with good companies and are valueless when attached to bad ones. The swastika is a case in point. Prior to its adoption as the Nazi party symbol in 1926 (and German national symbol in 1933), the swastika's history dated back to antiquity, when it signified good fortune. In the early twentieth century, it was a very popular commercial mark used on scores of products. But once it was adopted by a heinous regime, it was inextricably wed to evil. The design of the swastika is simple, pure, and memorable, while its symbolic meaning is forever tainted. Nevertheless, once the logo is decided upon, then designing the other elements of corporate identity must proceed.

Mark Fox

The Mark Maker

Mark Fox started working at the age of 17 as a printer's devil, a pasteup artist, a cameraman, and a stripper for offset presses. In college he found employment with Wasserman Silkscreen in Santa Monica and with the Communications Department of UCLA. Most of his post-college career has been spent as a designer, educator, and occasional writer. Today he specializes in the design of symbols: trademarks—including monograms and wordmarks—icons and avatars. The kinds of symbols he designs are all "compressed carriers of meaning," he says. From 1986 to 2007, Fox worked alone under the name BlackDog. Nowadays, he collaborates with Angie Wang at their San Francisco studio, Design is Play; currently he is an associate professor in the graphic design program at California College of the Arts (CCA), where he has taught since 1993.

Much of your work is making icons and logos. How did you get started?
I didn't study design in college—my degree is in fine arts—so I didn't have any school assignments with which to build a portfolio. As a result, I spent the year after college inventing projects I could execute on the cheap but that still looked good. One couldn't produce a convincing annual report by oneself at that time—this was 1984— but one could design a convincing trademark and present it as a clean black-and-white stat at little expense. I spent three days a week for a year designing fake trademarks for fake businesses in an effort to create a portfolio. Fortunately, my fake trademarks proved strong enough to get me a job with Michael Schwab.

What is a logo? A trademark? A symbol?
A symbol suggests rather than depicts; it represents not only itself, but also some larger, external narrative. This narrative may be religious, cultural, commercial, or personal in nature.

In his 1952 essay "On Trademarks," Herbert Bayer refers to the trademark as a form of "pictorial stenography." A good trademark is glyphic and functions as visual shorthand for a commercial endeavor (i.e., a company, product, or service). All trademarks are symbols, but not all symbols are trademarks. The term logo as applied to corporate identity is a relatively recent addition to the design lexicon, its first recorded use in English dating to 1937. (It appears to be a shorter variation of

Dog Lamp
Client: In-House
2001–2011

Trademark for UC Press
Client: University of
California Press
Studio: BlackDog
Designer: Mark Fox
Illustrator: Mark Fox
2005

Logo for Coffee Company
Client: Four Barrel Coffee
Studio: Design is Play
Designers: Mark Fox and
Angie Wang
Letterer: Mark Fox
2008

CCA monogram
Client: California College of the Arts
Studio: BlackDog
Designer: Mark Fox
Letterer: Paul Renner (1924–1927)
2003

the nineteenth-century terms logograph, logogram, or logotype.) As it originates from the Greek word for speech or word, the term logo is applicable to anything from a nonlingual symbol (such as the Nike "swoosh") to a corporate motto. Its range, therefore, is rather vast. Although more prosaic, I prefer the clarity of a trademark.

When you start one, what goes through your mind?
What is the client's point of differentiation? What makes their approach, service, or product unique or superior? What ideas or associations does their name conjure? What are the key letters that comprise their name? What would be an appropriate typographic "voice"? What aspect of the design problem excites me? Where in the problem can I find interest, amusement, or beauty? What typographic forms make me happy?

How do you know when it is right?
When the idea is smart or original; when the forms are beautiful or well crafted; when I like looking at it. When possible, I strive to create trademarks that don't simply identify but that pull the eye and hold it, that reward repeated viewings.

Is it better to use type or just image?
Either can work, but images have the advantage of being translingual and of occupying less horizontal space. (Paul Rand compares the trademark to a "coin," a self-contained unit.) When done well, the monogram seems to offer the best of both approaches: functions as type and image. (The Chanel mono-

gram is a good example: Its forms are both decoded as language and seen as abstract shapes.)

Do you think trademark and icon making is an inborn talent or a learned skill?
One may be born with "an eye" or with the facility to make marks, but these abilities will either be cultivated through practice or eroded through neglect. Our bodies are no different: One's muscles become stronger with use and weaker with disuse. Innate talent is only a benefit when there is a continual application of that talent.

You teach. What is the tenet or idea you teach most?
I believe that the primary idea I convey is authorship. My students develop their symbols from scratch, through iterative sketching. The final forms are executed the old-fashioned way, with a Rapidograph technical pen and a drafting board. The precision demanded by this process forces the students to pay attention, to be deliberate in their decision making, and to become "makers" and "authors" in the sense of being the origin (and thus the authority) of their own work. My curriculum celebrates the designer as maker or designer as author; it stands in opposition to the designer as reassembler of images lifted from the Internet.

Avatar for the CCA Graphic Design
Facebook Page
Client: California College of the Arts
Graphic Design Program
Studio: Design is Play
Designers: Mark Fox and Angie Wang
Illustration: Mark Fox
2013

Logo for L.A. Boulders
Client: L.A.B
Studio: Design is Play
Designers: Mark Fox and Angie Wang
Letterer: Mark Fox
2013

BO.LT
Client: BO.LT
Studio: Design is Play
Designers: Mark Fox and Angie Wang
Illustration: Mark Fox
2010

Logo for Indoor Climbing Gym
Client: The Studio
Studio: Design is Play
Designers: Mark Fox and Angie Wang
Illustrator and Letterer: Mark Fox
2011

Logo Emarko Restaurant
Client: Embarko
Studio: BlackDog
Designer: Mark Fox
Letterer: Mark Fox
1989

6 Books and Book Jackets

The publishing industry remains a major employer of graphic designers. Publishers use design to package and sell their merchandise, and while it may seem crass to discuss books as products, this is exactly how they are conceived and marketed. It is the book designer's job to cast the text and images in an accessible and pleasing manner; it is the book jacket designer's job to create an alluring wrapper. Book and book jacket designers have more creative license than most food and hardware package designers, but the goal is the same: to move a product off the shelves. As shelves become less important, there will be a change in the way book jackets and covers are designed, but the industry is not yet sure what that will be.

The book design profession is divided into two basic categories—book interior and book jacket—that have a number of subsets. The book designer is responsible for the interior design for books with text or with few or no pictures, such as novels and certain nonfiction. The jacket designer is responsible for the hardcover dust jacket, paperback cover, or paper-over-boards wrapper. Good typography skill is an essential skill for both.

It is useful to explain the genres of publishing, for each requires a different kind of design. Industry sectors are conventionally categorized as follows: trade or commercial, which produces fiction and nonfiction books aimed at a general

audience; professional, which caters its products to the needs of specific professional groups; and textbook, which produces educational books for school- or coursework. Within these basic categories, publishers might specialize in areas such as pop fiction, military biography, graphic design how-to books, and so forth. Perhaps the largest publishing genre, however, is the mass-market paperback—cheaply produced novels (romances, mysteries, science fiction, Westerns, etc.) that are marketed not just in bookstores but also in airports, drugstores, supermarkets, and the like. Some publishers are known for highbrow content, others for middle- or lowbrow content. Some publishers are enormous conglomerates that release hundreds of titles in a season (usually fall, winter, and spring); others are comparatively small proprietorships with a limited number of books.

Some publishers have a tradition of fine classical typography; others promote contemporary sensibilities, and a number do not have any house style or overarching design philosophy at all. Some publishers doggedly follow conventions imposed on their specific genre, while others are more inventive. When seeking employment in a publishing house art department, be familiar with the house's method (or lack thereof) in order to tailor your portfolio accordingly.

There are many ways to become involved in book design. The two most common are as an in-house or freelance designer. A publishing house art department includes a creative director or art director who manages other designers and also designs book jackets and interiors. In some houses, there are separate art directors for interiors and jackets; in others, one art director manages both. In some publishing houses, design services come under the aegis of the production department.

The larger American trade publishing houses, such as Knopf, Simon & Schuster, and Farrar, Straus & Giroux, can release as many as 150 or more titles per season, each requiring interior and jacket design. In instances where the art director and staff designers cannot handle the workload, or the art director requires a unique or special approach, freelance designers are commissioned. The freelancer may be the principal

or an employee of a design firm or studio or an independent contractor who specializes in book design. Most publishing houses maintain an expanding stable of freelancers, who are selected according to the appropriateness of their individual illustrative or typographic style. To become a freelancer specializing in book design, it is necessary either to show a portfolio or send a promotional mailer (each with mostly book-related work) to the art director.

Mass-market paperback houses often produce three times as many books as the average trade publisher, usually on a monthly or bimonthly basis. Their book covers are invariably more hard-sell than those of trade books, with screaming titles, authors names set large and in garish colors or metallic embossing, and seductive illustrations that leave little to the imagination. Most paperback art departments employ a few staff designers responsible for a specific number of covers on a list. Staff production persons routinely handle the interiors, which follow a more or less strict typographic format. Paperback designers often commission freelance illustrators to render cover illustrations and sometimes the lettering as well. Realistic or narrative paintings, mood photographs, and custom lettering are the usual design components for mass-market paperbacks, and specialists in these areas are often in demand for fairly fast turnaround work.

Publishing houses that produce professional, textbook, and subspecialty books more often than not use in-house art departments for the majority of design and production work. On the whole, these houses produce less adventuresome products but rather follow house styles and standards developed over time. For the neophyte, working in this environment provides considerable experience and perhaps an interesting assignment or two per season, but most of the work is fairly routine.

One other sector of publishing, book packaging, has exerted a strong influence on design. Book packagers are independent producers of books and related products who sell complete packages—text, illustration, design, and sometimes printed books—to publishers and distributors. Increasingly, large publishing houses purchase a certain number of book packages—usually the visual books on their lists. The larger packagers are likely to have their own art department, staffed by a creative or art director, staff designers, and production persons. These positions are excellent opportunities to do creative work because there is little or no separation of labor; a visual book must be designed from jacket to index by a single designer to ensure the integrity of the package. Smaller book packagers use a fair number of freelancers and select candidates based on the quality of a portfolio and experience in total book design.

Not every designer can do book design well, just as not every jacket designer can create an effective or inspired interior. Different skills and talents are required, and although many designers have both, desire must be supplemented by knowledge.

While the jacket of a book functions as a mini-poster, the design of its inside requires a different kind of knowledge: the nuances of type, and, in the case of a visual book, understanding the nature of visual flow. And flow is not as easy as following a grid in placing pictures on a page; it involves knowing what elements complement each other, which picture crops contribute to the dynamism of the page, and how the pages should flow to achieve melody, harmony, and dissonance. Sometimes on-the-job training is adequate, but intensive study in school or a continuing education program is best.

Ultimately, a designer in book publishing might choose to stay in this specialty for a long or short time, depending, of course, on the nature of the job. Many art directors and designers devote their lives to the field because challenges are ever-present; others find the specialties too limiting and look for new opportunities in other creative media.

Scott-Martin Kosofsky

Making a Living Doing Books

Scott-Martin Kosofsky develops, edits, designs, and produces typefaces for books. He does everything up to the point plates are made, and often beyond that. He tries to stay up to date on the latest developments in press technologies and likes to know the "language" of the buttons and dials, insofar as they influence the final product. "I like technology, both old and new," he asserts, "not so much for its own sake, but as toolboxes that have their own sensibilities." His work falls into two unrelated categories: Jewish liturgy and Hebrew Bible, intensely typographic books that reach a very large but restricted market; and image-driven books on widely diverse subjects. He works in a large converted garage in a heavily wooded neighborhood in Lexington, Massachusetts, about 12 miles from Boston, with his wife, Betsy Sarles, a designer and his chief consultant.

CCAR. Title Page.
The Sh'ma prayer in the forthcoming "Machzor Mishkan HaNefesh," the Reform machzor published by the Central Conference of American Rabbis, 2015

The large Hebrew type is Hillel, by Scott-Martin Kosofsky, based upon Ashkenazic manuscripts of the fourteenth century.

You design books in the digital age with precision and detail, but you come from an analog world. Was it hard to make the transition?
I spent a decade casting and composing metal type, which certainly informed my sensibilities, giving me a window into the working ways of the old masters and also a sense of how our reading habits were formed. I was aware that working exclusively in metal type would have forever restricted my possibilities, so I decided to bring what I learned to whatever was the current technology.

I'm very adaptable; if owned a time machine and found myself stranded any time after 1450, I'd be perfectly happy. I worked with film type to a small extent, and more in early digital (pre-PostScript). Through a friendship with the owner of a large commercial printing company, I was able to get a free slot in the Scitex training program in the early 1980s, so when Photoshop appeared not long after, I was able to use it for high-end work, even when the speed and capacity of early Macs was still limited. Similarly, I had done some consulting work on type quality for a company called Compugraphic (it later became Agfa), in which I could parlay what I knew about sidebearings and spacing into the digital realm. When Fontographer was introduced in the late 1980s, I was home free. Rather than complain about the inadequacy of other people's work, I could do it all myself. It was empowering and exciting—and it still is, as the possi-

OXFORD HEBREW BIBLE
התנ"ך אוקספורד
EDITED BY Ronald Hendel

Genesis 1:1-4 | Greek Septuagint

Compare With ▼

Views ▼

בְּרֵאשִׁית בָּרָא אֱלֹהִים אֵת 1
1 At the beginning of God's creating of the
הַשָּׁמַיִם וְאֵת הָאָרֶץ: 2 וְהָאָרֶץ
heavens and the earth, 2 when the earth was wild
הָיְתָה תֹהוּ וָבֹהוּ וְחֹשֶׁךְ עַל-פְּנֵי
and waste, darkness over the face of the ocean,
תְהוֹם וְרוּחַ אֱלֹהִים מְרַחֶפֶת עַל-
rushing-spirit of God hovering over the face of the
פְּנֵי הַמָּיִם: 3 וַיֹּאמֶר אֱלֹהִים יְהִי
waters—3 God said: Let there be light! And there
אוֹר וַיְהִי-אוֹר: 4 וַיַּרְא אֱלֹהִים
was light. 4 God saw that the light was good, and
אֶת-הָאוֹר כִּי-טוֹב וַיַּבְדֵּל אֱלֹהִים
he separated the light from the darkness. 5 God
בֵּין הָאוֹר וּבֵין הַחֹשֶׁךְ: 5 וַיִּקְרָא
called the light "day," and the darkness he called
אֱלֹהִים | לָאוֹר יוֹם וְלַחֹשֶׁךְ קָרָא

1 ἐν ἀρχῇ ἐποίησεν ὁ θεὸς τὸν οὐρανὸν καὶ
1 In the beginning God made the heaven and the
τὴν γῆν 2 ἡ δὲ γῆ ἦν ἀόρατος καὶ ἀ
earth. 2 Yet the earth was invisible and unformed,
κατασκεύαστος καὶ σκότος ἐπάνω τῆς ἀ
and the darkness was over the abyss, and a divine
βύσσου καὶ πνεῦμα θεοῦ ἐπεφέρετο ἐπάνω
wind was being carried along... the water. 3
τοῦ ὕδατος 3 καὶ εἶπεν... ...νηθήτω φ
And God said, "Let light come in... ...nd
ὡς καὶ ἐγένετο φῶς 4 καὶ εἶ... ...τὸ φ
light came into being. 4 And God saw...
ὡς ὅτι καλὸν καὶ διεχώρισεν...
that it was good. And G..d separated
μέσον τοῦ φωτὸς... ...
light and between the...
σκότους 5 καὶ ἐκάλε...
the light Day and the darkn...
μέραν καὶ τὸ σκότος ἐκάλ...

01:31 ◀◀ ▶ ▶▶ -00.53

Biblical Hebrew Demo
This is the way biblical Hebrew was cast and set in metal type, based on my measurements taken of justified matrices at the Plantin-Moretus Museum, Antwerp.

The type was made by Scott-Martin Kosofsky and Matthew Carter, after Guillaume Le Bé, 1567.

bilities of OpenType are still evolving, even though at present it can be a kind of ugly place, with klunky applications that lack decent interfaces and a lot of homemade Python scripting. (It's the revenge of the nerds, I tell you.)

What about the printed book is so appealing?
Texture is a quality that most people relate to "fine press" printing, not commercial work, but it can be an important factor in commercial work, too, and it's the reason I work closely with materials manufacturers on some projects. With the Conservative High Holidays prayerbook, *Mahzor Lev Shalem*, I cajoled Domtar, the paper maker, to make a very light stock (28#) that had good color, sufficient opacity, and a good "hand" that would create a pleasant sensation when people ran their fingers over the pages. The binding material, which was made in Rhode Island by Ecological Fibers, has an extremely warm, tender feel, which is a by-product of the top coat. Ecological is willing to work with designers to come up with new things, and their process, which sometimes involves

gravure cylinders, has endless possibilities. I've been the guest of a number of synagogues for High Holiday services, and time after time I'm approached by congregants who comment as much on the feel of the books as the typography. Men tend to talk about the typography, whereas women just as often talk about the touch. I'm very conscious of my engaging in an act of seduction, which is especially effective when it's unexpected. Needless to say, given the gravity of the High Holidays, it's only a psychological seduction.

Can you make a living designing books?
Not by design alone. You have to be able to do more things that create added value to your work in order to hold onto whatever money is in the system. High-end image prep,

Asylum: Inside the Closed World of State Mental Hospitals
by Christopher Payne and Oliver Sacks
Client: The MIT Press
Designer: Scott-Martin Kosofsky
2009

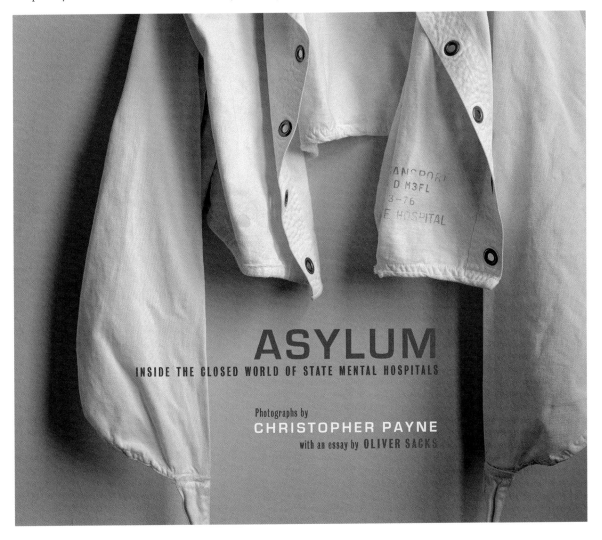

obviating the need for the printer to intervene, is one example; font work is another. Being a good compositor, providing better work than can be bought elsewhere, is a major one; specialty composition in multiple alphabets (non-Latin) is a very high-value skill. If you add to that serious editorial skills, you can develop books and sell them to publishers as complete packages. But if you divide up the income among a number of people, there might not be enough, unless you are able to work very fast.

You are what we are now calling a "content developer." How do you define your role?

Most of the books I produce originate with ideas that someone has brought to me, most often someone I know. They're "near ideas" that need further development but have the kind of subject matter I like to develop, something I'm happy to live with for two or three years. There's no unifying theme to these books, although I like topics that I think will become part of the public consciousness and conversation in some new way.

Do you take ownership in what you produce? Are you an entrepreneur?

I always have some ownership stake—at least two slices, perhaps three. The difference between the cost of manufacturing and the price I agree on with the publisher is mine. In some projects, grants are involved, and I get a share of them as part of my agreement with the author. As I mentioned, I am also the author's agent, through which I receive a percentage of the royalties or advances. Grants are one reason I prefer to work with nonprofit publishers, such as university presses, as most grantors are required to give only to nonprofit organizations.

How can designers make more than their fees?

If you work for fees alone, it's very difficult to make a living. I did that for years, then, after a bad experience, I changed my business model entirely. Somehow, everything came together after that. What's nice is that I continue to derive some income from projects long finished. I made the investment, I gave it my all, so it seems reasonable that there's some return while people are still buying the books.

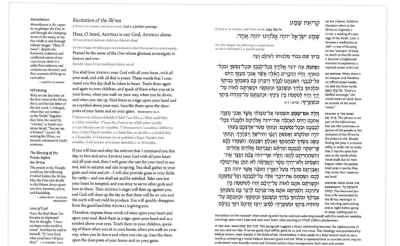

Michael Carabetta

Books and E-Books

A Wide Range of
Unique Offerings
Client: Chronicle Books
Art Director: Michael Carabetta

Michael Carabetta is creative director at Chronicle Books in the San Francisco Bay area. Initially, in 1991, he was hands-on, involved with every step of book design. Today, he is consulting across the board, offering his views on all print formats published by Chronicle—books, of course, but also calendars, notebooks, postcards, journals, stationery, and gift items. "But for books, I still take part in discussing and debating the finer points of cover design. Covers are critical because they are the last bit of marketing that a book can do, on its own, when it is on display tables in stores."

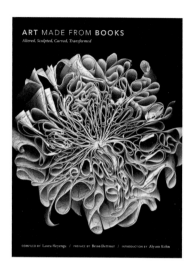

Art Made from Books
Client: Chronicle Books
Art Director: Michael Carabetta
2013

Half of my most favorite books on my shelves have been published in the United States by Chronicle Books. As the creative director of Chronicle, can you take credit for the pleasure I get from owning them?
I can take some credit for the aesthetic appeal of the Chronicle Books you own, though I would be quick to point out that all due credit should go to the design team, those who design and/or art direct the cadre of freelance designers we work with.

How long have you worked at Chronicle Books, and how has your work evolved over the years?
I've been at Chronicle for almost a quarter of a century! Back then there were three designers plus myself. Since the size of the design group has grown tenfold, and technology has become an integral part of how

we do things, I've taken on more of a global role in the look and feel of the company's brand. My work today can range from the design of our trade show environments and retail stores to conducting a Design Lab seminar with our design fellows, the recent graduates who spend six months working with us. Over that same period of time, I've proposed and implemented book ideas for Chronicle and for our sister company, Princeton Architectural Press. Of late, I have been instrumental in adding a line of letterpress stationery products to our list. I also teach, conduct workshops, and lecture on design at art schools and universities. And occasionally I will blog for the Chronicle website.

The titles of the books in your catalogue seem to promote a relentless and healthy optimism. Even one of your best sellers, *The Complete Worst-Case Scenario Survival Handbook*, is designed to make you smile. Is "good cheer" a value at the core of your brand?
I think humor, or "good cheer" as you put it, has always had a place in our

You Are So Loved
Client: Chronicle Books
Art Director: Michael Carabetta
2013

editorial hearts. Over the years, it has taken different forms and degrees of irreverence and subject matter, and today is sometimes augmented by available technology, namely, the sound chip. On the other hand, a good chocolate chip cookie made from one of our cookbooks can also bring a smile to one's face.

Am I wrong to assume that Chronicle Books celebrates what we all love in books: the thingness of it all? The enjoyment we derive from handling printed matter? The tactile implications?
In this day and age of everything digital, we value the tactile experience that handling a book can bring. It's an emotional experience as well. The choice of paper and binding materials, the printing, and the surprise that awaits you on the turn of every page is magic—and hard to replicate on a screen.

You have very few e-books on your website. The only one I could find had to do with cooking. Why this choice?
We recently published our 1000th e-book! We don't sell them on our site, though. The best place to find them and the few apps we produce, is on the Apple or Amazon sites for e-books. As I understand it, the facility for selling e-books is a complex one, and a lot of publishers are not equipped to handle transactions such as downloads, personnel, equipment, billing, and so on. It's better to leave it to those who

can readily fulfill the orders and are
in business to do so.

**I would love it if you could share with
our readers your insights about the
future of pulp-based publications. In
your opinion, is the power of print
here to stay?**
There is little doubt, especially here,
but also among those who write
critically about our culture, that the
physical book is here to stay. The
book has been and continues to be
an enduring artifact across time and
cultures. It's paradoxical that the
captains of the digital world—Jobs,
Gates, Ellison, Allen—all have had
books written about them, some of
them commissioned! The physical book
is an object of validation, in particular,
it seems, among technology leaders!
Of course, their books, and ours, are
available as e-books. As a business, we
need to respond to that segment of the
market that now consumes its books
electronically. So far we've published
1000 e-books—and counting.

**Each book published by Chronicle
seems to be its own thing. You do not
promote many series or collections.
Is this a strategy?**
You are mistaken. We have published
books in series form and continue to
do so, in particular in the children's
category. However, we have also
published cookbooks in series, going
back to the James McNair single-sub-
ject cookbooks and of late, a third
book in the Tartine series has just
been released. As for *The Complete
Worst-Case Scenario Survival Handbook*, it has over 30 titles in the line!

**What is the most important quality/
skill you expect from your designers?**
There are any number of qualities that
would make for a great designer, but
for me, the most important quality, is
curiosity. If you have curiosity, it can
lead to exploration, experimentation,
and insights to solve design or communication problems, whether in the
print or digital realms.

Restaurants to Check Out (top)
Client: Chronicle Books
Art Director: Michael Carabetta
2003

Books to Check Out (bottom)
Client: Chronicle Books
Art Director: Michael Carabetta
2001

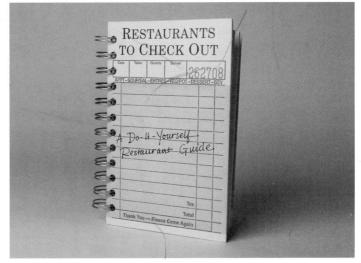

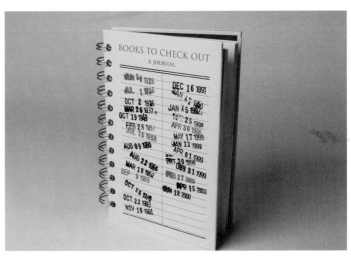

Paul Buckley

The Bookeeper

Paul Buckley is creative director at Penguin Books, overseeing the art and design needs for trade imprints, making sure Penguin's varied publishers have a talented art director and design team to match the tone and requirements of the types of books and authors they publish. From Thomas Pynchon to Jane Austen to John Le Carré to Terry MacMillan to Neil Young to Mike Tyson, they package a beautiful variety of authors. Buckley also personally art directs a few of the imprints, as well as designing some of the books and occasionally dabbling into illustration as well. He oversees a staff of 25 people and "a gazillion freelancers," he says. "I can barely type a sentence without being interrupted." He has never worked for another publishing house. "As a client, they embrace fun and creative work, and they treat me very well, so as a platform to show my wares, I could not be more lucky."

Choices
Creative Director: Mirko Ilic
Designer: Paul Buckley
Illustrator: Paul Buckley

What do you love about the book jacket and cover that you cannot find in other media?
I like tactile things that make a difference. Intelligent books are that for me. I could never be a web designer or design toothbrushes for a living or work for some soulless celebrity rag. With books, every day, every project, I get to explore different styles of art and design, and work with some of the best artists in the world. . . it is the perfect design job.

Do you have a "method" of art directing and designing covers?
Yes, as to art directing. . . find the right designer/artist/photographer/etc. that matches the tone of the writer . . . then convey the thoughts of my publisher

and editor, send them the manuscript, and insist they read it, and then try to be as hands off as possible—allow someone ownership of a project and they will try like hell to make you proud that you hired them. As to designing things myself, I mull . . . then hopefully a smart idea begins to form or serendipity strikes. If that fails, then panic sets in and I come up with something simply because I have to. As long as I put something fairly good in front of a publisher and editor, a constructive "let's maybe think about trying x, y, or z" conversation can take place.

You've created some beautiful series. How do you conceive of a series?
A lot of it comes from just being tired of going to the same well to solve a

Penguin Threads
Creative Director: Paul Buckley
Designer: Jillian Tamaki
Illustrator: Jillian Tamaki

problem and being aware of what outside influences are coming at me from day to day. . . What if we hired a slew of tattoo artists to illustrate a series of books; why not try embroidering covers and sculpt embossing them to feel every stitch; has anyone hired Jessica Hische to do a drop cap series A thru Z? No? Then let's think about that. Publishers are looking for good ideas—and not just from writers.

I am lucky that my Penguin publisher, Kathryn Court, and my Penguin Classics publisher, Elda Rotor, are open to collaborating on good ideas, and as long as what I'm

doing continues to succeed, then I maintain that trust and a steady diet of fun projects. So many people take design so seriously—that's fine, but I also want to have fun with it. This is key; people forget to take risks, to have fun. . . This is why everything looks the same, sounds the same, reads the same.

Book publishing is in flux. Have you had to morph into a digital designer?
To a degree, my staff and I do handle these needs. I understand, embrace, and go after this. The world is evolving as the majority chooses it to do so, and while I may love print best, I better embrace the capacity to be

able to provide whatever digital needs Penguin requires of me or become obsolete. It's a very small percentage of the job and simply not a big deal.

You work with various freelance illustrators and designers. What do you look for in their portfolio?
I look for stunning work and an individual voice. I look for visual intelligence and problem solving. I look for risk taking and those who clearly love what they do. Once I contact them, I choose to only work with driven, nice people. . . If they are not both, I move on to another artist.

You've given your artists some great opportunities. How closely do you manage their work?
Each book is different and comes with its own cast of characters and its own needs based on the content and players involved. Sometimes when I am being introduced to the material by the editor and publisher, an idea forms and I may choose to say, "You know, as you are speaking, I'm seeing . . .", and they may say "Yes! Perfect, let's do that" or "No, that does not feel right." Sometimes they say, "We have no idea; read it, have fun, and come back to us with an idea," or maybe the author has an idea that he or she wants to explore, and if we like that idea, we may try it. So any artists I contact to work on something will find themselves within some parameter I am communicating— all the way from "Go crazy; I want you to really go for it, anything you choose" to "I have this idea, and I'd like you to stick pretty close to it."

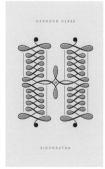

Drop Caps
Design and Coloring:
Paul Buckley
Illustrator: Jessica Hische
Art Director: Paul Buckley

Penguin Horror
Illustrator/Designer/Art Director:
Paul Buckley

Fear of Flying
Illustrator: Noma Barr
Designer/Art Director:
Paul Buckley

Jim Heimann

Making Visual Books

Jim Heimann's official title is executive editor of Taschen America in Los Angeles, and his primary job is to produce books for the publishing house. He is also an addicted collector with many of his own artifacts used for his book projects. He began his career as a freelance graphic designer and illustrator, and graduated college with a BA from CSU Long Beach graphic design program. After graduation, he was hired as an assistant to an illustrator, where he taught himself illustration, got an agent, and pursued a career as a freelance designer and illustrator for over 30 years. This gave him the confidence to do anything that the visual world offered: He made art, designed a line of jewelry, was commissioned to do a series of public art sculptural pieces, and published books. He is the definition of the multidisciplinary design "maker."

Car Hops and Curb Service
Client: Chronicle Books
Art Director/Designer: Jim Heimann
1996

You started as an illustrator but with a huge penchant for books; how and when did you author your first book? What led up to that?
I began my journey in publishing in 1980 with the publication of a little square book called *California Crazy*. In college I had seen a book called *The English Sunrise*, and at that time, there was a whole group of small square books that focused on arcane visual matter; that format resonated with me.

Most of your book work is as a documentarian of American pop culture. It's obvious that there are great riches, but did the material you collect have an impact on your illustration/design life?
Yes. It was a symbiotic relationship. The magazines and ephemera were

incorporated into illustrations and also inspired my design. The thousands of images I had never seen before informed me about vernacular design and would also lead me to investigate designers, illustrators, and art movements. Otis Sheperd, Lawson Wood, J. C. Leyendecker, WPA posters, postcard companies, and so on were all revelations. I reinterpreted type, borrowed color palettes from matchbook covers, and cut up magazine ads for collages.

How do you research your materials?
Most of my projects start with existing collections. The menu book I did several years ago was the result of collecting vintage menus for 20 plus years. That collection started because I as drawn to the graphic covers and I used them in my research when I started

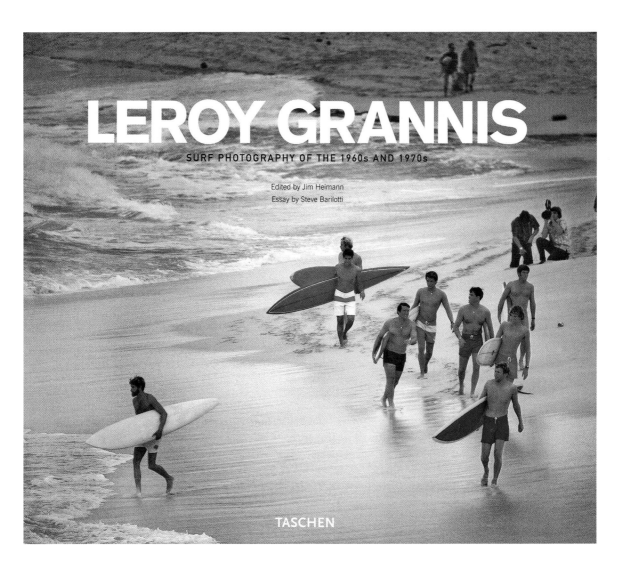

LEROY GRANNIS
SURF PHOTOGRAPHY OF THE 1960s AND 1970s

Edited by Jim Heimann
Essay by Steve Barilotti

TASCHEN

Leroy Grannis:
Surf Photography of the
1960s and 1970s
Client: Taschen
Designer: Paul Mussa
Art Director: Jim Heimann
2007

working on *California Crazy*. Often they would have the address of a building I was trying to locate. From there I couldn't stop. When Benedikt Taschen gave the green light for the project, I accelerated my collecting and leaned on other collectors for material that was hard to find. I do intensive research both online and in libraries for background material.

Would you call yourself an entrepreneur?
Absolutely. From the day I graduated from college, I felt I could and had to do multiple things. I felt being just a designer or just an illustrator was too confining. I wanted to do it all. And I did. I sought out clients and publishers. I licensed, lectured, and taught. Of course, I had several reps who also

helped me get a variety of jobs, but in general I was a bit of an anomaly for the time.

Do you believe that these kinds of career-building ancillary activities are what the design field is headed toward?

I think for many designers and illustrators this has already happened. Look at Milton Glaser. He has been doing this for over 50 years. In some ways, he inspired me to do any and everything. I saw that for him, design and illustration were not separate but part of a thing called "the visual world."

For those who want to go this route, what do you suggest?

Follow your passion. Whatever you love best you should pursue because that is where you are going to put your energy. That said, there are no guides or rule books, and it's harder than you think. Luck can play an important part. Get as much information about running a business as you can. Network like crazy. Lean on your peers or those whom you see as successes. Keep your eyes wide open and absorb everything. Read. Ask questions. It took me about 20 years to realize there were no dumb questions. I was intimidated that if I didn't know the answer, I would be perceived as stupid. Maybe it's age, but now if I don't know what someone is talking about, I ask, even if it makes me look dumb. I don't care; I want the answer.

All-American Ads: 40s
Client: Taschen
Art Director/Designer:
Jim Heimann
Cover Design: Sense/Net,
Andy Disl & Birgit Eichwede
2014

All-American Ads: 20s
Client: Taschen
Art Director/Designer:
Jim Heimann
Cover Design:
Sense/Net, Andy Disl
2004

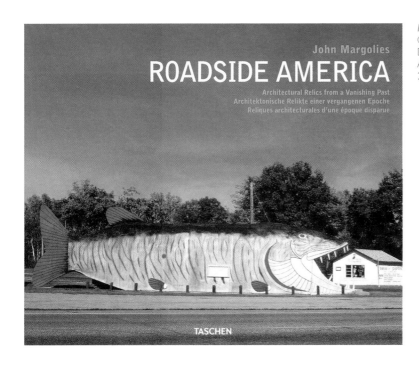

Roadside America
Client: Taschen
Designer: Marco Zivny
Art Director: Josh Baker
2010

Shop America: Midcentury
Storefront Design
Client: Taschen
Designer: Josh Baker
Art Director: Josh Baker
2007

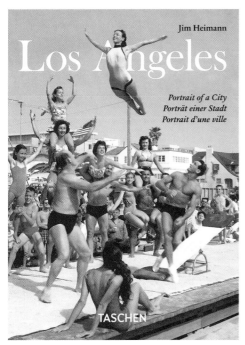

Los Angeles:
Portrait of a City
Client: Taschen
Designer: Anna-Tina Kessler
Art Director: Josh Baker
2013

7 Editorial Design

Magazines and newspapers once gave opportunities to a large percentage of junior and senior designers and art directors. There are fewer of them in print now, but digital needs have increased the positions for a slew of digital designers.

Within a magazine or newspaper infrastructure, design duties are often divided into two fundamental groups: editorial and promotion. The latter, which administers advertising and publicity, including the conception and design of ads, billboards, branded collateral materials such as "madvertising" rate cards, subscription campaigns, and promotional booklets and brochures, may be large or small, depending on the priorities of the specific company. Today, much of this work is being done in the digital space.

The former, however, is the creative heart of an institution. Editorial designers are the people who give the publication its aura, image, and format. And yet the editorial art department is configured differently from publication to publication, so it is not always possible for a job candidate to know the makeup of specific departments before interviewing for a job (which may or may not help anyway). The following are typical scenarios that illustrate the variety of editorial opportunities.

MAGAZINES

Design positions at magazines are frequently available for all experience levels. The intense and constant work flow that goes into periodical design and production demands many participants. A typical hierarchy begins at the top with a design director or art director, who manages the overall design department and design of the magazine, including the format (which either he or an outside design consultant originally designed); this may include overseeing the work of senior and junior page designers and designing pages and covers himself. It may also involve assigning illustration, photography, and typography. (When the budget allows, custom typefaces are also commissioned.)

In addition, the art director is involved in meetings with editors (and sometimes authors) concerning article presentation. Some of these duties are invariably delegated to a deputy or associate art director, who does many of the same design tasks as the art director and also may manage, depending on the workload. The deputy or associate may be on a track to move into the art director's position, should it open, or, after acquiring the requisite experience, move on to an art director position at another magazine. On the next-lower level, senior and junior designers are responsible for designing components of a magazine (features, columns, inserts, etc.). Some design entire spreads or pages and commission the artwork and photography; others design elements of a feature and use the illustrations supplied to them by the art director or the deputy. Some are better typographers than users of art. The difference between senior and junior designer is usually the degree of experience and talent. The former may have been a junior first or may have been hired directly as a senior from another job; the latter is often right out of school or was an intern while a student. Based on achievement, a senior or junior designer can be promoted to a deputy or associate position. There are no codified rules of acceleration other than merit and need. Therefore, it is not impossible for a junior to be so professionally adept that promotion to the next level is fairly swift. Conversely, merely competent progress in a job is rarely rewarded.

The junior designer position is often at the entry level. Some magazines have additional entry-level jobs, such as unpaid interns or paid assistants who do less critical, yet nevertheless necessary, support work. The most common task is production, such as scanning images into the computer or maintaining electronic files; occasionally, a minimal amount of layout or design work on tightly formatted pages may be assigned. In addition, the intern or assistant is invariably required to act as a gofer, attending to all the odd jobs that need to be done. This is actually a critical juncture for the wannabe because an employer can measure the relative competence or excellence of a worker.

The relative importance of art and design is often linked to the comparative strength and power of the design or art director. Whatever the hierarchy, it is important that editorial designers (at any level) be aware of the editorial process—not merely the schedule, but the editorial philosophy of the magazine. Even the lowest-level designer must have a precise understanding of what is being editorially communicated in order for the design to not only carry but also enhance the content of the publication.

NEWSPAPERS

Although the number of newspapers has been radically reduced, over the past three decades, newspapers have augmented hard news with soft news features, such as lifestyle and home sections. At the same time, printing technology has significantly advanced to allow more innovative visual display (including full-color reproduction). In the past, newspaper composition was carried out by editorial makeup technicians, people who were not trained as artists or designers; today, art directors and designers are responsible for the basic look and feel of the average newspaper.

Newspapers have introduced new job categories unique to this industry. One notable entry is the graphics editor, a hybrid of editor and designer, who is responsible for the information graphics (charts, graphs, and maps) that appear regularly in most newspapers. This new subgenre has become essential to contemporary newspaper content.

The newspaper industry has distinct hierarchies, but each newspaper has different jobs and job descriptions; the following are typical. Beginning at the entry level, the best way to start is as an intern. All newspapers employ seasonal (usually paid) interns as entry-level junior copy editors who act as assistants-in-training to the various newspaper desks. Likewise, the art department (which is often under the wing of the news department) employs a design intern to work directly with designers or art directors. Often, art department interns are selected from art schools or universities with publication design programs (the candidates need not have had newspaper experience, although some newspaper work is a definite advantage). The tasks given the intern vary depending on the publication; one newspaper may offer intensive training in design, production, and information graphics, while another may have the intern do gofer work (scanning, making copies, or whatever clerklike tasks are necessary). Internships sometimes lead to permanent employment; sometimes they do not. An internship is a kind of test for an employer to ascertain how well an individual fits, professionally and personally, into a specific art department.

The next level is usually more permanent. If a newspaper has junior designer or design assistant positions, these are often full-time jobs with various responsibilities. But every newspaper art department is organized differently, so the assistant in one may work closely with the senior designer or art director actually designing some of the pages of a hard or soft news section, or the junior may assist many designers in the daily process.

The next job designation is design director or art director. In some newspapers, the title graphics editor is also given to those who design hard and soft news sections. The responsibilities vary depending on the size of the newspaper. An art director may design a specific section of a newspaper, assign the illustration and photography, and design the so-called dress or feature pages. (An assistant designer or, at many newspapers, a makeup editor, may design the more routine pages.) The senior designer or art director works with text editors, picture editors, and others.

Newspaper design is essentially different from magazine design. It is expressed on a larger scale—more editorial components must be balanced on the broadsheet pages. It occurs at a different frequency—the luxury of a weekly or monthly magazine deadline allows for more detail work, whereas at a daily newspaper, little time is available for the nuances of design. Still, in the past decade or so, high-quality printing and production have improved the design potential. But the most revolutionary part of the newspaper business is its integration of online media . . . with video, interactive features, and responsive interfaces.

It is, indeed, a new design career playing field.

Len P. Small

Print Is Bouncing Back

Len P. Small is the art director at *Nautilus*, a monthly science magazine published online and in print. He directs a cadre of illustrators, who tackle the assignments with clever, narrative-driven art. *Nautilus* whittles down the best online articles and reworks them for a print quarterly. It also develops interactive content and videos, in-house marketing and campaigns, and expanding media, including designs and content for mobile and tablet platforms. Small began designing as a way to make money when he was attempting to be a musician. It took him almost a decade of working in graphic design to realize that he enjoyed the work. He worked up to an art director position but was also eager to make content himself. After attending the SVA Designer as Author MFA program, he graduated to publishing, "the industry everyone else is trying to flee."

Cover of *Nautilus* Quarterly 04
Client: *Nautilus*
Art Director: Len P. Small
Illustrator: Ellen Weinstein
Courtesy of *Nautilus* (nautil.us)
Summer 2014

You are the art director of a printed quarterly magazine. Didn't you hear that newsprint is dead?
"Greatly exaggerated . . ." Print is bounding back because people want a reading experience away from the glowing screens that demand our attention every minute of every day. *Nautilus* has tried to fashion a magazine that edges into book territory. Like vinyl records' roaring return, we clamor for the sensation of something real. We consumers want a finite, curated experience after the infinite lists of tweets and e-mails that blow out our heads daily.

I see many new niche magazines discovering that designing a more rarefied product allows flexibility in both content and demand. Instead of printing a large number of magazines that end up in a shredder, create a tighter, short-run publication that brings back something we all miss: finding something special that we can be the first to experience and share.

How do you balance the digital and analog requirements of *Nautilus*?
By taking a big breath! Actually, I find that there's a little passageway between the two, where you can get the immediacy and rush of working on digital content, while still retaining the slightly more measured presentation and formal thinking of print. Digital cascades into print well, with a little tweaking, though, interestingly, I find it tough to work in the other direction. Design and art begin to lock in more rigidly with print than digital.

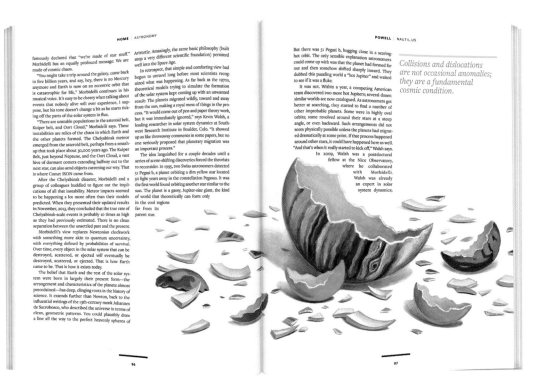

"The Madness of the Planets"
by Corey S. Powell (above)
Client: *Nautilus*
Art Director: Len P. Small
Illustrator: Chris Buzelli
Courtesy of *Nautilus* (nautil.us)
December 12, 2013

Curtain for the Web Issue 14:
Turbulence (opposite bottom)
Client: *Nautilus*
Art Director: Len P. Small
Illustrator: Josh Cochran
Courtesy of *Nautilus* (nautil.us)
July 2014

What is the difference between *Nautilus* online and on the newsstand?
Our online experience uses all of the shortcuts that make digital content exciting—quick access to new ideas that can be read quickly (for fast readers who skim through headlines and artwork) or slowly (deep-diving articles with links and online resources). We try to make the print experience more luxurious . . . the pieces that make it to ink tend to be more free of timing. We try to design the content to feel more available for any time that the reader chooses to pick up the issue.

Some people have said illustration is dying. You seem to have other plans. Why is illustration the backbone of your design style?
I have to start by giving props to two people: Our publisher John Steele laid out his intention to have illustration lead the visuals in my first meeting with him. And Alissa Levin of Point Five Design acted as consulting creative director as we were getting started (in addition to designing the logo and magazine template). She truly showed me the ropes during the first months of publication. Without those two, there would be no great *Nautilus* illustration.

What characteristics do you look for in illustration and illustrators?

I want illustrators to bring their own story to the piece. I enjoy style and attitude, but I need to know that they will not be afraid to try on something that's not in their wheelhouse. If you always draw people, why not try drawing a landscape? If all of your characters are naked and screwing, then you should enjoy the challenge of creating a cool image that could be hung in a school library. I'm all for the subversive. I don't need colors to be real. I don't need the science to be accurate (unless requested). What I desire is to see an odd but fastidiously considered twist on a familiar story or a complex concept made stunningly relatable.

You also hire designers for print and digital. What do you look for in each case? And is there any crossover?

I discovered that the best *Nautilus* designers don't get caught up in being defined as a print or web designer. Designers see visual puzzles everywhere, and the best are eager to solve them with whatever tools are present and necessary.

What must an editorial designer know today that is new and old?

Content is still king. Good readers can sniff out old ideas, but a whiff of familiarity can also help move things along. It pays to listen to your peers. You will make lots and lots of mistakes. Editors tend to be good at judging

Cover of *Nautilus* Quarterly 03
Client: *Nautilus*
Illustrator: Shout
Art Director: Len P. Small
Courtesy of *Nautilus* (nautil.us)
Spring 2014

artwork, but never let them sit in front of your computer and start moving things around in a layout. Whenever possible, only use three type sizes on a page. Foremost, make your deadlines. Don't forget about the words; they're quite substantial.

Since we began with *print is dead*, why is print alive for you and *Nautilus*?

I'm a bibliophile, raised by a librarian and a third-generation newspaperman, corn-fed on comic books, magazines, and novels. I might have blinders on, but it seems to me that there are lots of people like me who want print to live and thrive. Print doesn't have to succeed on the same terms as we expected 20–30 years ago, but it would be a crime to let it die.

Susanna Shannon

Art Director Becomes Editor

Announcement for
"Irregulomadaire" Calendar
Art Director/Designer:
Susanna Shannon
2014

Susanna Shannon, the principal of Design Dept., is an independent newspaper art director known for her bold modernist typographical sensibility. An American living in France since 1962, she maintains a very strict Anglo-Saxon approach to information architecture while working for some of the most avant-garde publications, *Libération* and *Les Inrockuptibles*, as well as the most conservative ones, *L'Expansion* and *L'Express*. "My parents both had this incredibly sharp artistic sense, and our houses were always beautiful wherever they were, and loaded with magazines and newspapers and books," she remembers. "To this day, my dad sends me packages of Bloomberg *Business Week* and *The New York Times*, and we talk about them over the phone."

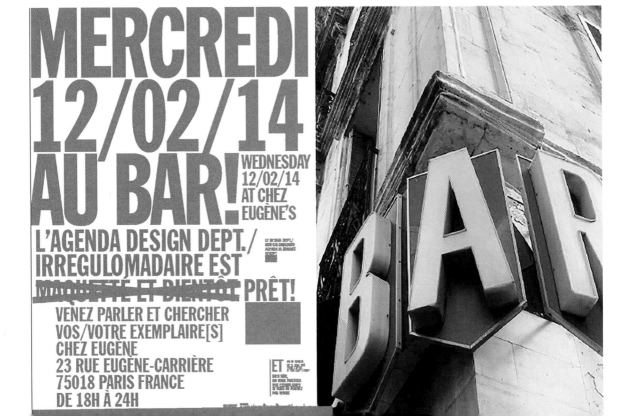

You are an American publication designer, living, teaching, and working in France. You've worked for a wide range of prestigious French newspapers. How did you get there?

I moved to Paris in 1962 with my family when I was four-and-a-half years old because my father was posted there as the first foreign correspondent for The *Los Angeles Times* in France. As for the design part, designing publications is something I just do naturally. When I came back to Paris in 1981 from London, where I had been studying at the London College of Printing, French editorial design had not really begun—it didn't really exist. I had no problem finding work.

In 2013, you had a chance to create your own newspaper, *La Life*—a daily newsletter produced in situ, for the International Festival of Graphic Design in Chaumont. Can you tell us about it?

We set up our temporary office/cabin in the cavernous lobby of a former bank. I brought my old computer, the one that I knew was about to crash and in which was stored tons of stuff I'd never had time to sort out: pictures, notes, things I'd been thinking about. It was my brain. We had the concept, the tools to produce the newsletter, a couple of volunteers, and a deal with a local printer—but basically it was a madhouse.

Were you acting as both the editor and the art director?

Yes, I was the official editor and AD, but the director of the Chaumont

Festival, Etienne Hervy, was the "curator" of the project. My friend Stefano Giustiniani was the designer, and his wife Maria did most of the writing. We decided that since we all spoke different languages, we'd write whatever we covered in the lingo of our choice: The paper would be multi-lingual. Events, reviews, comments, or last-minute news could be covered in French, English, Spanish or whatever.

How did you generate the content on short notice?

We had our list of ideas and interviews set in advance, but we also jumped on people who happened to stop by to ask them for articles, for their leftovers, for whatever they wanted to write.

Every one of the 13 issues had a different look, yet they were stylistically coherent. Did you have a consistent grid, a strict format, a few typographical guidelines?

We decided that all body text would be in Times New Roman because that's the best typeface for legibility—Stanley Morrison had designed it specifically for newspapers. We had a grid, yet considered changing the format of each issue. Not systematically, though—but whenever we got bored! Likewise, we changed logos to fit the feel of the editorial content.

In your experience, what makes a seat-of-the-pants newsletter like La Life an exciting editorial endeavor?

For us, it was the fact that the paper truly had a function: to inform every-one in Chaumont about what was going on, who was there, which event was scheduled that day, where and

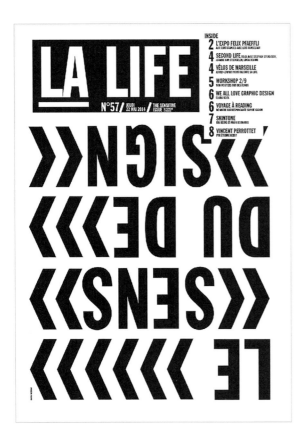

La Life, No 57, front page,
Festival de Chaumont (left)
Art Director/Designer:
Susanna Shannon
2014

La Life, No 57, page 6,
Festival de Chaumont (right)
Art Director/Designer:
Susanna Shannon
2014

when. People were racing to get their issue at 2:00 p.m. Everybody was reading it, commenting on it, photographing it, trading it, and making fun of it. It was truly the local paper for this particular two-week-long event.

Some designers would do a take on our multilingualism: They'd throw an article written in French about them into a Google translator in order to read it in their native language, mostly English. The result was always hilarious. Then they'd publish that wild translation on their website. La Life was so popular that we were asked to repeat the experiment in 2014. We were slightly more organized this time. Also, I cracked down on the typographical format, with a more exacting grid and rigorous use of Franklin Gothic Extra-Condensed All Caps for headlines. My team of volunteers didn't seem to mind. Truth be told, I am a tyrant when it comes to readability.

Ah, the smell of fresh ink on newsprint! Do you think that paper publications are here to stay?
There's something fundamental about the way you make newspapers and the

way they circulate, about the way they are used as wallpaper for the attic, about the way they are saved to make a fire in the fireplace, about the way they are stacked in the basement only to be rediscovered by grandchildren years later. Sure, we all love the smell of fresh ink, but more compelling is the old information on the surface of their pages. The printed matter is a record of our culture. Newspapers to me are like the paintings of Lascaux and the Gutenberg bible.

I don't know if pulp-based newspapers are here to stay, but their elimination would definitely be an attack against democracy and the cohesion of our society. It would impair our ability to live together and understand each other. A newspaper is an edited collection of daily information that readers can share the moment it is published but can also read the next day, and collect to be studied years later, in all sorts of different locations. Newspapers provide the social glue. They are tools for social integration—"instruments d'agrégation sociale," to use a French expression.

La Life
Editor-in-Chief: Susanna Shannon
Art Director: Susanna Shannon
Client: Chaumont International
Graphic Design Festival

8 Social Innovation

Doing good is not exclusive to graphic design; every profession wants to influence or bring about positive change. In recent years, the term "social innovation" has become part of designer jargon. It is not entirely specious: Designers routinely make innovations for social welfare. Like any buzzword (e.g., design thinking), its effectiveness diminishes with overuse. Still, for our purposes, terms like "social impact" and "social innovation" serve the same yet broader function than "pro bono" (which is often thought to mean "free work" but is actually derived from *pro bono publico*—"for the public good"—in Latin).

Social innovation can be a career path or not. It can be a means to build a portfolio or not. It should be a way to help others directly or indirectly. Graphic designers have long been seen as those who support social innovators through the expert organization of useful data or the rebranding of a not-for-profit organization. Yet graphic designers are finding ways to take an even more proactive role as "makers" and "producers" of socially valuable products. Here the term "social entrepreneur" is apt, for designers with easy access to digital tools are equipped to make significant contributions. This chapter will not provide the outlets you need to make a difference, but our interviews address the ways to find those outlets and to channel your inspiration for the public good.

Mark Randall

The Citizen Designer

Mark Randall is the founder of Worldstudio. In the seventh-grade, with a friend, he published a Star Trek fanzine called *Star Charting*, using a typewriter and the photocopy machine in his dad's engineering office. The boys were drawn to the show's positive social message as well as the cool spaceships, aliens, and adventure. "This was my only introduction to graphic design until I went to college, where I discovered that it could be a career," he recalls. The combination of strategy and structure around the communication of an idea, all within an artistically creative context, appealed to Randall. "The inclusiveness, optimism, and social messages that were contained in Star Trek sparked in me a desire to contribute to a positive future." In the mid-nineties, these two interests came together with the launch of Worldstudio, a strategy and communication's firm that uses the power of creativity to impact positive social change. Randall and his business partner at the time, David Sterling, wanted a studio that addressed social issues on a daily basis, utilizing the skills they have as graphic designers.

Logo for Worldstudio
Foundation's Signature Program:
Design Ignites Change.
Designer: Worldstudio

Worldstudio is a unique business model. So much of your work is in the area of social good. Please explain how this works.
Our goal was to create a studio that not only served clients but [was] one that would give us a platform to develop our own self-generated projects and programs around the social issues in which we were interested. There are two parts to the organization: Worldstudio, Inc., the for-profit side, and Worldstudio Foundation, which is nonprofit. We actually started the foundation first and then launched the design studio two years later. Because

of tax requirements, we needed two organizations—but in the end, we think of them as one, just Worldstudio.

Worldstudio, Inc. works like most traditional graphic design firms that offer client services, but our focus is on the nonprofit and civic realm. Working in this area supports our mission of using design to impact positive social change. We work on a wide range of projects from branding, interactive, and collateral to packaging and environmental graphics. This side of the business pays my rent and allows me to buy tickets to the most recent Star Trek movie.

Identity and Package Design
for a Socially Minded Tea
Company That Focuses on
the Triple Bottom Line:
Profit, People, Planet
Designer: Worldstudio
Photographer: Mark Randall

**Why did you launch a foundation?
What was your aim and goal?**

We established Worldstudio Foundation as a tax-exempt, 501c3 organization to create the social initiatives that we wanted to develop. We needed the tax benefits of being a nonprofit so that we could accept donations and receive grant money from our partners, which is how we fund these initiatives.

We believe that creativity holds enormous power for positive social change. Through the work of the Foundation, we focus our efforts on providing inspiration and support for designers, architects, and artists who want to use creativity to give back to their communities and the world at

large. Our initiatives have ranged from scholarship programs, professional fellowships, and grant making to educational opportunities, which include mentoring programs for high school students and social design workshops and intensives for college students and creative professionals. We have created a number of high-visibility public art and design projects, which unite communities around compelling social themes.

**How much of what you do is
strategizing for meaningful
projects and actually designing?**

Strategizing around a meaningful project is the best part of my job—but, alas, it is a small part. We're a small office; right now it's myself, two designers, and our foundation programs director. Everyone has to do a little bit of everything. My day-to-day responsibilities break down in two ways: For Worldstudio, Inc., I act as art director and client liaison. I usually have a range of disparate activities going on at the same time; because of this, I find it hard to carve out chunks of time in which to focus on the actual process of design. But when I do, I enjoy it. When it comes to our social initiatives, my role is that of a producer, developing the concept, building the strategy and partnerships needed to make it happen, and then managing the project through to completion. We believe in the power of partnerships, and everything we do through the Foundation is very partner driven; these relationships are critical to our success.

Talk about your favorite (and possibly most successful) project.
Drawing on my vast experience as the publisher of Star Charting, our first social initiative, in 1994, was a magazine called *Sphere*, which featured articles about artists and designers who incorporated a social agenda into their work. At the time, there was little to no discussion around design and social impact in the media. We decided that a publication would be a great venue in which to explore these ideas and generate a conversation around the subject.

We not only acted as the publisher, but we were the editorial and creative directors as well, bringing together teams of editors, writers, and designers for each issue. We produced seven

2003 Issue of *Sphere* on the Theme of "Tolerance" (bottom)
Editorial and Creative Directors: Mark Randall, David Sterling
Editors: Peter Hall, Emmy Kondo
Designer: Daniela Koenn
Cover Designer: Santiago Piedrafita

Sphere, "Wish You Were Here" Issue (left)
Editorial and Creative Directors: Mark Randall, David Sterling
Editors: Peter Hall, Emmy Kondo
Designer: Sven Oberstein
Cover Designer: Shawn Wolfe

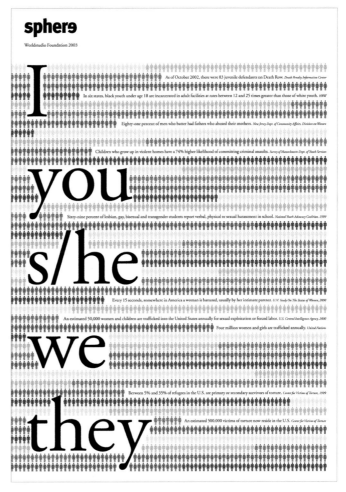

Urban Forest Project Lightpole
and Banner Tote Bag
Designer: Rob Alexander
Client: Jack Spade
Photographer: Mark Dye

issues over nine years, and each issue was sent free to 15,000 designers across the country.

That sounds quite ambitious. . .
Sphere demonstrated to us that we could launch our own initiative and make it economically viable. This also gave us visibility and street-cred in the design community, which we built upon for future opportunities. I think of Sphere as the foundation of our Foundation.

What do you look for when hiring someone to work at the studio or on specific projects?
For Worldstudio, Inc., a designer with excellent communication and typographic skills is critical. I am not interested in just aesthetics. I get excited when I see a combination of inventive creativity—which can be very cutting-edge and contemporary—mixed with clear and compelling communication. I like design that is playful and fun with the right note of seriousness when the message calls for it.

On the Foundation side, we look for creative individuals, often who come from a background in arts administration. They don't have to be designers, but they must have an interest in design and how it relates to social issues. This is a rare combination, but we have been lucky and have had great people working with us.

You not only run Worldstudio but also you direct a summer intensive, Impact! What is your goal here?
The profession as a whole is trying to figure it out. We need to create our own opportunities to work in this area

and demonstrate to potential employers, clients, or collaborators what we can bring to the table. Recent graduates as well as midcareer designers are looking for ways in which to pursue this type of work. There are not many opportunities for designers to learn about this emerging field, and there is no go-to list of social design jobs to apply for.

We launched Impact! in the summer of 2010 to give people a place to start, as well as an understanding of the field. We like to think of our program as graduate school crammed into six weeks. Many of our students have leveraged their Impact! experience into a full-time social design job or they have gone on to launch a business or project idea they incubated in the program.

In the not-for-profit world, is it possible to sustain oneself financially?
Socially minded work is not limited to the nonprofit world. There are a range of opportunities out there—all of which require research and perseverance to unearth. I see them breaking down broadly into the following categories.

You can get a job working for a nonprofit organization. Many mid-to-large-sized foundations have their own in-house design departments. Currently, foundations utilize graphic designers in the traditional way: to create their communication materials. I am optimistic about a future where these organizations will see the value of having a designer at the table as they develop the initial strategy around their programming. Designers should be more involved in the entire process, not just as an add-on at the end to make things look better.

Ringling Museum of Art Identity
Client: John & Mable Ringling
Museum of Art, Sarasota, Florida
Designer: Worldstudio
Icon designer: John Pirman

Corporations have money, reach, and power; many are engaged in corporate social responsibility (often referred to as CSR), recognizing that it directly affects their bottom line. They need designers to help them communicate their efforts. As with nonprofits, I'd like to see a future where we are at the table from the beginning to help with strategy. Our skills as creative problem solvers can be brought to bear, and we can work from within, as entrepreneurs, to help them make meaningful change. This may be overly optimistic—but a worthy goal!

Government desperately needs good design. This is an area full of opportunity, as it gives designers a chance to work on projects that impact the lives of millions of people. Right now it is an uphill battle but I believe one that is worth waging.

If you want to start your own design firm, you can create a client base from a segment or mix of all of the above.

There are successful studios that do this. Granted, it might not be as lucrative as a client list made up of Fortune 500 companies, but from my personal perspective, working for social change trumps the money.

Lastly, you can live the life of a social entrepreneur and create your own socially minded nonprofit organization or social enterprise. This is the area that expands the most on what designers can do. Design is often not the end result, but the skills of a designer are brought to bear on making the concept reality.

Is there a business model for being a "pro bono" designer?

I have mixed feelings about pro bono work. We should get paid for the work we do, even if the work is socially motivated. Pro bono is not sustainable if you want to engage in this type of work over the long term.

One business model that is often cited is to take a percentage of your time, ranging from 1 to 10 percent, and dedicate it to pro bono work. Based on a 40-hour work week, 1 percent represents a modest 20 hours per year per person, and 10 percent represents 200. It is important to treat pro bono work just as you would a paying client. Create a proposal with a clearly defined scope of work, outlining expectations on both sides. And, sign the contract!

I don't believe that you should do pro bono work without getting something in return: deep personal satisfaction, an opportunity to learn a new skill, introductions to a new community, or a great piece for your portfolio that you can leverage for future opportunities. I allocate my pro bono services to my own efforts through the Foundation, and I can easily say that I get a return on this investment from all of the benefits I just outlined.

Bob McKinnon

Socially Impactful Design

Bob McKinnon is president of GALEWiLL Design. One hundred percent of their work addresses social issues, ranging from childhood obesity to climate change. He has led teams that have redesigned the food stamp program for the state of California, transformed the way we talk about social factors and health for the Robert Wood Johnson Foundation, and created new ways for youth to stay above the influence for the White House Office of National Drug Control Policy. He has also partnered with leading organizations such as the Bill and Melinda Gates Foundation, the U.S. Centers for Disease Control and Prevention, Sesame Workshop, and The William J. Clinton Foundation, among many others, to help millions overcome obstacles on their way to a healthier and happier life. His book *Actions Speak Loudest: Keeping Our Promise for a Better World* is but one of the ways he has spread the message of social innovation.

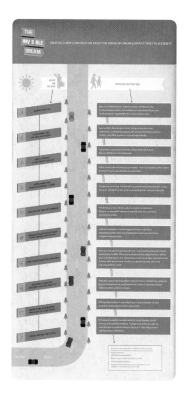

Invisible Dream
Client: GALEWiLL Center
for Opportunity & Progress
Studio: GALEWiLL Design
Designers: Bob Mckinnon,
Tyler Mintz

What is your definition of social innovation in today's design scheme?

I see social innovation as anything we create or design that can move the world forward. It can be for one person, one community, or the entire planet. "Does this make someone's life better?" is a simple question we should always ask ourselves when designing anything. If the answer is "no," we should respond by wondering whether we should be doing it at all. If the answer is "yes," then we should think about how to get this out to more people who could benefit by it.

What is different in today's design world than 10 years earlier regarding design for social good?

Ten years ago, design for social good was less an explicit goal and more of an implicit choice. Even then, within almost any design choice we make, we could either move the world forward or set it back—in ways imperceptible or grand. Today things are much more open and accessible. There are more opportunities to explicitly focus on this kind of work. Firms such as ours do 100 percent social change work. Others open up smaller practices within larger organizations. Platforms and tools come on the scene that promote social entrepreneurship and make it more attractive. The explosion of opportunities in this space has been incredible and much welcomed.

How should designers get involved with public welfare projects?

In some ways, we create a false choice when we position public welfare projects vs. commercial projects. Everything we design has the potential for social impact, regardless of whether it's designing for a public cause or making better choices for a company.

Practically speaking, there are more entries into this space than ever before. You could tackle a cause you believe in on your own, volunteer for a small nonprofit, get an advanced degree in design for social impact, work for a company you believe does good things for the world, even go into government. There is more and more demand for people with great design skills and a passion for making a difference.

Is this still called "pro bono"—the occasional free job—or have we reached the point where this kind of work is not the exception but the norm?

I think we've reached the point where pro bono is becoming less and less the norm, and I think that's a good thing.

We pay for things we value. And what is more valuable than designing something that could solve major societal issues and improve lives? There is a unique skill set that comes with designing for social change. And like any other field within design, extensive experience and knowledge command a premium.

Now, of course, if you're a small nonprofit with limited resources and there is a designer looking to con-

tribute who is passionate about that cause, then this can be a match made in heaven.

But, alternatively, if you have large organizations with significant resources that are trying to tackle critical issues, then they should pay for expertise. This is no different than what you would do if you were hiring an engineer or architect to build your headquarters, an accountant to do your finances, or a lawyer to manage your legal issues. Design for good shouldn't be charity work, unless it absolutely has to be.

How are social impact jobs solicited and funded?

The good news is that increasingly people are seeing the real value good design can bring to a cause. It can be the difference between whether an organization fails or succeeds or whether one life is saved or a million. So within organizations, you can begin to see the return on investment that comes with good design.

More and more organizations are making investments in this space, and I think there will be increased demand for talent as a result. The White House has an Office of Social Innovation and Civic Participation. There are media outlets like Good and Fast Co-Exist that increasingly feature design for social good. Schools like SVA create stand-alone programs to meet the increasing demand. Large foundations and nonprofits are increasingly investing in design for themselves and their partners. And this is to say nothing of the people who are creating viable businesses, like Tom's Shoes, who are proving that doing good and making

Redesigning California's
Food Stamp Program
Client: California Department
of Social Services
Studio: GALEWiLL Design
Designers: Bob Mckinnon,
Jennifer Kaye

money don't have to be mutually exclusive pursuits.

What should a designer do to make a viable project?

Start by designing for one. We can fall into the trap of "I want to change the world" and forget that this still happens at the individual level. What does one person need to improve their lot in life? I love to talk to social entrepreneurs about their origin stories— what was their inspiration for getting started. Almost without exception, they tell me a very simple yet instructive story about how they were looking to help one person. Whether that's Sal Khan whose Khan Academy began by tutoring his cousin Nadia or Adam Braun who started Pencils of Promise as the result of an interaction with a child while he was traveling, it always starts there. If you want to change the world, design for one.

At the same time, we must remember that a person's life is not a problem for you to solve. We make the mistake of designing down, thinking we know what people need. We should design up, first seeing if we can be of some help, asking them how and letting them be the agent of their own success.

9 Branding and Packaging

Branding is storytelling. "It's that simple," Brian Collins said in the previous edition. "And storytelling is always interesting because it's driven by one question: What happens next?" That's what consumers want to learn. It's why they turn the page, why they enter a store, or click online—to see what happens next. The anticipation of being drawn into a new world or experience guides us all. Collins adds: "We are all in the what-happens-next business." People lose interest, fast, when nothing interesting happens next. So branding people—designers and writers—evolve stories to retain the public's interest. It is the job of advertising and design to help shape brand stories into something truthful, meaningful, and useful. When branding is done with sincerity and imagination, the outcome can be beneficial to the corporation and the individual. Design is a tangible, immediate kind of storytelling because it touches people's actual experience. "It isn't the promise of experience—like an ad," Collins notes. It is experience." Design is a brand's promise made visible, and ultimately, personal. And once an experience becomes personal, it can become a meaningful part of someone's own story.

Take the example of pirates and their skull and crossbones flags. That black flag—the logo—was the pirate brand identity, and it sent an unmistakable brand promise to other ships and sailors. The flag prompted distinct brand expectations, which if you believe the movies, the pirates consistently delivered. "Each time they acted ruthlessly," Collins says, "the pirates delivered on their brand promise—and deposited more legends and meaning into their flag. In fact, they were so bloodthirsty so consistently that by the eighteenth century, all a pirate ship had to do was hoist its Jolly Roger and the crew of the victim ship would often drop their cargo and flee."

Designers today are principal participants in the branding business. This means going beyond the design of one-off artifacts and creating as much of that broader experience as they can. If you are asked to design a package, for example, try to create such a big idea—a big story—that it could inspire the design of a great store, an ad campaign, a film, an event, a game, or a series of books, all based on the product idea. That is the branding idea.

Sharon Werner

Approachable Design

Sharon Werner created Werner Design Werks, Inc., 20 years ago in Saint Paul, Minneapolis. It's a small branding, packaging, and design studio that handles a variety of projects for firms that range from small start-ups to larger corporations. The studio attracts clients who are personally invested but may need a bit of coaching. It also caters to large companies that understand the design process and have a very streamlined or layered approach to problem solving. With her senior designer, Sarah Forss, Werner can tackle all types of design needs, "but developing the brand language for consumer products has been the core of our business for the past few years," she says.

Labrats Work Kits
Designers: Sharon Werner
and Sara Forss

How did you come to define your field of expertise?

This has not been a planned path, but, rather, one project led to another and to another. We don't call ourselves experts in any specific category, but, rather, we are observant, curious, intuitive consumers and observers. This curiosity has led to projects in the wine and spirits industry, fashion, [and] children's and personal care products, to name few.

How are Sarah Forss, your senior designer, and yourself are able to share the workload so seamlessly?

Sarah and I have worked together for over 18 years. Maybe that answers the question best. Basically, we have a process that works well for us. We share most projects in the beginning phases. We're open to criticism from each other and don't feel overly protective of our ideas. We can see potential opportunities or pitfalls in each other's rough sketches.

At some point in the process, one of us takes the lead, and the other becomes supportive. This can flip back and forth throughout the project. We each grow very familiar with the broad overview and fine details of the projects. At the end, it's often difficult to remember exactly whose original idea it was.

Part of your philosophy is to enter into a collaborative relationship with clients. But that's dangerous, isn't it? Do you sometimes have to "crack the whip" and let them know that, as far as design is concerned, you are in charge? Now more than ever, clients want to be part of the process. Dangerous?

Yes, definitely! But it's a reality, or at least it is for us. Many of our clients are financial stakeholders in the project. They want to see the process at mul-

dp Hue Shampoo and
Conditioner Bottles
Designers: Sharon Werner
and Sara Forss

tiple points in order to protect their investments. I can't say I blame them.

There are designers out there who approach and present design as if it's "magic" and there is only one rabbit in the hat. For us, the magic is in the design process—albeit not necessarily a linear one. Solutions need to be challenged at multiple steps to make sure they can hold up and stand the test. We can do that ourselves, but a client should also get involved. Clients need to take ownership of the brand—particularly small brands. They need to believe in it and live it for the result to be authentic and successful. They're often putting their homes or savings on the line. If they've been part of the

process, they're more likely to be able to embrace the solution and find success. But collaboration doesn't always work smoothly. We have had to remind clients why they hired us.

You've kept your studio small for two decades! You don't waste time in staff meetings. But how do you avoid the stigma of being a "mom-and-pop" operation?

I'm not certain that we always avoid that stigma. But who cares? We have successful work to show and maintain a professional method of working. It's our feeling that if a client feels they need a larger agency with more manpower, then they probably do need that, and we're not a good choice for them.

Clients have gotten considerably more savvy in the past few years and realized that even in a larger studio, their project is generally handled by two or three people at most, although the meetings may be propped up with three or four extra people for show!

You create, manage, and package your clients' brand image, but how about your own brand? What do you do to keep it vibrant?
We have a difficult time with this. It's definitely a case of the shoemaker's kids having no shoes scenario. We're attempting to launch a new website with a ton of new work, but it always takes a backseat to client work. However, I do believe that a successful project is as good for WDW as it is for our client, so that helps a little. But if anyone has the answer to this question, without working 120 hours a week, I'd love to hear it.

Compared with digital communication, print is now a luxury that fewer clients can afford. In which situations do you think print makes most sense?
Well, obviously packaging! Yeah! I love packaging. A few years ago, everyone touted the fact that websites created THE experience, which they can, but print has the potential to be as much or even more experiential. Think about cracking open a new book, the sound of the spine creaking, the smell of the fresh ink on paper wafting up, the smooth texture of the laminated jacket in contrast to the toothy, text pages. That's an experience that can't be replicated with an iPad.

As designers of print, we need to create those touch points within other areas of print. We need to use print to make an impression that involves all the senses. We need to create experiences, whether it's opening an envelope or a Hermes box.

Meyer's Clean Day,
Cleaners and Soaps
Designers: Sharon Werner
and Sara Forss

Octopus, from Alphabeasties and Other Amazing Types (above)

AlphaSaurs and Other Prehistoric Types (left)

Bugs by the Numbers (right)
Published by Blue Apple Books
Authors and Designers:
Sharon Werner and Sara Forss

10 Illustration Design

In previous editions of this book, illustration was ignored or downplayed as a component of an overall design. Arguably, illustration—the making of images by hand or computer in two and three dimensions—has returned with a vengeance. Or shall we say, many illustrators combine their drawing and vectoring skills with what can only be described as design.

This is not a new phenomenon. Graphic design was an outgrowth of illustration. Posters were large illustrations that incorporated type and lettering. Building on this foundation of the "complete work of art/design," as we call it, various designers and design firms became popular for the integration of these elements. Styles and methods were often recycled. While a few decades ago typography was its own art form, today the illustrated letter, the drawn image, and the designed message are once again, one again.

Editorial illustration may not be as robust as it was, but illustration for many more media and platforms are pronounced. If you call yourself and illustrator, you can also be a designer. If you call yourself a designer, you can still illustrate. This may be a renaissance—if only for the moment.

Michel Bouvet

The Citizen Designer

Michel Bouvet is a French poster designer, in the tradition of Savignac: He is first and foremost an illustrator, whose slightly quirky sense of humor appeals to the man on the street. "My goal is to intrigue, surprise, and amuse as many people as possible," he says. "Savignac was a master of that genre." Bouvet, who is a member of the Alliance Graphique Internationale since 1997, is one of the last proponents of The Conceptual Image. His clients are, for the most part, cultural institutions such as theaters, festivals, and museums, but he is also a prolific and tireless curator of special events promoting graphic design, illustration, and artists' books.

Poster for *Mélodrame*(s)!,
La Pépinière Theater
Art Director/Designer:
Michel Bouvet
2013

Today, you are one of the best-known poster designers in France. You can juggle visual concepts like no one else. Why do you think that your style has such visual appeal?
Like Savignac, I try to express things simply, directly, in a way that is instantly understandable by everyone. I put my talent at the service of the message or the event I am supposed to promote—but, more importantly, I put my talent at the service of the public.

Your most popular campaign is for the Rencontres d'Arles—an international photography event that you promote with posters featuring bold illustrations! Illustrations? Why this counterintuitive choice?
I've got nothing against photography—a medium I use from time to time—but I figured that illustrations would be more provocative. My mandate was to avoid at all cost an overly sophisticated approach. We wanted the

d'Arles photography festival to shed its elitist image. The event was losing its appeal and needed a shot in the arm. I decided to inject color and controversy into the campaign—and illustrations allowed me to do both.

How did you convince your clients that it was the right choice?
The president of the festival at the time was a visionary man who had been in charge of the Pompidou Center. He liked my radical approach. His director was equally supportive. Together, they should be credited for turning what was a losing proposition into a huge success.

The posters you designed are reminiscent of Pop Art. Why?
The simplicity of the image was important, but also the subject matter had to have a universal appeal. I used bold strokes and bright silkscreened colors, à la Roy Lichtenstein. I even added the suggestion of a dot pattern.

The posters represent animals or things that are totally incongruous.

Not so incongruous: The fruit and vegetable make reference to the still-life style so popular in artistic photography, while the portraits of animals are spoofing formal portraiture. It's a little far-fetched, I admit, but it works. And the images are popular with the 100,000 visitors each year who come to the festival and buy licensed products like T-shirts, mugs, notebooks, bags, and badges, all stamped with my bold drawings.

What role does absurdity play in your creative process?

Since a young age, I have been mesmerized by fine art, paintings in particular. But I was also reading books all the time. Both art forms were for me a way to escape into strange lands and discover unexpected things. Today, my challenge as an illustrator and a graphic designer is to use familiar and easily recognizable images to evoke weird, uncanny, and sometimes absurd situations. But that's just it: Poster designers are people who can break and bend rules to transform commercial messages into magical images.

You are also a prolific curator of shows and events on the theme of graphic design. You are a tireless and passionate communicator. What motivates you?

I want to give back what I have received: I have been invited all over the world to show my posters, a process that had been humbling in some way. The graphic designers I would meet on those trips were often exceptional artists whose work was

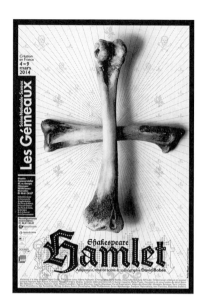

completely unsung. I have been to poor countries: Paraguay, Uruguay, Bolivia, Albania, and Cuba, just to name a few. There I saw posters that took my breath away. I decided to create events to feature the production of those neglected designers, along with that of their better-known colleagues. I like to combine graphic design with geopolitics.

In your own graphic design practice, you seem to make very little use of digital technologies. Yet you are prosperous. Do you think that, in the future, people like you will be the exception?

Believe me, I am stuck in front of my screen all day long, even though my work doesn't look like it was generated by a string of codes. Some of my posters—for the Gémeaux Theater in particular—are photographic images that have been manipulated digitally. Technology is magical, but it's only a tool. In that sense, we are all in the same boat.

Poster for *Hamlet*,
Les Gémeaux Theater (Left)
Art Director/Designer: Michel Bouvet
Photographer: F. Lahazzague
2014

Poster for *Othello*,
Les Gémeaux Theater (right)
Art Director/Designer: Michel Bouvet
Photographer: F. Lahazzague
2011

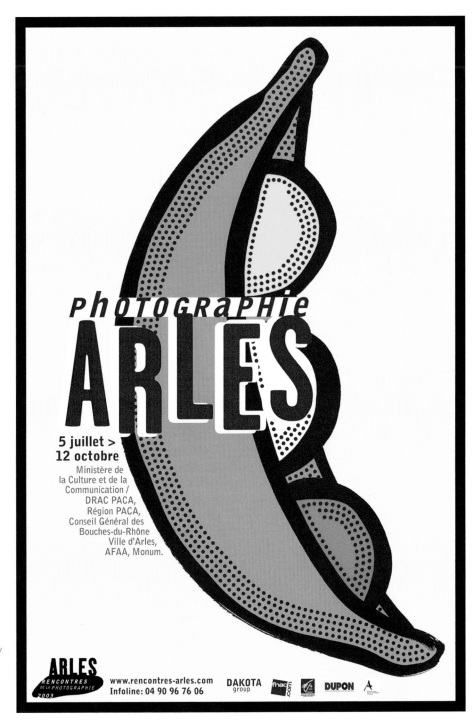

Poster for the Photography
Festival, Les Rencontres
d'Arles
Art Director/Designer:
Michel Bouvet
2003

Mirko Ilic

Design Is Like Classical Ballet

Mirko Ilic was born in Bosnia. In Europe, he drew comics and illustrations, and art-directed posters, books, and record covers. When he arrived in the United States, he became the art director of *Time* magazine International Edition and later art director of the Op-Ed pages of *The New York Times*. He got his first Mac in 1991 and soon afterward was creating illustrations with it, for publications such as *Time* magazine. By 1995, he had established his own firm, Mirko Ilic Corp. In the course of his career, he has received countless awards: from the Society of Illustrators, Society of Publication Designers, the Art Directors Club, I.D. magazine, *Print* magazine, *Graphis*, the Society of Newspaper Design, and others. But that's not all: Ilic is the coauthor of several books with Steven Heller, including *Genius Moves: 100 Icons of Graphic Design, Handwritten*, and *The Anatomy of Design, Stop Think Go Do*, and *Lettering Large*. With Milton Glaser he coauthored *The Design of Dissent*. He teaches in the MFA Illustration as Visual Essay program at the School of Visual Arts.

Canada
Client: Time International
Art Director: Rudolph Hoglund
Illustrator: Mirko Ilic
June 18, 1990

You've transitioned two times, from pen-and-ink illustrator to digital illustrator and from illustrator to graphic designer. How difficult was it to make these transitions?
Actually, there were a few more transitions. I was constantly trying to change styles in order not to draw in exactly the same way, time after time. A few years later, I became a designer working closely with photographers, an experience that turned out to be very useful later, when working in computer 3-D, with camera angles, width of lens, lighting, all that stuff. Transitions for me were quite smooth. I was curious;

I wanted to try things. When I got my first computer, in 1991, the first illustration I managed to produce in Illustrator was published in *Time* magazine. [The] first illustration I managed to produce in Photoshop was the cover of *Time* magazine.

Did your clients know who they were getting at any given time?
I just mentioned my first illustration created in Adobe Illustrator and my first cover created in Adobe Photoshop. In those instances, I was quite lucky because I was my own art director, and as a client, I didn't give

Not Much Has Changed
in a System That Failed
Client: *The New York Times*
Art Director: Tom Bodkin
Illustrator: Mirko Ilic
September 8, 2002

Knowledge at a Higher Price
Client: *Start no.293*
Designer: Mirko Ilic
1980

myself a hard time. Most of my clients see diversity in my portfolio, and so they expect diversity, unless, of course, they specifically tell me they would like a certain look.

Did you have to market and sell yourself differently to fit different needs?

Yes, the better known you are as an illustrator with a certain style, the harder it is to change directions. Big ships require much more time and energy to turn around.

Is this a field for specialists or generalists?

Things go both ways. When the economy is not doing well, if you are an established specialist, you are going to do fine. But if you are an up-and-coming designer or illustrator, you are better off being a generalist. You must take whatever you can get.

Do you integrate your illustration with your typography?

Whenever it is needed. It is not my primary goal. Sometimes it just works out that way.

What is the best part of being an illustrator?

As an illustrator you can play much more than as a designer. Of course, it depends on what kind of illustrator you are. Playing with forms, colors, shapes, techniques is a little bit closer to our perception of artists from the

The A.D.L. Under Fire
Client: *The New York Times,*
Op-Ed
Illustrator: Mirko Ilic
May 28, 1993

past. That is probably why they are still calling that artwork.

What is the best thing about being a designer?

Being a designer is much more restrictive than being an illustrator. What is the medium—electronic or print? If it is print, is it a poster, a book, a business card? Each piece of the puzzle has a different set of rules: the text, the logos, the photographs, or the artwork furnished by the client. How many colors? And what about the special effects? Are you embossing, varnishing? All that depends on the clients and their budget. Only when you have all these elements, when you know under which conditions they can be used, when you understand who your target audience is, can you start thinking about design. And that is when the best part begins. It's like classical ballet: known composition, strict limitation of motion, but it can still be beautiful and inspiring.

SVA To Help See Possibilities
Client: The School of Visual Arts
Creative Director: Anthony Rhodes
Art Director: Michael Walsh
Designer: Mirko Ilic
Illustrator: Mirko Ilic Corp.
2008

Steve Brodner

Graphic Commentary and Design

Steve Brodner is an illustrator and caricaturist. "But I think you can say that I am a storyteller," he notes. To tell stories, he depicts popular icons because "that's an effective way to get points across." He claims to be at the nexus of a tradition of print parody and the world of hypocrisy and pain. During 1979–1982, he published his own journal, the *New York Illustrated News*. In 1981, he became a regular contributor to *Harper's* magazine with the monthly feature, "Ars Politica." He has also contributed to *The National Lampoon*, *Sports Illustrated*, *Playboy*, *Spy*, and *Esquire* (as an unofficial house artist). He began doing portrait caricature, art journalism, and a back-page political cartoon, "Adversaria." This all served to convince him that illustration was an important part of the mix of any journalistic enterprise. His work appears today in *The New Yorker* and elsewhere.

Does art echo life or change it?
I think the answer is yes.
Illustrator: Steven Brodner

Your work tells stories. What stories do you tell?

My work is sensitive to current affairs. It tries to get behind news and examining who's involved and what makes them tick. Portraiture employs insight, which drawing, painting, writing can sharpen. The very act of rendering forces more precise examination.

How do you see illustration surviving in this era of democratic technologies?

The thing is to understand that the old rules are being radically revised. In the distant past (15 years ago), there were just a few big media venues that determined how we saw things and how we expressed reactions. Now the big ones have been shattered into many smaller pieces. You're right, the media world is more democratic; it is flatter. If you start a comic blog, it's possible someone will see it and give you a publication opportunity. If I post something on my site, an opposing political group may organize 100 people to flood it with comments, many of which I couldn't quote here. If I do a piece for a publication, that piece may be put on Facebook by the art director to show the world what he is doing. And then I get to see how many people "like" it. There is much more to be attentive to, but it is very easy to lose track of what's important.

You make videos. Does this mean you've adapted well to the new technologies?

Videos are an interesting aspect of the Web. Who would have thought that

Obamaloon
Client:
National Journal
Jan Zimmeck CD
Editor:
Ron Brownstein
Illustrator: Steven
Brodner

computers would make posting and watching video as easy as writing a Post-it note? But making a video is still extremely time-consuming. Unless you have a handle on how much time will be involved and how much you can afford to give it, it could consume you! I made video shorts for a few years and came to the conclusion that it wouldn't be a major component of my work.

Can illustration be a separate field any longer?
I think it has always been a collaborative art. That will continue. What we call it may change. What doesn't change is that people are driven to communicate with each other. They are delighted when that communication can be done with art. People are

going to keep figuring out how to stay engaged and entertained, and will be willing for pay for some of it.

What must an illustrator know now to succeed?
An artist must be free, first of all, to be true to him/herself. Know what you love and in what neck of the creative woods you want to spend your time working. Second, find your markets. See who's working and for whom. Target your work, promotion, and pitches so that people are seeing a comfortable person with ideas, very available to be even more brilliant. Third, know that you are an author. Always be working on a project that has a real shot of getting people interested in it and will also reinforce your (I hate the word but here it goes) "brand." This is nothing more than an association of content and form with yourself. Make sure it's real and you will be fine.

What do you look for in a solid illustrator? Is it more than art or craft?
Thinking, drawing, imagining, selling. Illustration will honor those people who can combine talents, skills. They will always land on their feet, coming up with a new, great thing.

The Mad Men of Climate Change
(opposite top)
The American Prospect
Creative Director, Designer:
Mary Parsons
2013

Ron Paul, Hero of Israel
(opposite bottom)
The Nation
2012

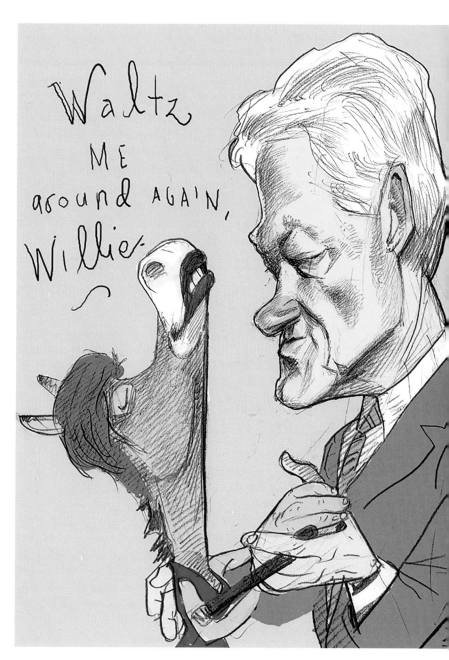

Bill Clinton Woos the
Democratic Convention
The Nation
Illustrator: Steven Brodner
2012.

Steven Guarnaccia

The Old New Illustration

Like most illustrators today, Brooklyn-based Steven Guarnaccia is a hyphenate: an illustrator-educator-writer-designer–kid's book author/illustrator. He illustrates children's books and [does illustration] for magazines and newspapers. He is a full-time faculty member at Parsons, where he was the illustration program director. He writes regularly for the illy coffee company blog. He is currently designing wine and olive oil labels for a small producer in Italy. And he is always working on his next children's book. *Cinderella: A Fashionable Tale* was published by Corraini Editions and Abrams in 2013.

Cinderella: A Fashionable Tale
Editors: Marszia Corraini,
Howard Reeves
Designer: Maurizio Corrraini
Publisher: Abrams
2013

You've been an illustrator for over three decades, but your work is very youthful. What is it about your style or method that stays on the curve rather than behind it?
First, I'm restless. I'm very distractible, and I constantly need new stimuli. I ravenously trawl for old books and unfamiliar visual imagery in the online and analog worlds. I've also never felt particularly virtuosic in any one medium, technique, or style. I didn't go to art school; I'm pretty much self-taught. So I try a lot of new things. These days I'm painting on old pieces of wood.

You define yourself as an illustrator, but you are also a designer—maybe not of books or magazines, but of things where you can apply your art and lettering. What prompted you to break out of the illustration mold?
I don't know that I ever broke out of the illustration mold. Rather, I'm not sure I ever fit very comfortably into it. When I was in college, Milton Glaser's seminal book, *Graphic Design*, had just been published. It was called *Graphic Design* but it was filled with illustrations, typeface designs, toy designs, a design for a cocktail. My parents really didn't understand what it was I wanted to do. I showed them that book and said, "This is who I want to be."

Having started out as an editorial illustrator, do you believe it is a sustainable career?
There's wonderful work being published in magazines and newspapers— both ink on paper and online. But I realized early on, quite some time before the so-called decline of illustration, that it wasn't going to be fulfilling to me for very long to plug holes in text columns in magazines with my drawings. At a certain point, I wanted to initiate the word-image conversation rather than just respond to it.

Busy Bust City Street
Design Director: Denise Cronin
Designer: Steven Guarnaccia
Illustrator: Steven Guarnaccia
Publisher: Viking

You've created products galore: ties, pencils, textiles, clocks, etc. How did you enter this field of objects?
First, I had already started making one-of-a-kind objects, often painting on something that already existed— a lobster buoy, a salad bowl, a piece of doll's house furniture—vas a break from my full schedule as an editorial illustrator. The impulse to make something that had form and a reason of its own for existing was very strong. I had written about my collection of Rooster brand ties from the fifties and sixties for *GQ*, and the company contacted me to design a line of ties. I think the illustrator-designed product was a new and exciting area for me and others. It certainly helped expand the definition of what an illustrator does.

Were you to start over, would you follow the same route?
The world of illustration today is very different than it was when I entered it. So I don't know if a route similar to the one I took even exists anymore. I would, however, probably make more

personal work, one-of-a-kind work, from the beginning, rather than wait as long as I did.

Is digital media part of your creative, professional life?
Only when I research something online, either specifically for a job, or for general creative inspiration. And I deliver much of my work digitally.

What do you advise that illustrators do to have a viable career?
I've always felt that having ideas is more important than having talent. I tell young illustrators to pursue what interests them most, what they're passionate about, and to initiate projects from the start. I teach a zine class, and I encourage young illustrators to self-publish, to get their work into the world directly, without the filter of the editors and publishers.

Brogue
Painted Found Shoe

'L LAC/Wine Label
Designer: Steven Guarnaccia
Art Director: Simone Barlottini
2013

Buzz Saw
Painted Found Saw

Berlin Guitar
Painted Found Ukulele

Neil Gower

Fraudulent Graphic Designer

Neil Gower from Newport, South Wales, UK, calls himself a freelance graphic artist, not a graphic designer. And why not? He studied at Ravensbourne and Brighton Schools of Art, graduating in 1984, and works in a range of disciplines, from book jackets to magazine covers, illustrated maps, and garden plans. Within each of these, he employs a wide range of graphic styles, but the single factor that unifies all of his work "is an exploration of the interplay between images and words." He produces all of his images by hand, using traditional media, but says he "delights in the modern technology that allows him to communicate with and supply his work to clients in Europe, North America, Asia, and Australia."

Pigtopia
Client: Faber & Faber
Illustrator: Neil Gower
Art Director: Shona Andrew
2005

You have said you don't think of yourself as a graphic designer. What else would you call combining image and letter?
I feel something of a fraud calling myself a graphic designer. I imagine graphic design "proper" to involve far more discipline and complexity than what I do, which feels essentially like having fun with words and paint. I often feel as if I do paintings of graphic design. Maybe that extra degree of detachment is my way of dealing with the "impostor syndrome" that most creative people feel.

My work is too illustrative to be graphic design, yet it is too graphic to be pure illustration. And, as my degree was in illustration rather than graphics, I feel that disqualifies me from displaying the brass plaque, as it were!

You appear to have a variety of styles. Is style important to you?
I have a magpie approach to style, which I hope transcends mere imitation. I like to create designs that take elements from several disparate sources and combine them to form something surprising that is more than the sum of its parts. The way that different techniques, styles, and letterforms can be folded together to elicit a particular response from the viewer is something that one can never stop learning about. I have a vast collection of ephemera, which I turn to for inspiration, including countless old atlases, maps, and guidebooks—and even 120 espresso cups, each of which is a typographic jewel.

Underlying this approach are three concerns: firstly, a fear of being

Appointment In Samarra
Client: Penguin Classics
Deluxe Editions
Illustrator/Designer:
Neil Gower
Art Director: Paul Buckley
2012

typecast and of being a "flavor of the month." Secondly, that impostor's fear of being caught out—I figure a moving target is always harder to hit. Third, and most important, is the need to avoid complacency: I have to keep scaring, surprising, and reinventing myself in order to keep things interesting and fresh.

How would you categorize your manner or method? Is it conceptual, formal, or what?
"Formal" and "rigorous" are the first words that spring to mind, involving

exhaustive preparatory sketches and, in the case of book jackets, reading. I would love to respond more spontaneously to a brief and to count on a last-minute flash of genius, but that just isn't me. My ideas have to develop slowly, percolating through page upon page of notes and thumbnail sketches. These apparently repetitious thumbnails are helpful, as their inevitable subtle differences allow one to judge nuances of scale and line within the frame.

There can be a conceptual element to what I do, to the extent that illustra-

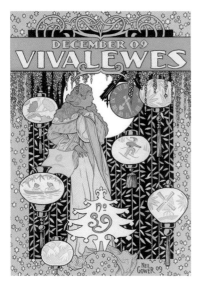

tion need not be literal depiction. For example, when putting together my 50th anniversary cover design for *Lord of the Flies*, I was asked to avoid the hackneyed imagery of broken spectacles, conch shells, pigs' heads and so on. I chose to devise something based on ancient Aboriginal/Oceanic art because that immediately conveyed a sense of the atavism explored in the book and also hinted at the exotic location. It was also very visually striking and ultimately sang out from the bookstore shelves.

What have been your goals? How have you pursued them? And have you gotten there?

I always wanted to be a "commercial artist." I love the discipline imposed by the limitations of a brief, and developing the skill of responding to a brief is as important as improving on one's drawing. Often, what a client DOESN'T say can be as telling

as what he/she does say. One then has to respond by devising a solution that meets all the client's requirements whilst allowing you to express yourself fully, which will ultimately give them a wow moment. It's also worth bearing in mind that the person briefing you is taking quite a leap of faith and spending considerable amounts of money for which he/she is answerable.

Are you happy with what you do?

I suppose I can say I've gotten there if "there" is still working and occasionally receiving prestigious commissions. Underlying this, however, is not satisfaction that the phone is still ringing after 30 years, but the continuing fear that I'll be caught out and it will stop ringing in a few weeks. Those prestigious commissions STILL bring with them the sense that there's been some kind of error and that this lovely, coveted project is now somehow tainted by my involvement.

Do you work alone or with others, like interns or apprentices?

I work alone. I'm often asked if I could use an assistant/apprentice but, as clients pay for my brushstrokes and lettering, I've never seen how it could work. The best analogy I can offer is that of an actor getting someone else to act in the easier scenes, which would be patently absurd. When students contact me for advice, I am always careful to respond, but I'd like to engage more with young people starting out in the profession, and I'm hoping to find opportunities to talk more often at colleges and so on.

Do you see illustrating and lettering as being a viable future?

Absolutely, provided, that is, that one remains sufficiently flexible and alert to changing technologies and media. As long as people need to communicate— and they seem to have an increasing desire and need to do so—there will be a need for images and words crafted by professionals to help them do so.

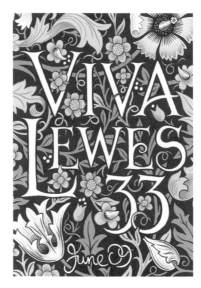

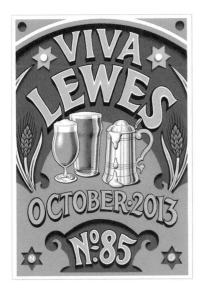

VivaLewes
(opposite and above)
Client: *Arts Listing Magazine* in
Lewes, Sussex
Illustrator/Designer: Neil Gower

One Summer
Client: Doubleday UK
Illustrator: Neil Gower
Art Director: Claiare Ward
2013

Craig Frazier

Designing Pictures

Craig Frazier, from Mill Valley, California, started as an illustrator/designer in 1978. In 1995, he focused exclusively on illustration and is commissioned by national and international design firms, advertising agencies, and publications to create distinct illustrations. "I think of myself as an illustrator who brings a designer's expertise to his work—and a designer who can draw," he says. A frequent contributor to *The New York Times* as well as business publications like *Time* magazine, *Fortune, Business Week, Harvard Business Review,* and *The Wall Street Journal,* Frazier also collaborates with design firms and ad agencies to promote and brand major corporations. Among those companies are Adobe, American Express, Boeing, Chevrolet, Deloitte, MasterCard, Navigant, The Royal Mail, the U.S. Postal Service, and United Airlines. He has created seven postage stamps, including the 2006 Love stamp and the 2010 and 2012 commemorative Scouting stamps. He has published a monograph, titled *The Illustrated Voice* (Graphis Press, 2003) and 11 children's books.

Listairs, Personal
Illustrator: Craig Frazier
2013

What triggered your foray into illustration?

Though I love design, the practice of running a design studio is relatively inhibiting to personal expression compared to illustration. Illustration requires many of the same problem-solving skills that I practiced in design —but permits, (and demands) a level of subjectivity and style that is absent in design. As a designer, I was creating design solutions that gave away the primary visuals to other illustrators and photographers. I wanted some of that fun for myself. The other simple fact is that I like to draw, and that was not getting nurtured as a designer.

Who are the influences in your work? Do I see a bit of the German Expressionists and Sachplakat too?

I think that since my DNA is [that of] a designer, I am drawn to the poster as influence simply because of its intention to create a singular message. I am influenced by Sachplakat primarily for its boldness and simplicity. The idea of the representation of elements in graphic terms never goes out of style, especially in these visually polluted times. As an illustrator, I am probably most influenced by some of the great conceptual illustrators and designers like Paul Rand, Ivan Chermayeff, Guy Billout, Christoph Neimann, Luba Lukova, and Shigeo Fukuda.

Stanleyfish, Stanley Goes Fishing
Illustrator: Craig Frazier
2006

Do you work alone?

I do all my illustration and production alone, and I have an assistant who runs the day-to-day operation of the studio.

In fact, how do you work? Is the computer a primary tool for you?

I'm a big sketcher and work almost exclusively with a Micron .01 pen in Moleskines or on vellum. I then cut my illustrations out of Amberlith, scan [them] into the computer, and color in Photoshop. Start analog; finish digital.

Can you give me an example of how the "idea" comes to you? Is there a sketch process?

For me, ideas come in the form of answers to the problem. I sketch a lot, very small, looking for a compelling visual that asks the viewer to get involved. I don't think "what does this look like?" Instead I think in terms of "what does this say?" This approach tends to lead me down roads that make for surprises and odd juxtapositions in reality. Sometimes

I can sketch immediately what my mind sees, and it becomes one of those satisfying solutions. However, most of the time, I am trying to get down a lot of little visual notions that drive me toward a solution. I'm looking for some cross-pollination or collision of notions that measure up to a new idea. You can't get there without squeezing it out, pure and simple.

You've engaged in many entrepreneurial projects. Is this necessary for sanity or security?
I suppose this is the benefit of being a designer first. I am interested in thematic work, like books, websites, and series. I recognize that the world of an illustrator has a certain limitation because the work typically grows out of a client-driven context. I feel it is my responsibility to try new things and put some of that work out for consumption if I want to grow my business. For example, I built a series of animations as an experiment and ended up getting viable animation assignments. My first kid's book grew out of one of those animations. That being said, I have dozens of personal projects in progress that will never be anything more than "satisfying practice."

What do you look for in other artists' work?
I look for the same thing I want my work to aspire to. I want to be surprised, inspired, consumed—and a certain measure of envy. I want to see work that makes me want to up my own game. In the same week, I saw the Hockney show and the movie *Nebraska* and both inspired me in similar and different ways. Both had

artistic qualities that I could relate to and easily aspire to. Both of them touched me in very simple and sincere terms. That's good work.

Late for the Sky (above)
Navigant Consulting
Illustrator: Craig Frazier
2009

Spikeclimbing (opposite)
Personal
Illustrator: Craig Frazier
2012

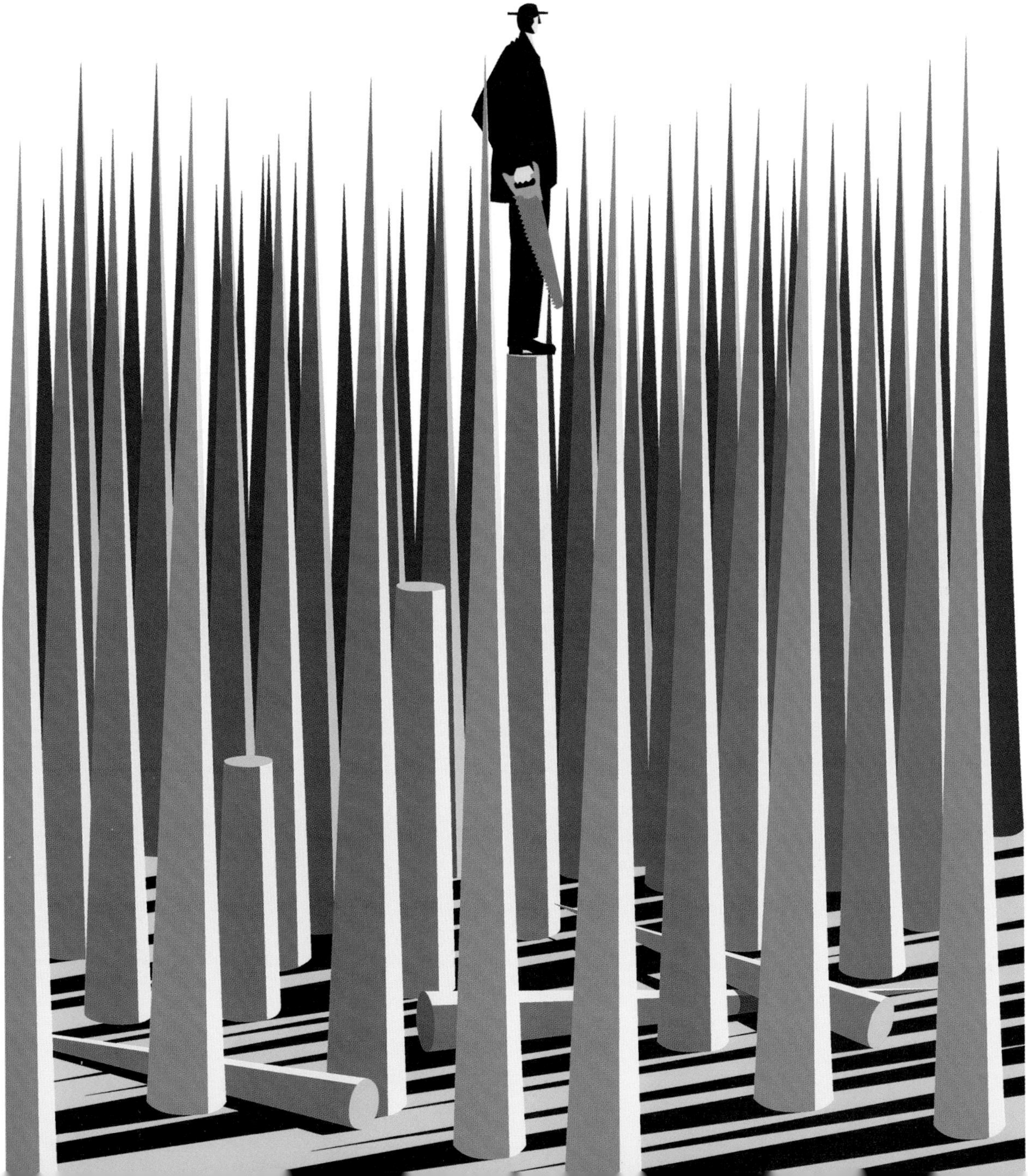

Transitional Design

The introduction of digital media was, for many graphic designers, a major disruption of geological proportions. While some reaffirmed their allegiance to printed matter, considering that the new technologies were nothing more than advanced production tools, others, driven by curiosity, chose the path of experimentation. But there were no signposts along the way. Words had to be crafted to describe choices and options. Transmedia projects. Creative ambidexterity. Data visualization. Integrated thinking. Experience Design. The new jargon did nothing to explain what was happening. The first graphic designers who ventured outside the boundaries of the known analog realm were speaking in tongues!

However, their work was quite sensational. If they had trouble naming what they did, the results spoke for themselves. Even though their practice was "transitional" (another word that doesn't say much), these designers won big awards, were invited to participate in juries, spoke at international conferences, made headlines, and had museum retrospectives.

Today, there is a new generation of graphic designers who haven't experienced this transitional phase firsthand but who have retained the multidisciplinary approach pioneered by their peers. One can count on them to usher in new ideas and unexpected practices. Most of them are self-taught and entrepreneurial in spirit. To join their ranks, graphic designers don't have to be fluent in programming codes or even technologically proficient, but they must be fast learners. Critical is an ability to hit the ground running and get up to speed in no time at all.

If you happen to be this type A individual, the number of opportunities for employment can be mind-boggling. You can join teams of Web designers who are exploring novel ways to navigate information and interact with it. You can find work in the field of motion graphics, where you will be prompted to develop your storytelling skills. You can he hired by advertising agencies to work, in their "lab" department, where researchers explore new media options and concoct alternative tactics for social networking marketing.

How do you break in? By having a passion and doing something about it, whether it is claymation or bookbinding, prototyping or broadcasting, information graphics or wayfinding. Develop projects that demonstrate how you approach the topic of your choice. Bring a product or a service of your own making to the market. Raise money for a venture with a crowd-funding campaign. Design an app. Initiate a cycle of conferences. Open a small gallery. Make mini-documentary films.

The measure of success in this space we call "transitional design" is not how things look but how things "work."

Needless to say, no one aspires to job security in this career path! As the saying goes, "The ink doesn't dry in the digital age." But, as confirmed by the next series of interviews, there is no shortage of successful people in this category. What these innovators have in common is a certain amount of charisma, not because of their personality, but because of their attitude—a fearless disdain for preconceived ideas.

11 Understanding Change

Today, initiating new interactions is often more productive than generating new products, new forms, or new styles. Graphic designers who collaborate with people in other disciplines—architects, choreographers, linguists, mathematicians, chefs—are discovering that they can expand their practice beyond the confines of the conventional boundaries for their profession and still retain their distinctive competence. Truth be told, there are very few domains in which the input of graphic designers doesn't enhance the end result and elevate the conversation.

Richard Saul Wurman

The Architect of Understanding

Richard Saul Wurman, an American architect, is best known as the cofounder of the TED conferences, (Technology Entertainment Design), the 16-minute presentation format in which charismatic speakers pitch new ideas that will change the world. He also created the TEDMED conferences and the e.g. conferences. A new format, the WWW suite of gatherings, is now in development. Wurman is also credited for having coined the term "information architecture." He demonstrated how to present data effectively with a series of travel guidebooks in which vast amounts of information were dissected into smaller maps, graphs, and text blocks. Along with more than 40 Access guidebooks, he authored *Information Anxiety* (1989), *Understanding Healthcare* (2004), and 33: *Understanding Change & the Change in Understanding* (2009). One piece of information he has trouble sharing with others is his motivation. "I want you to understand something," he says. "I do not have a message. I do not have a mission. All I am trying to do is not be boring."

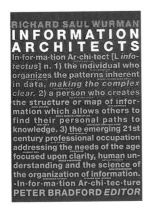

Information Architects
by Richard Saul Wurman
1997

Back in 1984, when you put together your first TED conference, what was your objective?
All I was trying back then was to create a conference I would personally enjoy—one featuring people who intrigued me. I wasn't trying to "share" my interests with others, but rather satisfy my own curiosity. Granted, it was egocentric and self-serving. I just wanted my programs to be "good." And they were.

My very first conference was amazing. Among the speakers were Frank Gehry, who wasn't famous yet;

Steve Jobs, who made public for the first time three working prototypes of the Macintosh; Nicholas Negroponte, who announced the MIT Media Lab; and the president of Sony USA, who distributed shiny little disks—the first CDs anyone had ever seen. I wasn't trying to change the world—but my guests did!

I sold TED in 2003 to a gentleman who, unlike me, is trying to "change" the world. There is a fundamental difference between him, who wants to "do good"— and me, who wants to "be good" at whatever I happen to be working on.

Your mission might not be to change the world, but isn't it to make information more understandable?

I have written many books on the topic of "understanding"—too many titles probably: *Understanding Healthcare, Understanding USA, Understanding Children, Understand Change & the Change in Understanding*, and so on.

Let me put it succinctly: Usually, to make things understandable, graphic designers illustrate words. They put pretty pictures on words. That's not what I suggest you do. You should use words when words are better; you should use pictures when pictures are better. And you should marry them both when that's better.

You were one of the pioneers of data visualization with your ACCESS books—graphically intelligent city guidebooks published in the 1970s. In fact, aren't you credited with coining the term "information architecture"?

Yes, however, people give me credit for a lot of things, but really my passion is to try to understand what it's like NOT to understand. That's all I ever do. I sell my ignorance.

But I cannot go to a publisher, or to anybody for that matter, and say: "Here is a topic that interests me, but I don't understand it. Can you give me money so that I can find out?" Needless to say, I would never get the money. That's why I generate my own projects.

The Urban Observatory Exhibit
San Diego
2013

My mission is not to make information more understandable. My mission is to go from not knowing . . . to not knowing. I never try to sell my expertise. In fact, rather, I sell my ignorance. When I am finished with a book or a project, it's over. It's done. I have no interest in it. I am on to the next thing—to the next thing that I don't know anything about.

And what is the "next thing" today?

There is a bunch of next things. Last year it was a conference format called "www," in which presenters were paired in improvised dialogues. There is also my "Urban Observatory," a new graphic initiative to compare information on urban centers, and something called "The Orchard of Understanding." It's a lot to explain!

But my latest-latest project is called "555." It's a series of conferences to try to satisfy my curiosity about the future. The format is: five cities, five speakers in each city, giving predictions for the next five years. I am 78 years old; what am I curious about? I am curious about "next"—next being the next 5 years, not the next 10, 15, or 50 years.

What will be the format?

I'll improvise, as I always do in these situations, but within an extremely well-curated nebula of visual information, including cartography, diagrams, interactive maps, and so on. We'll start in Australia and go around the world. Then Berlin, Singapore . . . and within a year, all 25 speakers will have had improvised conversations with me about what we can expect in the next five years.

You improvise! You are fearless!

I am absolutely comfortable saying whatever is on my mind. I feel that there is no filter between my brain and my mouth. Now, that looks like being fearless. Maybe it's because I am primitive, immature, childlike, egomaniacal, not too bright. Maybe I am like the *Emperor Who Has No Clothes.*

I don't know another way to be— but I can tell you, it works well. I am successful.

Crossing Diciplines

Many graphic designers are content to design beautiful lettering, splendid pages and packages, or smart logos for the course of their entire careers. Developing such skills over time is both personally rewarding and professionally satisfying, to be sure. But others are not content about having only a single specialty. Some view specialization as offering too few challenges and therefore explore numerous options as a matter of personal pride and preference. Still others believe that specialization equals limitation, and limitation in this expanding field is professional suicide.

Well, suicide may be too gruesome, but variety informs longevity. And the secret to longevity is not a marketable style but, rather, keeping abreast of shifts in all media and incorporating as many of these as possible into your own repertoire.

Crossing disciplines is not an exception to the rule—it is the rule. If one is unable to solve problems in more than one discipline, a client will eventually go to someone who can. Survival of the fittest demands versatility. Crossing disciplines means that a graphic designer must be something of a chameleon. Today, crossover disciplines are woven into the graphic designer's education or daily routine, yet they also must be sought out, learned, and practiced.

The most common crossovers involve aspects of all forms of digital media for television, film, video, and exhibitions, requiring both interest and skill in complementary media, including music, lighting, and editing, for example. Graphic designers have also become more proactive in the process of conception and management in a variety of areas. The quintessential cross-disciplinary graphic designer is not merely a subcontractor serving the needs of so-called higher-echelon designers but is an active participant in an overarching planning and design scheme, a valued member of a team that integrates several media into one entity.

How To Talk About Your Work: The TED Model

By turning business pitches into 16-minute cabaret acts, the high-spirited TED conferences have changed forever the way we talk about our work.

The "E" in TED stands for "entertainment." Long gone are the days when audiences sat still while lecturers lectured and speakers spoke. "I didn't want to have to listen to boring people," says Richard Saul Wurman, who came up with the TED concept back in 1984 (see page 189). How do you make sure that no one yawns while you speak? Regardless of the topic, you have to present ideas that have a potential to change the world.

That's why, before being allowed to walk on the TED stage, presenters are coached by professional media trainers. Regardless of their accomplishments, scientists, activists, pioneers, astronauts, survivors, humanitarians, inventors, Nobel laureates, ex-presidents—and designers—are taught to perform.

It's a grueling experience, according to people who lived to tell the tale. Even Chip Kidd was terrified. Milton Glaser and Paula Scher took it in stride. Stefan Sagmeister turned out to be a natural. If it were your turn, how would you feel knowing that every word coming out of your mouth was going to be translated into 100 languages?

You might as well be prepared. Here are tips, just in case you get a call from a member of the TED conferences selection committee.

1. Make it personal: Briefly, tell your audience who you are (self-deprecation is an option).

2. Have a snappy name for your project. Recount how you came up with it.

3. Explain the problem you propose to solve.

4. Back to you: why you can do something about it.

5. This is the storytelling part of your presentation: Take your time, use your hands, walk around, build suspense, show pictures.

6. The moment has come to ask your audience one or two rhetorical questions. Answer them promptly.

7. As you are about to conclude, bring one last visual on the screen—a quote or a chart.

8. Describe your next step—what you will do tomorrow.

9. Take a deep breath before saying "Thank you."

Petrula Vrontikis

Creating Interactions

Petrula Vrontikis is the owner and creative director of Vrontikis Design Office, in Los Angeles, and a leading voice in design education for over 20 years. Like most graphic designers who have been practicing for many years, her work has transitioned from creating artifacts to creating interactions. She still does the occasional catalog, brochure, or poster, but mostly she's designing for online communications. What she calls her "creative ambidexterity" allows her to move around freely between worlds—between traditional and "transmedia" communication strategies. "Southern California is a great place to practice design because it's a great place to live," she notes. "It's a place where creativity is valued and crazy ideas can find like minds."

Why is Southern California a great place to practice design?
Los Angeles has been primarily an entertainment industry town, but designing for that sector has become intolerable and no longer lucrative. However, fresh, dynamic tech companies have created Silicon Beach in the Santa Monica and Venice areas. Pasadena is aggressively fostering innovative companies and venture capitalists. This has cultivated a start-up culture that's energizing young entrepreneurs to create their own products and services. It's a very exciting time to be a designer here. It's been terrific to see so many pioneering firms flourish here.

How has the culture of Los Angeles influenced your design sensibility?
To some, it may sound trivial, but the great weather here helps me keep a sunny disposition and a clear outlook.

I'm a seriously happy person in a seriously lovely place. Plus, Los Angeles attracts wildly talented young people who choose to start their careers in graphic design. It's made teaching at Art Center College of Design so deeply meaningful.

You are a teacher, a lecturer, and a writer as well as a graphic designer. Is your love of words related to your love of typography?
Yes, absolutely. I love the power that letterforms have to both clarify and abstract messages and meaning. I love the play of words in both writing and design.

In your spare time, you are an underwater photographer. Back on dry land, you "swim" between various design cultures. Is transmedia graphic design a little bit like scuba diving?

UCLA Extension Fall Quarter Poster
Designer: Petrula Vrontikis
2013

The Changing Landscape of Philanthropy
Designer: Petrula Vrontikis
Photography by Susan Burks
2013

Scuba diving is certainly a cross-media multisensorial experience! To survive, you must be agile—equipped with everything required in an ever-changing environment. An accomplished diver attains something called neutral buoyancy—a kind of mastery of the underwater "formal skills" where you float weightlessly without effort, neither sinking nor rising. The equivalent for a transmedia graphic designer could be called "creative ambidexterity," which combines the skills, equipment, and mind-set for her/him to swim confidently between print, digital, dimensional, interactive, motion, and environmental media.

For both the designer and the diver, this toggling becomes second nature, so we no longer have to think about barriers anymore. We become free to make left turns, travel upside down

and sideways—becoming fearless and playful. Interacting with a well-crafted Transmedia project feels spontaneous and delightful.

Processing—the software—can generate incredible visuals. It's critical for students to immerse themselves in it (the underwater metaphor is unintended). In your evaluation, is generative design an important new discipline—and why?

Generative design is so powerful that I believe it will enable an entire generation of young designers to create motivations and circumstances that could never have been imagined. Its power as a medium to engage and interact with both individuals and communities is only in its infancy. Graphic designers are at the forefront of this unique expressive science experiment. It's an entirely new language that transcends cultural and communication boundaries.

What would you say is the main advantage of being a woman in the design field?

I believe women have greater access to empathy—which is the successful designer's secret weapon. Empathy energizes the design process, builds trust, and connects people to ideas emotionally.

Many women designers and educators I know inspire others and bring meaning to what they do personally and professionally. It pleases me to see women in more leadership positions than ever before. Attributes considered "female" seem to be the emerging keys to effective creative leadership.

Lemonade Restaurant Website
Designer: Petrula Vrontikis
2013

Lemonade Restaurant Signage
at LAX Airport
Designer: Petrula Vrontikis
Photography: Bill Brown
2011

Erik Adigard des Gautries

The Experience of the Information

Erik Adigard des Gautries is a media artist and graphic designer who studied in France and in the USA before creating M-A-D, also known as "madsx," a brand and communication studio with Patricia McShane in the San Francisco Bay area. Remarking on the fact that he is a consultant on projects that include branding, print, Web, video, exhibits, and multimedia, he says: "It feels like Sisyphus. We are immersed in forever shifting media— the tools, supports, networks, languages, cultures—and therefore the nature of our commissions is continually changing." His design solutions have always been surprising: from his visuals essays for *Wired* magazine in 1992 to his involvement with the U.S. pavilion for the Venice Architecture Biennale in 2012.

Venice Architecture Biennale
U.S. Pavilion
Designer: Erik Adigard
Studio: M-A-D
Art Director: Erik Adigard
2012

I think of you as someone who "curates" projects at the boundaries between emerging medias. But how do you describe what you do?
Our profession is full of ambiguities, and that is perhaps where the notion of "curating" might often be more relevant than a mere focus on typography, imagery, and other core graphic design functions. At the end of the day, our job is to help bring the ventures of others into specific parts of the world. These specificities demand that we be adaptive, accurate, and relevant to cultural and technological conditions. For the last two centuries, technology has been the driver of culture, with designers as tentative catalysts to keep it on a constructive track.

You relish projects involving complexity, like branding IBM software and redesigning their icon systems. Only two or three people on the planet really understand what you are trying to explain. Is it fun?
Branding IBM software was an epic and extremely interesting assignment, and a puzzle to tackle in that we had to create a cohesive system for five software initiatives that thousands of IBM designers could easily apply to communications, ranging from websites to packaging and exhibits. The original brand architecture of IBM software was dated, messy, full of meaningless brand gestures, and expensive to maintain. We had written a short letter to raise our concern: It influenced them to include M-A-D in the competition for the rebrand campaign.

You are a maven when it comes to abstract thought. What's your secret?
I don't buy the pretense of "design thinking" but do believe that thinking is inherently a part of design, as abstraction is part of thinking, even if necessarily complemented with context and objectives. My time studying semiotics and linguistics in Paris did help to develop an analytical mind, but I also am inspired by and learn from others with critical thinking skills: architects, sociologists, journalists, philosophers, theorists, and so on. Much of my thinking is the outcome of due process observations and interpretations. In that sense, it is more a craft than an art and more a matter of influences than one of instinct.

You said once that graphic design can help us "reframe the information that matters most." In your work, the information that matters most is often the experience of the information. Do you agree?
That is such a great way to put it! I am beginning to surrender to the idea that in this world, "experience" matters more than information. I mean this in two ways. First, experience can be a meaningful sensorium of ideas, some poetic and others empirical, but mostly this is an artistic point of view, and second, with interface design user experience factors are at the core of our practice yet are meant to be transparent and at the service of information.

Chapter 50: AirXY Venice
Architecture Biennale
Designers: Erik Adigard, Chris Salter
Studio: M-A-D
Art Director: Erik Adigard
2008

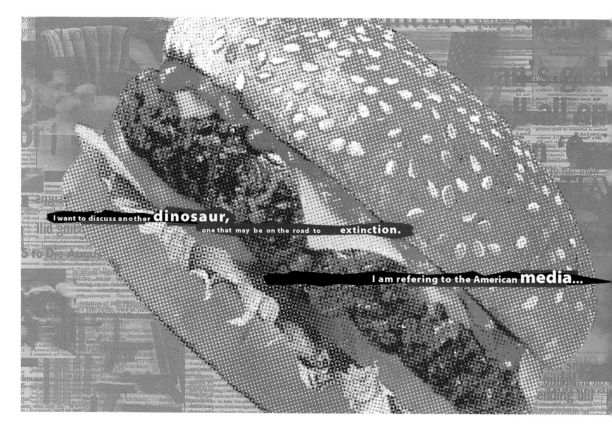

I want to discuss another **dinosaur,** one that may be on the road to **extinction.**

I am refering to the American **media...**

Spreads from *Wired* Magazine
(1993–2000) (above)
Designers: Erik Adigard, Patricia
McShane, Philip Foeckler
Studio: M-A-D
Art Director: Erik Adigard
1993–2000

AGI Save the Bees Poster
(bottom opposite)
Designer: Erik Adigard
Studio: M-A-D
Art Director: Erik Adigard
2010

There is a striking difference between your 2008 and your 2012 Venice Architectural Biennale installations. The first one was highly technological, while the second one only used paper shades and pulleys. Were you trying to make a point?

My 2008 Venice Biennale installation was a creative commission—an experimental design exploration about media and the environment in all its dimensions. It was conceived as a physical and emotive sensorium, with sounds, sensors, lights, rhythms, flows, and even an atmosphere. The use of sensors, fog, a strobe, and a vertical projection gave the whole a peculiar sculptural quality.

In contrast, the 2012 U.S. Pavilion installation was a commission from the State Department, whose concern was information more than formal expressions. The curator, Cathy Lang Ho, the Guggheneim's David Van Leer, and Freecell architects also played a role in the interactive analog approach. One of my key contributions was to set the massive contextual information on the floor below the visitors and the 124 projects hanging from the ceiling. The simple interaction, combined with the idea of displaying the entire body of information, was a gamble enthusiastically embraced by the visitors and the Biennale judges.

I use the term extinction **literally.**

To my mind, it is likely that what we now understand as the mass media will be gone within ten years. **Vanished**, without a trace."
– Michael Crichton

You always work in network, with designers, architects, researchers, editors, programmers, and so on. Is your role in the team that of a "cultural mediator"?

Architects, writers, programmers, composers, theorists, curators, and other experts have played an important role in M-A-D's evolution in bringing their distinct perspectives. These are usually complementary, but sometimes they introduce creative disconnects, which is when the big questions are raised. Regardless, the outcome is sure to be surprisingly interesting. The grass is always greener on the other side, yet learning from others can result in ending back on your own turf!

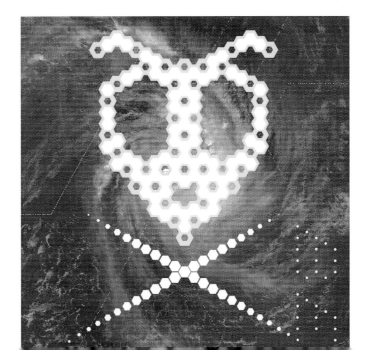

Véronique Marrier

Graphic Design as a Cause

Véronique Marrier is graphic design project manager for the CNAP (Centre National des Arts Plastiques), the French national center for visual arts. After graduating in literature in Bordeaux, she opened in 1996 the first gallery in France that was exclusively dedicated to graphic design. She then moved to Paris in 2000 and worked freelance for the Chaumont Poster Festival, the Graphic Design conferences at Echirolles, and a number of other cultural institutions before getting a job at the Ministry of Culture. "On top of my day job, I have always been involved in a half-dozen other projects," she says, "a newsletter for an Italian paper company; the launch of B42, a small publishing venture; plus all the events, juries, initiatives, and conferences I organize, assist or attend."

L'épreuve du temps, Graphisme
en France
Publisher: CNAP
Graphic Designers: Léa Chapon,
Mytil Ducomet/Atelier 25
2011

Can you tell us about your work so far?
Right out of graduate school, I worked in a gallery in Bordeaux, Galerie 90 degrés, an art space specializing in graphic design. I was creating exhibitions and events, doing everything from finding sponsors, curating collections, booking speakers, and supervising the design of catalogues. In 2002, I worked in the press office of the contemporary art museum of Rochechouart, a chateau in the Southwest of France that is home to an important archive of the work Raoul Haussmann—about 700 pieces, including collages, photograms, and experimental films. Two years later, I got an assistant position at the Ministry of Culture, where I had an opportunity to develop a series of cultural publications on the theme of graphic design.

Do you now have an opportunity to help shape government policies toward graphic design?
In France, graphic design is not a profession as much as it is a form of social, political, or philosophical engagement. The concept of official "policies" doesn't exist. The way I can help shape the future of graphic design in France is by being "engaged" myself on a number of fronts. My "causes," if you want, include issues of language, the role of the new digital tools in defining how we communicate, the history of graphic design, and contemporary French typography.

Were you ever tempted to become a practicing graphic designer?
I am not a "practicing" graphic designer; however, "practicing" graphic

design is exactly what I do! I "practice" by being an actor in the field, by creating opportunities for events, conferences, publications, acquisitions, proposals, and research projects. My "practice" consists in developing, analyzing, decrypting, interpreting, curating, art directing, managing, and promoting. All those different activities are what most graphic designers do today on a daily basis. The profession is no longer just about communicating specific ideas or messages—it is the coming together of various strategic pursuits having to do with visual expression.

From your point of view, what is the main contribution of graphic designers to the digital culture?
I am glad you asked this question because graphic designers have a very special talent: They think from the top down rather than from the bottom up. They come up with ideas that are all-inclusive rather than deductive. In other words, they have a capacity for integrated thinking.

That's why the digital age is the age of graphic designers! The merging together of experimental techniques involving visualizing, processing, computing, coding, scaling, and modeling comes naturally to them. If I give a graphic designer a brief for a publishing project, for instance, he'll turn it around on its head and come up with something totally unexpected. The technological component is just one of the many factors a graphic designer will incorporate in order to be truly creative. By "creative" I mean inventive, uninhibited, willing to propose a different world altogether.

Les Graphistes Associés
Group Show
Galerie 90 degrés, Bordeaux
1996

"<code><outils><design>"
Graphisme en France
Publisher: CNAP
Graphic Designers:
Guillaume Allard,
Johann Aussage,
Vanessa Goetz/Pentagon
2012

How do you define your mission as a government-appointed advocate for graphic design?

I want to help define graphic design as a "practice." I want clients, patrons, and users to think of it as a discipline for taking advantage of new opportunities and technologies, but also as a chance to reimagine how society functions. Because of the phenomenal number of innovations today, graphic designers are no longer limited by technology. Their unique experience, their personal vision, and their particular history are just as much part of their métier as their proficiency when using this or that software. Today, you experiment—for better or for worse. You take chances. You come up with hybrid solutions. You collaborate with unlikely partners. You work without safety nets.

It sounds exciting—but how do you keep it all together?

Paradoxically, the new generation is incredibly disciplined, intellectually. As I mentioned earlier, the credit for this renaissance goes to French design schools. In the last decade, they have required that all students write elaborate research papers before they can graduate. Design history and criticism are now part of the curriculum. By the time they hit the job market, young graphic designers are not only creatively mature and technologically savvy; they are also better informed than their potential employers and less isolated culturally. I love working with them: They are a very articulate group.

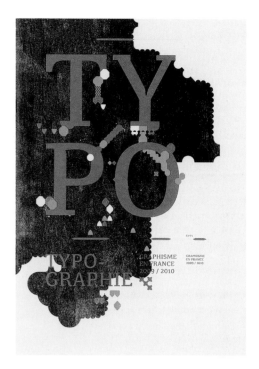

Typographie, Graphisme en France
Publisher: CNAP
Graphic Designers: Capucine Merkenbrack and Chloé Tercé/ Atelier Müesli
2010

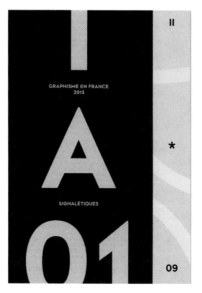

Signalétiques, Graphisme en France
Publisher: CNAP
Graphic Designers: Anna Chevance, Mathias Reynoird/ Atelier Tout va bien
2013

Making Transitions: Returning to School with Barbara DeWilde

Barbara DeWilde is a former book cover and magazine art director/designer. These days she says, "I'm a designer. Period." After many successful years in print design, she returned to school, the SVA MFA Interaction Program. She deliberately left her comfort zone, feeling that otherwise she would stagnate: The print business was narrowing, physical books were selling in smaller quantities compared to digital editions, printed magazines were losing ad revenues. The creative opportunities were narrowing. But figuring out her next professional step, and how to go about it, hadn't been easy.

She saw User Interaction Experience (UIX) as an opportunity, but returning to school after 25 years of professional experience was incredibly hard. "I was concerned that the learning curves would be steep and that I wouldn't have the digital chops to keep up with my classmates," she said. "I was concerned that I would embarrass myself with my knowledge gap. I worried about what my peers would think. And, finally, returning to graduate school would not guarantee anything in my future creative life. It was a leap of faith."

Leap she did, and what she learned was critical to her future: "In interaction design, you're not designing to communicate; you're designing for human behavior," she explained. "The designer needs to do research, make observations, design, and iterate. More often than not you are working in teams. With the exception of typography for magazines and book interiors, which has information design at its core, the cover design work I had been doing was largely emotional and intuitive. Now, I've learned to alternate these two approaches, methodical and intuitive, and to articulate my ideas more through models, diagrams, and writing."

She learned how code works, about business, entrepreneurship, and the Internet. She learned that to create a new digital product or service, it's essential to develop an online persona, to be known on the Web, and to network throughout the community. Interaction design is an open-hearted, open-source environment. People share. In the graphic design world, there's a lot of finger-pointing about who made what first, credit, and ownership. In the digital world, everyone can make a photo-sharing service and users can flock to the one that appeals to them. First to market or first to have an idea does not mean the best or the one-and-only.

DeWilde would like to launch a digital product and bring it to market, to contribute to a team that makes digital product designs, and to shift away from print unless it is the best medium for a design project. "To use a David Foster Wallace descriptive," she said. "I no longer want print design to be my default setting. I'm sorry I didn't make the switch sooner. I'm so anxious to clock in my 10,000 hours and to become an expert. I may not have enough time to reach that goal."

AIGA Exhibition
Designer: Barbara DeWilde
Client: AIGA

NY Times Mobile Opinion App
Designer: Barbara de Wilde
Photographer: Creative Time
Client: *NY Times*

12 Eccentrics and Design Quirkiness

The digital age, paradoxically, breeds quite a few eccentrics. Unlike "originals," who initiate trends that others may adopt, imitate, and exploit, "eccentrics" defy categorization. You cannot replicate what they do— nor would you want to. Eccentrics are not leaders because they do not have followers; neither can they be described as pioneers, pathfinders, torchbearers. Their role in society is to be "different." Free-spirited, self-motivated, with the courage to do their own thing, they also possess a mischievous sense of humor. Where would we be without these famous eccentrics: Pythagoras, James Joyce, Peggy Guggenheim, or Oscar Wilde?

Oddball graphic designers fall between the cracks, so to speak, but are able to develop unique approaches, never realizing that they don't fit into any identifiable niche. They take advantage of every new technology, fiddle with it, and make it work in ways that are unusual and offbeat. Mad collectors of vintage artifacts, obsessive hobbyists, stubborn software tinkerers, connoisseurs of cultural trivia, former musicians, chefs, or athletes, with or without political agenda, they were probably not trained as graphic designers, but when they stumbled on this discipline quite by chance, they were quick to embrace it.

These relentless inventors seldom take the time to explain what they do and why. But when they do, as is evident in the next candid interviews, they demonstrate that the difference between a graphic designer and an artist can be very small, indeed.

Charles S. Anderson
Celebrating Commercial Art

Charles S. Anderson is a product, packaging, and brand designer living in Minneapolis, Minnesota. Established in 1989, his company is famous for the graphic identity of his main client, French Paper, but also for its prodigious stock of original illustrations—the celebrated CSA Images. Although the majority of the collection was—and still is—created by in-house designers and illustrators, many are commissioned by independent designers worldwide. "I find inspiration in nearly everything ever designed or printed," says Anderson, "from diverse sources, some well-known, others from obscure artists, designers, and illustrators. The majority of this inspiration comes from the past because (for now at least!) it's more accessible than the future."

CSA Images
Art Director: Charles S. Anderson
Designers, Illustrators,
Contributors: Numerous
1989–2014

One of your goals is to keep alive the heritage, look, and feel of ink printed on paper—online! Paradoxically, in the digital age, the status of paper and paper products is greatly enhanced. How do you explain this phenomenon?

I'm fascinated with the idea of bringing paper into the digital realm and vice versa. Print on paper used to be perceived as ephemeral, but now, compared to the pop-up-and-delete nature of digital, it feels real and everlasting.

I own a perfectly legible, bound library of newspapers from various countries around the world spanning the 1850s through the 1980s. Although a bit tan around the edges and somewhat brittle, they still retain their clear and crisp print, which is more than I can say about my own archive that is preserved digitally, since the beginning of the 1990s. We had to migrate the images forward, over and over, to keep up with the latest technology for digital storage—otherwise, they would have become irretrievable and, as a result, completely lost.

You are putting all this effort into conserving a digital record of images from the past. Isn't it a little anachronistic?

Just as anachronistic are the fake 3-D, bubbly, glistening, gleaming, shiny, drop-shadow logos, and icons populating the Web. They are not more modern or dynamic but, rather, more gimmicky, usually in an attempt to jazz things up. The millions of cyber-slick, mathematically perfect, soulless vector images, with gradients in every quadrant, are often created because it's quick and easy, not because it's good or necessary. The fact that you can make something 3-D doesn't necessarily mean you should.

In contrast, digital images that mimic nostalgic printed matter, complete with their dot screens, misregistration, and transparent overlapping inks, have the ability to trigger powerful visual and tactile associations of past memories.

For you, technology is just a tool, isn't it?
You bet. I've been ranting against phony rendered 3-D type and logos for the past three decades. Finally, Google and Apple realized how lame this fake "skeuomorphic" 3-D approach is. They switched to flat and legible design (like the traditions of ink printed on paper). In doing so, they jolted out of their complacency every lemming agency, marketing company, design firm, and corporation that had mindlessly followed the 3-D trend. We are in a profession that has lost its focus, is fragmented, and has become

enamored, addicted, and distracted by technology.

Your creative output for French Paper is prodigious, and so is your ever-expanding contribution to the CSA Images collection. Can you tell us how you manage it all?
Over the past 40 years, more than 100 different artists, designers, illustrators, photographers, keyword specialists, software developers, and rights clearance attorneys have worked for us and with us at CSA, to create the CSA Images collection.

We've spent a staggering amount of time searching through every conceivable type of historic printed material to find the small percentage of images that are aesthetically interesting. They are then simplified and made more graphic, and are, in some cases, redrawn, colored, or combined with other elements to change the context and convey new ideas. The constantly expanding CSA Images collection is continually inspired by the entire history of graphic design and illustra-

tion, from their origins in printing and commercial art through the digital age—and continues to expand into new applications and mediums.

I assume that you are an obsessive collector of graphic artifacts?
I am not a "real collector"—but I do collect graphic artifacts, most of which occupy a substantial portion of the endless French Paper warehouses in Niles, Michigan. They have been crated up and shipped there over the decades. Many haven't seen the light of day since they were put into storage. I honestly don't even recall what most of the crates contain or exactly where they're located in the vast warehouses—possibly somewhere next to the Ark of the Covenant!

What type of collectible attracts your attention?
I used to purchase individual paper graphic artifacts from collectors, and also plastic objects, which I view as sculptures. Over time I began to realize that I was using up a large amount of my life collecting and that I would run out of time before my collections were complete. Either I had to collect more efficiently or somehow extend my lifespan. I devised a way to do both. From that point on, I no longer collected individual artifacts, but, instead I collected collections of artifacts. With this approach, I gained the

Poster Design
Clients: AIGA, Pacific Design Center, *Entertainment Weekly*, De Pree Gallery
Art Director: Charles S. Anderson
Designers: Charles S. Anderson, Jovaney Hollingsworth, Sheraton Green, Todd Piper-Hauswirth.
1989–2014

years spent by each collector whose collections I purchased. Meanwhile, my collection of plastic stuff has been growing for nearly half a century . . . 100,000 objects and counting. Our next project will be to scan these plastic objects in 3-D, to make products like jewelry, lamps, and the world's most bizarre lawn ornaments.

Beyond vernacular images, what else inspires you?

In addition to images, I've also been collecting letters, numerals, and words—handwritten or typeset. We have 10,000 unique individual words (not fonts) on the CSA Images site, searchable by keyword. They come from every imaginable printed source and span the history of wood, metal, and phototype, including thousands of hand-lettered words that we've created and compiled along the way. We've also recently added nearly 2,000 of the most unusual individual letters and numbers to our site. These are all different single letters and numbers that don't contain any matching alphabets.

Are designers who purchase CSA images predominantly targeting an American audience? Do you have buyers in Europe and Asia? In other words, is U.S. pop graphic sensibility now truly universal?

The CSA Images collection, although firmly based in American pop culture, has grown more international and eclectic over the years. In fact, today, we license more artwork outside of the USA than inside. Our images are popular in Asia and Europe. I'm not sure if this means that the U.S. pop graphic sensibility is universal or, rather, just a pop graphic sensibility. Or maybe amazing, unique, diverse illustrations created by hand are universally popular everywhere.

How do you imagine the future of graphic design in the digital age?

I see a different modernism in design evolving, one not based on anti-septic minimalism and an absence of humanity, but one that is rich in cultural vocabulary and personal expression; one that is equally at home on the printed page, the store

Product Design
Client: Pop Ink
Art Director: Charles S. Anderson
Designers: Sheraton Green,
Jovaney Hollingsworth, Erik Johnson
Illustrator: CSA Images
Writer: Mike Nelson
2001–2014

shelf, or the digital realm. It is a design philosophy and approach that first acknowledges where we came from and uses that understanding to create a new path to the future.

Antoine Audiau and Manuel Warosz

Over-the-Top Digital D.I.Y.

"I look like I should be Antoine," says Manuel. "And Antoine looks like a Manuel to most people." Coprincipals of Antoine+Manuel, the two Frenchmen do nothing to clear the confusion—they want their work to bear a unique signature. Illustrators and type designers, they are best known for their theater posters, brochures, invitations, and wallpapers. But they do not limit their practice to print. All along, they have been developing video installations, 3-D environments, furniture, and creative playthings. Their decorative approach is highly original—and often controversial. There is always something sensory about their design solutions: A+M like things to be emotional and tactile, as well as visual.

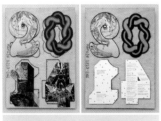

New Year's Card,
Musée des Arts Décoratifs, Paris
Studio/Art Directors: A+M
2014

Since 2008, when you published Volume One of your anthology, your work has drastically evolved. In what direction are you moving?
A: Back then, we were preparing our retrospective at the Paris Musée des Arts Décoratifs. We were exploring a number of different supports and venues, including theatrical sets, furniture, housewares, and art installations. Many of our clients were—and still are—theaters, dance companies, museums, and contemporary art galleries. What is new today is the range of techniques that we are exploring. To our existing assortment of skills and calligraphic styles, we have added motion graphics, photography, and glass design (for the Corning Glass Museum). But drawing, painting, and printing are still the basis of our practice.

In your creative process, are you influenced by new technologies and new techniques—data visualization, interactive media, and so on?
M: You bet. Digital tools help us a lot. Thanks to computers, we feel free to go wherever our imagination takes us.

You also design floor lamps, chests, storage units, and ceramic pieces. Are you thinking of experimenting with 3-D printers?
M: We used laser-cutting technology quite a lot in the past to fabricate parts of our creations. The 3-D printers are probably very similar, yet, somehow, they seem more whimsical.

A: As soon as these printers become available, we'll have fun with them!

But is your aesthetic sense influenced by the digital language of forms?

M: We must generate our own imagery, without interference from sophisticated software—otherwise, we cannot experiment freely. We are always playing with existing functions, tampering with systems, and pushing the limits of whatever digital program we happen to be using in order to come up with visual innovations. That's how we created the grandiose animated decor for the monumental ceiling of the Cartier show at the Grand Palais in Paris. The "Cartieroscope," as we called it, was the product of our digital D-I-Y approach.

Why do you think that your idiosyncratic imagery appeals to people who are in the world of luxury and high fashion?

M: We have so few fashion clients, it's hard to generalize. The fact that we have worked for Christian Lacroix and now Cartier is not enough to draw conclusions. One thing is sure: The codes of graphic design are very different from the codes of high fashion. Crossing over is not easy—few graphic designers are invited into the closed world of luxury brands.

A: I am sure that there are quite a few designers who are image makers and create visuals for fashion clients, but we don't know them.

The images you created for the Cartier exhibition were very "graphic"—they were over the top, yet they didn't interfere with the jewelry displays below. How did you come up with this design solution?

M: We were selected for this prestigious project because we were thinking like graphic designers, not like decorators. The other candidates had come up with grand schemes to spotlight the display cases. In contrast, our proposal was subdued at eye level, while dramatic overhead. Apparently, the judges of the competition were seduced by our approach. They liked the idea of a tapestry of baroque images unfolding slowly like a huge psychedelic canopy. We were lucky to have come up with a solution that appealed to both the museum curators and the exhibition sponsors. Dealing with tricky situations such as this one makes it fun. As a graphic designer—and as a child of divorced parents— I am a good negotiator.

A: When Manuel first walked into the monumental space in which the exhibition had to be installed, he felt tiny, like a child. He wanted to replicate, for the visitors, this impression of being dwarfed by the grandiose environment. We played on the contrast between the diamond necklaces in the cases (which one wishes to look at with a magnifying glass) and the colorful, oversized motifs looming on the ceiling.

Video Installation (above)
Nuit Blanche Mayenne
Studio/Art Directors: A+M
2013

Side Table (below)
Studio/Art Directors: A+M
2007

Ludovic Houplain / H5

Getting an Oscar for Graphic Design

Ludovic Houplain has always been a pioneer in the visual communication field. In the 1990s, his name was associated with the "French Touch"—the celebrated record covers look for techno music. In 1993, he founded a creative agency, H5, with Antoine Bardou-Jacquet, and they soon became known for their innovative animated music video clips. They've received many awards, gold medals, and accolades, including the prestigious Médaille de Chevalier des Arts et des Lettres. But most gratifying was the Oscar they got for *Logorama*, the ironic short animation film in which logos are heroes and villains in an apocalyptic Los Angeles setting. "It's pathological!" says Houplain. "At H5, we are endlessly testing the limits of our curiosity, discovering new fields of experimentation and mixing genres recklessly."

Poster for Hello Exhibition/
Installation,
Gaîté Lyrique, Paris
Designers: H5 (L. Houplain)
2012

You have always been ahead of the curve. Today, what sort of things interests you? What gets you up in the morning?
What interests me is how meaning engenders form—but I care little about "aesthetics." Not only are we all saturated with images, we have access to tools that allow us to create even more images. The result is overwhelming, fascinating, and, for the most part, well produced—but lacking in content. That's why I am more interested in generating concepts than forms.

Beyond this statement, I don't quite know what to tell you about my work. It's so hard to explain what one does! The French newspaper *Liberation* recently wrote that the specificity of my design agency, H5, was "décalage"—a word that can be translated as "deliber-ately different." Indeed, as a rule, at H5, we pride ourselves in being slightly out of synch with the prevalent trends—in that sense, we are "precursors." We can go from doing a short artistic film like *Logorama* to creating a politically subversive installation (Hello™), while at the same time working on advertising campaigns for major luxury brands (Hermès, Cartier, Dior, Moët & Chandon).

Among my favorite projects is *Röyksöpp* (*Remind Me*), a music clip using lame instructional drawings, and Alex Gopher's *The Child*, a musical typographical cab ride from Brooklyn to Manhattan, using words instead of images. We like improbable visual associations. And if we screw up, it's not the end of the world. It's only graphic design, after all. It's a game.

In terms of seating arrangements, 67% of you expressed a desire for an increased feeling of personal space.

Remind Me
Client: Royksoop
Production: Black Dog Films
Directors: H5 (H. de Crécy
and L. Houplain)
Label: Wall of Sounds/Labels
2002

Are you inspired by new technologies? Which one in particular?
I love them all! Not for their techy dimension (I am not a geek) but because I always welcome disruptions. New technologies will influence the way we think, react, and live our daily life. New technologies will force me to reassess my work constantly. The recent "Hello™" conceptual installation at the Gaité Lyrique, Paris, new media museum, is an example. We were able to blend seamlessly irony and technology—at the service of an idea: a full-scale parody of corporate branding.

Are your clients tech-savvy? Or do they come to you for advice in this domain?
Our clients are on top of the latest technologies! They do not come to us for our digital know-how, but for our conceptual approach—for our ability to think outside the box. We never feel compelled to create an interactive display of sorts, but when we do, we

hire multimedia specialists as outside consultants. As a rule, we assemble different teams for different projects.

With entrepreneurial projects like *Logorama* and Hello™, you have established the reputation of H5 as antiestablishment. Is this positioning detrimental? Does it drive away corporate clients?

Frankly, our corporate clients are clueless when it comes to our more "artistic" projects. Maybe they read about it in the press, but it didn't register as being something to worry about. They are slightly impressed by our media presence and perhaps more likely to listen to us. But, ultimately, what they like about us is our professionalism and creativity when it comes to delivering concepts, services, and results.

Outside the corporate world, we are a brand. However, it is not the result of concerted efforts on our part. We had no "brand strategy"—only a desire to succeed, to do great work, and to be independent. Our fearless ignorance of conventions and "legal" issues is probably the reason we got an Oscar for *Logorama*. We had ignored the warnings of our lawyers and had not gotten permissions from brands to use their logos. We were lucky: It worked.

Are parody and irony still effective modes of communication today?

Irony is here to stay. It is particularly effective today, in this age of conformity. Irony is a mental exercise, a way to question banality and subvert conventional wisdom. We like to poke fun at marketing techniques, for instance,

and try to expose the way they are now ubiquitous in politics, in particular.

Are you working on some new subversive entrepreneurial venture?

We can't help trying to subvert platitudes. And we are given more and more opportunities to do so, in public places, for various festivals, or in the context of artistic events. I am bored unless I have got something to say, some point of view to assert. But there is always a risk involved when you are speaking up: The *Los Angeles Times*, when we got the Oscar for *Logorama*, accused us of being card-carrying communists! We thought that their comment was funny!

Logorama (opposite)
Short Animated Film
Production: Autour de Minuit
Designers: H5 (A. Alaux,
H. de Crécy, and L. Houplain)
2009

Logo in Peace (L.I.P.) (below)
Client: Chaumont graphic
design festival
Designer: H5 (L. Houplain)
2010

Cary Murnion

Designing Cooties

HONEST, NYC is a graphic design firm founded by Cary Murnion. In 2004, Nike approached Murnion and his directing partner, Jonathan Milott, with the opportunity to write, produce, and direct a short film as part of their film series, *The Art of Speed*. That led to directing more live action short films with both Nike and other brands as well as TV commercials. "Essentially, we went to on-the-job film school that was funded by our clients," says Murion. In 2009, a film production company, Blowtorch, approached them to develop some short films to play before their feature length movies. HONEST made their first R-rated short film, *Boob*, the story of a boob that comes alive and terrorizes the people in a hospital as it tries to escape, but not before it falls in love with a sexy nurse. They have now produced a full-length feature film.

Muppets
Art Director: Honest
Agency: Vanksen
Date: 2009

How did the film, *Cooties*, about a virus that takes over an elementary school, take shape?

My directing partner, Jon, and I have always been interested in directing film. We idolized Mike Mills, who made the transition from graphic designer.

Boob went to SXSW attracting some attention in the industry. It was passed along to the producers of *Cooties,* who were looking for a director. *Boob* had a similar mix of comedy and horror as *Cooties.* They contacted us, and we went out to LA to pitch our directorial approach. They loved our vision and brought us on board when they got the finances in May 2013. We filmed the movie over 25 days between July and August.

While working on this project, was studio work put on hiatus?

Not at all. We had multiple projects going on at the studio while we were directing the movie. We have a great team who handled the studio work, allowing Jon and me to devote our full attention to the film. We had been doing this on a smaller scale when we'd direct the commercials and short films, so it wasn't completely foreign to the way our studio works.

I love the title. What was the process of conceiving, creating, directing, and producing *Cooties* to make it a viable property?

Well, first off, *Cooties* is not our idea. The basic story was conceived by Josh

Waller, who's one of the producers of the film, along with his partners, Elijah Wood and Daniel Noah. The script was written by Leigh Whannell, who created the *Saw* and *Insidious* franchises, and Ian Brennan, who along with Ryan Murphy, created *Glee*. So you can get a feel for the tone of the script if you mash *Saw* and *Glee* together.

When we were brought on board, we started working on bringing the movie from the pages of the script into the real world. Explaining what a director does can be confusing to people not involved with the industry, since we don't hold the camera or act. In a way, it's a lot like a designer. In our minds, the designer is a director in many ways, since every decision and detail is led by both. The most important starting point is finding the theme, subthemes, tone, character arcs, story arcs, visual style, and overall approach.

You took it to Sundance, which is no mean feat, and it was picked up by Lionsgate, a major distributor. What did they see in the film to make it ready for prime time?

I think they saw a film that was an original approach to the zombie/monster genre. There have been lots of films and TV shows that fit into this genre, but the ones that have been successful put a unique spin on it, whether it be *The Walking Dead*, *Zombieland*, or *Warm Bodies*. *Cooties* is one of those ideas that makes you ask, "Hasn't that been done before?" It seems so obvious in hindsight, but somehow it's never been done till now. It's also an amazing cast that will bring in an audience that might not normally be interested in a film like this. We

also like to think that we had a big part in Lionsgate's interest in the film. We were able to walk that fine line between delivering stomach-hurting laughs, while still keeping it grounded enough to deliver real scares and emotional moments. These kinds of elements are what attract people to theaters these days—to laugh and scream together.

You got some fantastic cast members for this comic horror film. How did this happen for two relatively new directors?

Elijah Wood is a producer on this film and he was attached to play the main character, Clint. So having him on board, and having the great script that Leigh and Ian wrote, helped get a lot of the other actors interested in the film. It was an interesting part of the process, since the director usually does casting and is clearly in charge of this choice, but in this case, it was clear we were also being evaluated. One of the ways we won the pitch was creating an extensive look book to clearly express our vision of the film. This helped show our clarity of direction. We also met with each cast member to make sure we were on the same page. We had to make them feel comfortable coming on board with us, while at the same time, we were interviewing them to make sure our needs could be met. We were very fortunate to get such a talented and eclectic cast.

What did you have to learn to be directors?

Directing is a strange thing, because you don't necessarily do something specific. You don't have to be an actor, cinematographer, producer, art

Boob, a short film about an experimental breast implant gone wrong.
Director: Honest
Date: 2008

Cooties, a feature film starring Elijah Wood, about a Zombie virus that effects pre-puberty kids.
Director: Honest
Date: 2014

director, editor, wardrobe designer, or stunt man, but you have to have a deep understanding of everything. For example, a great cinematographer will add a lot to the visuals of the film, but the director has to tell him where to put the camera and how to move it. It's the director who says to shoot a close-up of the hands, instead of the face.

The director should also know how different lenses will affect each shot. This doesn't mean the director has to be a good cinematographer, but if he doesn't know the difference between a wide and telephoto lens, his options are detrimentally limited. With a professional and creative cast and crew, the director's job becomes easier. Being a good director means balancing being very confident in yourself with welcoming collaboration from others. What's so fun about being directors is that you get to dip your toe into so many different disciplines,

which in turn you're expected to have very definitive opinions on. Yet it's the times when you find an opportunity to include someone else's opinion that will inevitably save the film.

What from graphic design could be used in your directorial toolkit?

Graphic designers are directors, which is why they are called art directors or creative directors. Being a graphic designer trained us to be a jack-of-all-trades. Designers work with all types of artists, writers, marketers, and clients. The designer combines many different puzzle pieces to communicate a certain message. That's what directors do with a film. From a rough sketch to final product, whether it's a designer explaining an idea to a client or executing an idea through discussions with a programmer, there are many crossovers with a film director.

Despite your impressive new credit, are you still graphic designers?

Yes, definitely, we'll always be graphic designers. We just get restless and like to try out new things and find different outlets to express our ideas. Maybe next we'll want to express ourselves through knitting.

Nick Ace
Speaking Frankly

Nicholas Acemoglu, a.k.a. Nick Ace, is an art director for whom the separation between editorial and advertising is a moot point: As far as he is concerned, creating a culturally relevant and distinctive content is what matters. "I don't think most younger readers care whether the content is advertising or not," he says. "They are educated enough to recognize that, in a magazine or on the Web, ads pay for some of the products they love." After graduating from the SVA MFA Design/Designer as Author + Entrepreneur program, he landed a job at *FRANK 151*, a small format, tablet-sized, hybrid magazine that lives both in print and online. For more than four years, he was responsible for managing all visuals aspects of its brand, its magazine and its website. Recently, he joined Collins, a brand and design-thinking agency in New York.

Leaders
by Jake Scharbach
Art Director: Nick Ace
2012–2013

How did you land a job as art director of a magazine, almost right out of school?

The summer after graduating from SVA, I had attended a release party for *FRANK*. Around three in the morning, some of the gang who worked for the magazine at the time asked me what I was up to. I responded, "Going home to work on a logo for some website that will never go live." Seemingly impressed by my late-night work ethic, my new friend, Bongi, who happened to be the art director of the magazine, got my phone number, because they needed help on their agency side.

FRANK also operates an advertising agency to service clients like Scion, Sailor Jerry, and Casio. My first project was for a liquor company—videos, print campaign, cocktail waitress uniforms, coasters, table tents, recipe books, and banners. The look and feel had been somewhat determined, and it turned out to be a nightmare. Working on the liquor business was bumming me out, but I needed money, having just graduated, and had to let it ride. Meanwhile, I familiarized myself with *FRANK's* aesthetic and began working on the magazine's layouts in my downtime. After a few months, I had written, designed, illustrated, photographed, and edited pieces for the "book," as we called the magazine. Before long I was given the job of art director.

When did you begin to shoot short videos for the magazine's website?

It didn't take long. I got the idea the day I was invited to an illegal boxing

Chapter 48: Doom Lyrics
by Mr. Kiji
Art Director: Nick Ace
2012–2013

match at a Dim Sum restaurant in the Lower East Side. The fights began after midnight. I managed to get two interns in with me to film. The next day they edited a visually stunning piece that went well beyond typical sports coverage. This was my first foray into producing short documentaries for *FRANK*. The process was so gratifying that I began to create more shorts, including the infamous video of me getting choked out by MMA fighter, Renzo Gracie.

To be a good art director, hanging out with the right people and taking amazing pictures at parties is just as important as sitting in front of a computer. At *FRANK*, we presented derelict culture around the globe in a sophisticated manor. A "derel" lifestyle may involve things like vandalism, street fashions, drugs, and partying. We use Instagram to promote the lifestyle of our brand and test what our audience responds to.

Is the tablet size of the print magazine a factor for the "culturally acute agitators" who constitute the bulk of *FRANK's* audience?
We spend extra on giving the magazine the look and feel of a "luxury" object,

one that readers would want to keep permanently, alongside any other special books or magazines in their collection. Our placement in stores like Colette in Paris and Opening Ceremony in New York has helped establish *FRANK* beyond a throwaway mag.

What does it take to be able to art direct both the print and the digital editions? When you are putting together stories, whether you are assigning illustrators or shooting videos, are you favoring one more than the other?

It's never one or the other. Basically, you have to be able work like a creep and let everyone in your creative circle know what you're up to. Jobs in this industry aren't nine to five; I might get called to shoot a piece at two in the morning. Most importantly, you have to delegate tasks and constantly search for new talent.

Things are happening so fast, it's hard to favor anything. Recently though, I've found writing treatments for videos and watching them come to life to be what I love most.

What is the most enjoyable part of your job?

A 60-year-old gentleman wrote a soccer piece for our Brazil issue. We were introduced online through a mutual friend, and when the book came out, he dropped by the office to pick some copies up. He told me that he "got it" and that our book was a sort of "*National Geographic* for street culture." He nailed it. When anyone, especially someone in his sixties gets it, I am enjoying my job.

You art direct the magazine and its website, yet you also design campaigns for some of your advertisers. Does it bother you to tamper with your editorial integrity?

We've been fortunate to work with like-minded brands that see it more as a partnership. They don't want to spend money and look like jackasses, and neither do we. Brands don't come to us looking for a generic audience, that's for sure. Our social media numbers aren't as big as some similar publishers, but our readers are completely engaged and demonstrate that they are into some really specific stuff and that they know what they like to do, when, and where.

The contemporary art scene, as much as the music scene, seem to provide a lot of content for *FRANK 151*. How do you keep up with it all?

I carry an iPhone, so there's no excuse for me not to keep up with everyone I've ever worked with. Again, if your friends know what you're up to, you get invited into a lot of different situations. Anytime I've written about a happening on the *FRANK* site, I've been invited to write about others. On any night, I might end up at a hip-hop show, gallery opening, or random ass dinner with other people who are doing "cool" shit.

I'm fairly nerdy about music, but our interns put me on to every new record the moment it is released. No offense to my background, but design school interns are pretty much the worst— they are great for production work, but they only listen to "designy" records and go to "designy" events. I try to hire kids who don't even go to college and

are trying to start their own music or fashion-related business—they know EVERYTHING.

Do you actually sit down and "design"—or is your job to keep the visual direction of the publication on track?

During a late-night session a few weeks ago, I was told that I'm "not a designer anymore" and that I need to just "direct these fucking kids." While my ability to delegate tasks gets stronger every day, there are still things that I obsess over—widows, orphans, odd photo crops, and lame typography. However, if I take over after a designer has been working on something for a while, I'll show them step-by-step what I'm adjusting and why.

Chapter 43: Bug Out
by Ricky Powell
Art Director: Nick Ace
2012–2013

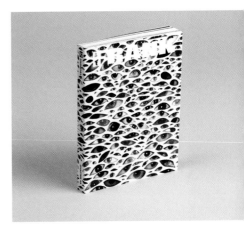

13 What Comes Next

The thing about transition is that sometimes it is not clear what's coming around the corner. Transition is as much about shifts in society, culture, and technology as it is in personal directions. Yet, there are societal trends that are more likely to create new opportunities. Among them is the changing role of words in our culture: Long explanations and text-heavy dissertations are a thing of the past. People will have less and less time to read, yet their curiosity will expand as a wider spectrum of information is available to more individuals. One can imagine that the graphic language will speak deeper than words and that "understanding" as we know it will become more intuitive but not necessarily less penetrating.

Another trend that concerns us even more is the democratization of the design discipline due to the proliferation of user-friendly design tools. People with no training in design principles, typography, color theory, or even marketing will solve the kind of problems traditionally handled by graphic designers. More cacophony is sure to ensue before the dust settles! Badly designed publications will strain the eyes of more innocent readers, and ill-conceived interfaces will leave more unwary users stranded in cyberspace. But on the upside, consider the influx of talent when truck drivers, eye doctors, plumbers, sculptors, and third graders will begin to pitch in and propose design solutions.

The interviews in this chapter are for individuals who are not afraid to alter what is comfortable and attempt something radically new. In order to do that, however, you have to have an initial direction. You have to have something to rebel against. Once you have a foothold in your creative career, what comes next should be different from what came before. Or, as Franco Cervi says about himself, be reckless—at least once.

Timothy Goodman

Disposable Ideas

Timothy Goodman, a graduate of SVA/NYC, sees himself as the 1980s version of the once popular 1930s *Dead End Kids* films made up of wise-arse street kids. Growing up in Cleveland in a family of modest means, Goodman learned how to be scrappy as a youngster. His heroes were characters like Ferris Bueller and Zack Morris, and he reveled in the idea of pulling a fast one on somebody in authority. "That's kind of how my graphic design career started," he admits. "In high school, I stole hall passes, replicated them in Microsoft Word, and printed out whole packs of them; later, I forged teacher's signatures." After graduating college, Goodman painted homes and hung wallpaper and drywall for 4½ years before going to SVA in NYC, which showed him how fortunate he was to be doing "what I love, and how lucky I am to do it in New York."

Women's Health:
Designer and Art Director:
Timothy Goodman
Creative Director: Theresa
Griggs
Photographer: Lucas Zarebinski
Prop Stylist: Ariana Salvato
Body Makeup: Lauren Cole

You've spoken in public about your own voice; you don't have a particular style, so where does the voice come in?
A couple of years ago, I made a decision to redirect my career and push myself into new, scary, and unexpected territory. It's been six years since I graduated, and I've been at the cross section of design, branding, illustration, and content creation. Even though I adopted one sort of drawing style, I have no interest in making work for solely aesthetic reasons. As my former boss, Brian Collins, says, we're not in the "kind of nice business." Meaning, we're not here to make pretty pictures; we're here to be provocative, to be memorable, and to tell great stories.

Comedy is a large part of your voice. Can all design be witty and funny?
I work hard to get my voice and my humor in my work. I've watched Winnie-the-Pooh many times the last couple years. Christopher Robin says, "You're braver than you believe, stronger than you seem, and smarter than you think." What an idea! I'm currently trying to be more naive with my work, as graphic design books and blogs will only get me so far. It's important to stop thinking like a graphic designer. We should think about other platforms and different narratives. I believe that's the first step to connecting with an audience.

Ace Mural
Illustrator and Art Director:
Timothy Goodman
Assistant: Andreina Carrillo
Producer: Jou-Yie Chou
Photographer: Mark Dye

New Yorker
Designer and Lettering:
Timothy Goodman
Art Director: Jordan Awan
Creative Director: Wyatt Mitchell
Photographer: Grant Cornett
Prop Styling: Shane Klein, Theo
Vamvounakis

You've worked for some major brands. You speak "brandspeak" if you need to. Where does voice enter into this?

That's the difficult balance. A real tragedy for so many young designers is that they have to have the voice of whatever client or studio they're working for; rarely do young designers get the chance to put their own voice or humor or sensibilities into their work. In the movies they say, "Do one for them. Do one for you." Early on I understood that it was important to do work for me—whether it was editorial illustrations or a personal project— and that ultimately began to inform my branding work, and vice versa. Luckily, I had bosses and mentors who

supported this. I became a quicker thinker and a more eclectic image maker because of this.

Influences are key in your work. How do you acquire the specific influences that drive your varied approaches?

I'm a big believer in having mentors. I think it's paramount to find someone who will help guide you, even beyond design, in a way that teaches you more about life. I always tell my students, "Don't worry about what you want to do as much as who you want to work for." I'm proud of the work I've been able to do, and I feel fortunate to have so many inspiring and encouraging friends, mentors, and colleagues who have supported and encouraged me.

**You work as an art director and
a designer? What do you look
for in those you might hire?**
Ideas are totally disposable and
constantly in flux for me. I learned
that while being in branding. Anything can spark an idea, and you
better have at least 100 of them. I
like those who have 100 ideas.

Tupac Mural
Lettering and Art Director:
Timothy Goodman
Producer: Andy Song
Photographer: Daniel Rhie

Ryan Feerer

Making Design Meals

Ryan Feerer, a graduate of the SVA MFA Design/Designer as Author + Entrepreneur program, is a designer and illustrator from Abilene, Texas. He is the program director of the Graphic Design/Advertising concentration at Abilene Christian University, ACU, where he attended undergraduate school. In addition, he runs the eponymous Ryan Feerer Design & Illustration. For the past couple of years, he has also been in the restaurant business, a coowner of Abi-Haus, with his friend Jimbo Jackson. Together they run the eatery and develop food products for the market. But illustration remains his stock and trade. For Feerer, creating brand-marks and icons are the simplest forms of illustration. In the traditional sense, illustration makes up about 25 percent of his business. "I pride myself in the craft of hand-made marks," he says. "I will always do something by hand if it is appropriate for the audience."

Abi-House
Designer: Ryan Feerer
Photographer: Nil Santana
2012

Can an illustrator/designer make a good living in Abilene, Texas?
Abilene is a wonderful place to live. There are so many opportunities here, but most of them you have to make yourself. I rarely take on jobs in Abilene unless it is something I'm directly involved with. The main issue I have come across is budget constraints. Most of my work comes from either the East or West Coast, or is international.

Is illustration somehow connected to starting your cafe?
I haven't really thought about it. I would guess you could say that. As creative people, we should have a passion to create. What I find magical about being a designer turned restaurateur is that you have the opportunity to touch all of the customer's senses. You can design their experience with the visuals of murals and menus, the smell and taste of the food, the touch of our hand crafted tables, the sounds of good music and conversation. Nothing feels better than to sit back and watch all of these elements come together, knowing you played a major role creating it. It is the ultimate design high.

You've used some great hand letterers to decorate your restaurant. How did this happen?
I wanted the restaurant to give the community a strong sense of pride with the phrase "Long Live Abilene" as the focus. I'm fortunate enough to be good friends with Jeff Rogers, who

Abi-House
Designers: Ryan Feerer,
Dana Tanamachi, Jeff Rogers
Photographer: Nil Santana

lived in Abilene while attending ACU. I approached him about the project and he was immediately on board. He asked if we should bring on Dana Tanamachi, also a fellow Texan and friend, to collaborate with us. I gave them my vision and what I was hoping to accomplish. In return, they helped me create something much more beautiful than I could have ever imagined.

Are you able to do commercial design and illustration whilst being a proprietor of an ancillary business?
Yes, quite a bit. I manage my time pretty well, so that's been helpful.

What will be the measure of your success?
As for the restaurant, we're coming up on our one-year mark, and we haven't closed down, so that's a huge success in my eyes! Actually, Abi-Haus is doing incredibly well. There isn't anything like it in town. It definitely has a New York vibe, which a lot of people haven't experienced. It is refreshing for our customers to have a nice in-town getaway. We have had many folks from Austin and Dallas tell us that they wish we would open one in their cities. Our locals see this and have a great sense of pride that something like this exists in their town.

Abi-House
Designers: Ryan Feerer,
Dana Tanamachi, Jeff Rogers
Photographer: Nil Santana

Are there other entrepreneurial activities happening or on the horizon?

For almost two years, a friend and I have been brewing BBQ sauce. I would love to take that to the next level, but the time isn't right.

How's the restaurant business these days?

Everyone wants and needs a good, unique meal on occasion. Our emotions play a big role in that. We want to give our patrons a home away from home. We have several customers who frequent Abi-Haus three or four times a week. They feel loved, needed, and part of the family. We are all about developing lasting relationships and having a good time.

Design Entrepreneurship

What is a design entrepreneur?

Would not a designer who opens an independent studio, firm, or office be considered an entrepreneur?

In the strictest sense, the answer to the second question is yes. But to be more specific, graphic design studios and firms that offer only client services are not truly entrepreneurial because service businesses do not create, supply, or distribute their own products. Conversely, as an answer to the first question, a graphic designer who in addition to providing services also initiates products (or "content") is indeed entrepreneurial. What's more, many designers who have the ability to skillfully package and promote other people's products have discovered that it is more satisfying and at times more lucrative to develop their own wares.

Over the past decades, enterprising graphic designers have engaged in various forms of entrepreneurism, from small cottage industries to large retail establishments, from balsamic vinegar bottling to book packaging. A graphic designer is not locked into products related to graphic design alone but, rather, is free to develop any kind of merchandise, from candy to furniture—or whatever the imagination conjures. Entrepreneurial activity is either a supplement to an existing design business or an independent subsidiary of one, yet in both cases, new products contribute to creative and business challenges that add value to a designer's personal and professional worth.

All that is required is a good idea, some capital, a business plan, a means of manufacturing, a method of distribution, and a modicum of chutzpah. Being an entrepreneur is not a viable direction for the designer who lacks the confidence to test the limits of creativity or the stamina to take business risks, but almost everyone with creativity has at least one idea that is worth developing as a product. For the faint of heart, as an alternative to starting an entrepreneurial business, many graphic designers develop products for other businesses, and they either retain rights to or obtain royalties from the sale of their products. Although, in this scenario, the graphic designer is still working for a client, the result is not a framing of a client's product or idea with a brochure, package, or other service-oriented item but, rather, providing the client with an entity that adds value to the product line.

Entrepreneurism offers the graphic designer insight into the nature of business as well as the satisfaction that simply toiling as a service provider will never generate. If the future of graphic design is greater involvement in the means and result of production, then we will see a lot more design entrepreneurship from now on.

Franco Cervi

"I'm Reckless!"

Franco Cervi graduated from Milan Polytechnic University in 1994 with a degree in architecture. This gave him a critical approach to design. He worked for 10 years in multidisciplinary studios (architecture, industrial design, graphic design) on an international level, including Atelier Mendini (Alessandro Mendini), Sottsass Associati (Ettore Sottsass), and Matteo Thun & Partners (Matteo Thun), "which over the years gave me the chance to work in close contact with hundreds of designers from four different continents. I found my own career path, that of graphic design," he says, referring to projects for international clients (Alessi, BMW, Citigroup, DuPont Corian, Hugo Boss, Lavazza), concentrating, among other things, first on corporate identity and, later, on interactive design. He is also the head of 279 Editions, a publisher of design books.

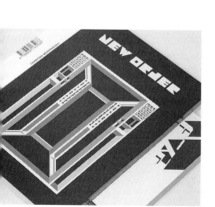

New Order
Art Director and Designer:
Franco Cervi
Writer: Ferruccio Giromini
Published by 279 Editions, Milan
Copyright 279 Editions, Milan
2010
All photographs are by
Fabrizio Nannini.

When, how, and why did you launch 279 Editions?

The first step was to publish 500 copies, in 2005, of a book entitled *Design Code*, which was a sort of summary of my creative language (which was still rather immature at the time, to be honest). The book had an interesting format, like a sort of "missal" for "graphics addicts." Its content was unusual, too, because instead of taking the form of a portfolio, it presented a series of "project fragments" aimed at illustrating how a very coherent graphic language can solve a very wide range of different design needs. So I had understood that the "book object" could be an interesting way to express my personal creative vision.

Had you experience in publishing before this?

No. I know, I'm reckless! After having gained the necessary experience as a graphic designer, the prospect of a publishing company seemed like a possible, natural evolution. Based on strong personal motivation, I leapt into it, in a totally instinctive, enthusiastic way, putting up with all the specific difficulties of the field . . . and at first it was very difficult indeed.

Do you have a business model that is sustainable?

The recipe is necessarily a simple one: high quality, small print runs, an engaged, faithful international audience. It might seem banal, but the famous "Made in Italy" has always seemed like a fascinating and, at the same time, mysterious concept for me, because behind the excellence of the final product, there are always people with important knowledge, devoted to their work, which they do with great passion and sacrifice. Today, everyone talks about quality, but to actually do it can turn out to be an endeavor that is beyond your means. It is a difficult challenge, but I like to emphasize the fact that while a balance sheet in the black is necessary, the main objective is not to make money, but to produce quality publications, books capable of improving with time and sometimes of becoming international collector's items. In the end, there is something spiritual about all this.

Your books are beautiful. Do you have a staff, or is it just you?
Anything that has to do with creative work comes exclusively from me. In this sense, my publishing house is a direct emanation of my taste, my cultural background, my creative research and technical capacities (and also my mistakes, obviously). In any case, necessarily, I have a very good staff for all the other strategic and operational aspects.

You've released a typeface called "Base." Is this an extension of your publishing business or another independent venture?
Over the years, I have concentrated on publishing the creative work of others, staying in the background; to compare this to cinema, I often feel like the director who, among other things, works on bringing out the qualities of

the actor. I remove every graphic sign from the publishing project that is not strictly necessary, and I try to avoid irritating "visual cacophony" between container and content. But this does not mean that I haven't continued with my own personal research, and the "Base" typeface is just one example.

You are based in Milan, but you have international reach. What is your goal?
Today, there are many large publishers that can spread their books through immense distribution channels, but very few are really interested in supplying the capacity for the production of books that will bring out creative work in a context of formal quality, books that can be developed and customized like a tailor-made garment, where the content and the container enhance each other.

*Mono Baseman
(A monograph on the pictorial work of Gary Baseman)
Art Director and Designer: Franco Cervi
Writer: Ferruccio Giromini
Published by 279 Edition, Milan, Copyright 279 Editions, Milan 2013
All photographs are by Fabrizio Nannini.*

Digital Design

In digital design, the word *digital* is vestigial. To be a "communications" designer these days implies working in digital space with digital formats. We've already examined the impact of digital tools on design practice, design thinking, and design production. Now we will survey the opportunities in the digital arena(s) and how others have mastered them. While a dwindling majority of graphic designers still describes their practice as "problem solving," a growing number of newcomers have declared that instead of looking for solutions to problems, they are going to be designing programs for solutions.

4

Not a breakthrough idea, this concept was pioneered 50 years ago by Swiss typographer Karl Gerstner, who wrote *Designing Programmes*, a book about systems in graphic design. It features four illustrated essays on a systematic methodology that is particularly relevant today, in the context of the most recent developments in computational design.

So, why all the excitement?

The big difference between then and now is the technology. Whereas back in 1964, when Gerstner was articulating his principles, the most advanced piece of engineering was the ill-fated Picturephone, today people, but also products, events, and services are digitally intertwined into a vast substrate of pulsating data.

The designers interviewed in this chapter all enthusiastically embrace technologically driven interconnectivity as the source of endless creative opportunities and career building. Jeoren Barendse, a Dutch graphic designer who was one of the first in his field to see in this new paradigm a huge potential for reinvention, affirms that today designers "must become creators of the very design rules and processes that will allow them to come up with innovative solutions."

In other words, today designers are on their own! No longer can they rely on tried-and-true formulas and techniques. To keep up with the proliferation of new devices, new software upgrades, and new usages, they hold on to the only thing they still can trust: the design process itself and the methodology behind it. "The most important part of designing is thinking," remarks Frieder Nake, a professor of computer graphics in Bremen, Germany.

All over the globe, and in every corner of the digital realm, designers are developing a keen analytical mind. Whether they are designing apps or multimedia installations, venturing into e-commerce or investing in start-ups, joining user experience teams, or specializing in generative design, they are redefining their professional practice as they go. "The focus of design has expanded from the form of objects to the behavior of systems," remarks Hugh Dubberly, a San Francisco software and service consultant.

This is good news for graphic designers who, until now, often played second fiddle to product designers whose creative output had easy consumer appeal. Industrial designers might not be able to make the most of the digital revolution, whereas graphic designers, who are no stranger to grids, templates, graphic standards, and visual identity guidelines, are better equipped to manage abstract complexity.

Lo and behold, as this next series of interviews demonstrates, graphic designers are emerging as the framers of a new way of thinking, one based on how we experience life rather than produce goods and sell services.

14 Interactive Multimedia Installations and Interfaces

How do you make sure that viewers and users, who are exposed to at least 3000 unsolicited messages a day, are actually remembering what they survey, read, hear, see, or touch? Interactive communication designers have an answer: They create immersive, open-ended narratives that turn passive spectators into active participants. On giant screens, on kiosks and on all sorts of stationary or mobile devices, the latest technological innovations are probed and tested to elicit the most dynamic response from the audience.

Exhibit designers, like interface designers, create information pathways with multiple options. The goal is to propose open navigation scripts for visitors and viewers to explore a given topic as they please. To create these learning experiences, you don't have to be an information technology (IT) expert. More critical will be your curatorial role—your ability to select artifacts, orchestrate programs, and develop sequential visual narrations. That's why visual designers hired in this specialty must have a general level of education allowing them to handle a broad range of topics— including medical, retail, automotive, finance, history, music, or mass media.

Today, no cultural exhibit, art installation, fashion show, promotional event, or industrial trade show is complete without some sort of interactive display integrating two or more media. To manage this type of project, visual designers work in teams, with people who are specialists and have the technical savoir faire, the UID experience, the engineering skills, or the scientific expertise necessary to complete the task. You don't spend much time sitting by yourself at your desk. Cross-disciplinary interaction between highly competent professionals makes this multimedia career path particularly rewarding.

Debugging the Language of Digital Job Titles

The main reason job titles are confusing is the employer's lack of precision. Understandably so. The field is evolving so fast, and competencies are so diverse, it's practically impossible to predict how to best fill a position.

However, there are three key words to watch for: (1) *developer*, (2) *designer*, and (3) *programmer*.

In most cases, developers are on the top of the pecking order: They develop the overall strategic vision. Next come designers, who shape the creative and visual content. Last are programmers, who are in charge of the technical dimension of projects.

Other designations within titles attempt to narrow down the field of expertise: multimedia, software, Web, user experience, and so on. Often, there are different words for the same specialty. What is the difference between a motion designer and a video graphic designer? Only the context can tell you.

And just to keep you guessing, there are job titles that do not fall into any preexisting grouping. They sound exotic, though. Among them are content strategist, digital curator, UX architect, and CDO (chief digital officer). Here is a tentative glossary of titles to help you sort out the job listings.

Digital developers create and program creative content for websites and all types of user interfaces, including tablets and mobile experiences.

Digital media developer

Web developer

Software developer

User interface developer

Interactive developer

Digital designers are responsible for supporting Web development and creating other digital media products.

Digital designer

Digital content designer

Digital brand designer

Marketing digital designer

Digital production designer

Experience designer

Web designer

Interface designer

Interaction designer

Multimedia designer

Information designer

Motion designer

Video graphic designer

3-D designer

Digital programmers encode, test, debug, revise, update, and document programs.

System programmer

Application programmer

Device programmer

Jeroen Barendse

Subverting the Mental Map

Jeroen Barendse is one of the founding partners of LUST, a Dutch multidisciplinary design studio established in 1996 at the cutting edge, where new media and information technologies, architecture, and urban systems and graphic design overlap. That "cutting edge" was wishful thinking 20 years ago, says Barendse. However, today, at long last, it's a reality. "Today, you can easily switch between media, connect to different systems through open formats and connectors, and create something new out of it, something that functions in a real-world environment." LUST keeps sharpening that same cutting edge, and today the studio is at the forefront of innovations in abstract cartography, data visualization, and interactive installations.

At Random? Interactive Media
Installation
Museum De Paviljoens, Almere
Designer: LUST
2008

From your vantage point, what is the greatest change you have observed in the last 20 years?

The current mantra that everybody is a designer or, more recently, that everybody is a curator, is true to the extent that there are now tools available by which almost everybody can design reasonably good-looking works. But those designs are most of the time re-creations of things somebody once saw. There is no innovation, no conceptual value in them.

The greatest change today is the way designers must reinvent their role if they want to be truly creative: On the one hand, they must develop a more research-based approach, and on the other hand, they must become creators of the very design rules and processes that will allow them to come up with innovative solutions.

What is the philosophy of LUSTlab—the more experimental division of LUST?

When we start a project, we let the project guide us. We have no preconceived idea what the outcome will be. We just design the process and react to that. We believe in creating a lot of different sketches, visually and in code, in order to familiarize ourselves with the material we are working with.

This also means wandering around, similar to the idea of a Flâneur in a city. This wandering allows us to look at things in a different way, to apply different gazes to the same problem. At LUST & LUSTlab, we often talk about the "vocabulary" of a project. During the research phase, we don't shape or design. We just try to build the "vocabulary"—with each sketch, idea or experiment embodying a new 'word'.

The richer the words are, the more elegant the sentences we can speak.

In an interview, you said that, for LUST, interaction design is the new literature. Would you say that interaction design promotes open-ended narratives?
We indeed see interaction design as the new literature. For us, it is not only about the interactive aspect of the effect; it is also about the narrative possibilities: narrative structures that go beyond linear or nonlinear. This new literature is also about literary aspects like references, analogies, structures, points of view, time—all contributing to the complete narrative. A visitor does not need to grasp all possible readings of a work at once; instead, multiple story lines unfold over multiple readings. All aspects from content to movement, interaction, data collection, and collaboration contribute to this new literature.

Does semantics play a role in your research process?
Yes, it does. We are very interested in literary anthropology. A lot of our projects deal with language, or the construction of a metalanguage, that can be expressed in type, but also in images.

Type/Dynamics, Interactive Installation,
Stedelijk Museum, Amsterdam
Designer: LUST
2013

Do you define interaction as providing open-ended narratives that can be interpreted and, if need be, finished by the user?
We believe that something that is open-ended is far more interesting in terms of experience than a clear end. When we just started LUST in 1996, we always used a text about the missing piece of the puzzle as a metaphor for what we wanted to achieve with our work. If you almost finish a puzzle and the last piece is missing, you will probably always remember that experience. Translated to interaction design, one can say that the viewer is needed in order to finish the puzzle.

Do you think that viewers of interactive media tacitly understand that they are part of the information flow?
If you mean that people are more and more aware of different media, I would say "yes." My current students, for instance, can read and write in all kinds of media; they understand the medium they work in almost naturally. Even a few years ago, this was different. Current generations are born with the Internet around, allowing them a natural understanding of its implications and how we communicate with each other.

How do you define the role of graphic designers if the end product of their analytical process is a series of forms that design themselves?
Here, the design of the rules comes into play. Too often design is used to solve problems: real-world problems, but also editorial problems, organizational problems, and so on. We think it's better to approach something by not only looking at the problem but by looking at the opportunities as well. Only then can we define the task.

What quality or skill does a graphic designer need in order to be able to connect strings of codes with self-generative forms?
Coding can totally absorb a designer, as the possibilities are endless as well as the variations that can be rendered. The solving of minor problems can easily become a day job. A good creative coder can take a helicopter view once in a while, reassess the work done, and focus on the conceptual ideas that need to be achieved. In that sense, we think the conceptual goal is still the most important, independent of the medium you are working in.

In the future, will graphic designers design rules rather than outcomes?
Yes, simply because the message that people need to communicate will be more and more media-independent. No longer printed, many graphic design works are formatted as PDFs and can be viewed on tiny mobile screens, on 30-inch monitors, or on multi-million-pixel screens. This calls for a different type of designer, who not only can design a PDF, a book, or a website, but who can also grasp the implications of the medium they are working with.

In our work, we explore the metaphorical difference between a symbol itself and the meanings a set of symbols may signify. Instead of being concerned with what these symbols should look like, we should probably be concerned with developing a new design morphology to fit the contemporary world we live in.

At Random? Interactive Media
Installation (this page)
Museum De Paviljoens, Almere
Designer: LUST
2008

Julien Gachadoat

Demomaking for a Living

Julien Gachadoat is the founder, with Michaël Zancan, of 2Roqs, a design studio in Bordeaux, France. Specialized in interactive multimedia installations, they are at the forefront of a design practice often described as "demom-aking"—digital "demos"—that mix graphic design, music, and animated films. Gachadoat is an adept of Processing, the open software, and a member of the community around it. Algorithm thinking is his design methodology.

Interactive 3-D Vintage Postcard
Client: Office du Tourisme, Ville-
neuve-sur-Lot
Designer: Julien Gachadoat/2Roqs
2013

How did you discover your passion?
My dad brought home a computer in the 1980s. I was drawn to the machine instantly. You had to type in a series of instructions to launch a program of games. It was my first encounter with programming.

Later, in the '90s, as a teen, I was lucky enough to have an Atari ST—I was still fascinated by the interactive games. I joined a network of "pirates," with different "crews"—kids competing to crack open the protective codes of the games, to duplicate them, and to share them around.

Cracking open a game was a matter of seconds for the most talented hackers. To broadcast their exploits, they would create a personalized home page with special "greetings" to introduce themselves and the game to friends and members of their posse. They would also taunt competitors—the "lamers." Eventually, these "intros" became more sophisticated, with logos for each group, animations, scrolling texts, and even music.

These special effects, as displayed on "intro" screens, soon became more interesting, more intricate, and tech-nically more advanced than the games themselves. I was mesmerized by the technology of this parallel universe. I knew enough programming to appreciate the sort of achievement they represented. And I loved their peculiar aesthetics.

I began to collect games—not for themselves but for their "intros." I would try to reproduce the same visual effects I saw, even though my pro-gramming notions were rudimentary. I was self-taught. I was lucky to meet a friend at school, Michaël Zancan, with whom I was able to share my passion for graphic interfaces and algorithmic thinking. Eventually, Michaël and I went into business together.

Looking back, what were the major breakthroughs in your field?
From my point of view, the Internet changed everything. It allowed people to share ideas, to communicate, and to talk to each other in a democratic manner. For me, it was a break-through as well: I was able to access a lot of information, all of it crucial to

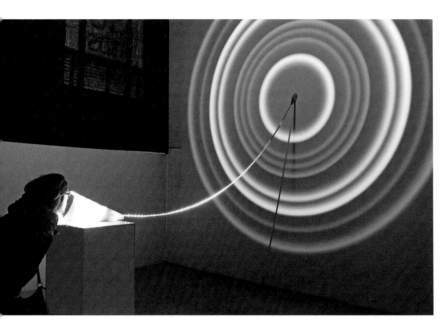

Murmur, Interactive Installation,
Client: Mirage Festival, Lyon
Designer: Julien Gachadoat/2Roqs
2014

acquiring an understanding of the new technologies as they evolved. That's how I discovered Processing, the open software, and the community around it. Soon I was able to create my company, 2Roqs, and focus on interaction design.

One of the first projects I created in 2005, in partnership with a London studio, came about as a result of connecting with someone on the Processing network. To this day, I keep up with all the various ways in which I can interact and connect with other communities, *Kinect*, for instance.

Can you explain to our readers why open-source software, such as Processing, is a superior creative tool?
I am not sure that "superior" is the right word. "Different" is more accurate. Programming software like Processing offers users a way to code their own tools, whereas traditional software

programs propose ready-made, preprogrammed computer tools. Open-source software promotes freedom but requires users to have methodology and be willing to engage in a more time-consuming learning process.

But in return, people who use open-source software such as Processing or Openframeworks have access to like-minded users who are ready to help them and encourage them on a variety of ways: project evaluation, suggestions for improvement, or sharing programs, for example. It's reciprocal: You also help others by constantly sharing your progress and discoveries with members of your community, adopting the "release early, release often" principle. This system is a lot more flexible than the closed system of regular software. The ground rule of open-source software is lateral sharing. All users are contributors, constantly sharing knowledge for the benefit of everyone else.

Along with your fascination for codes and programming, you are also interested in graffiti and typography. Can you give us examples of how you mix these disciplines?
The discovery of the graffiti universe was an experience on a par with the discovery of the "demos" world because it involved the same components: graphic design, typography, and underground cultural codes.

Our project, "Gravity," is a good example of how we integrate everything we love. In this particular installation, on the façade of a building, we project texts that people send with their smart phone. That's our trademark at 2Roqs: We try to be surprising, amusing, and intriguing, while at the same time interact with spectators by getting them involved.

You have developed a number of "real-time" interactive installations. What next level of interactivity are you exploring?
I am right now developing a wearable tech project with NORMALS, an independent creative group devoted to the practice of speculative design. It's a virtual garment, conceived to be seen on a tablet. Its appearance morphs according to data relating to the persons who "wears" it.

Michaël is working on an application that allows viewers to actually enter into a photograph to see it from a number of different angles. It can be

viewed as a projection, with the specta-
tor moving about to look at the image
from different perspectives, or it can be
viewed on a tablet with a similar and
startling result.

**You have quite a few clients—
mostly cultural institutions but also
commercial ones such as wineries,
electronics, or car manufacturers.
What specific type of multimedia
installations do you create for them?**
We are offering our clients three types
of interactive installations.

Full-size immersive installations in
which spectators, by their movements
and gestures, are able to transform the
display. An example is the permanent
installation at the Aquarium of
La Rochelle, in which visitors can
interact with schools of fish projected
on the floor.

Interactive kiosks such as tables or
vertical display units, popular with
museums and cultural institutions,
and particularly adapted to present
educational content to a wide audience. Our clients include museums
whose exhibits deal with science
and technology.

Interactive applications for tablets
that interpret, enhance, or visualize data.

**You are French, but English seems
to be the language most used by you
and your colleagues to communicate
in your field. Are codes also written
in English? Is programming a truly
idealist community?**
The question of the "language" used
for programming is complex. English
is the universal language of programming, simply because it was originally
developed in the United States in 1945.

However, the language used to talk to
a computer is not English—machines
only understand a very short list of
instructions, spelled out in a machine
code, thanks to a compiler.

To program you must learn to
write algorithms. In other words, you
must learn to write a finite number
of instructions to solve a problem
in a reasonable amount of time on
a given machine. Let me quote Ber-
nard Chazelle, the famous Princeton
University computer science professor:
"Algorithms open new perspectives on
science and technology. They are not
simply useful tools— they truly herald
a new way of thinking."

Textopolis, Interactive Installation
Client: Semaine Digitale, Bordeaux
Designer: Julien Gachadoat/2Roqs
2012

Ada Whitney

The New Motion

Ada Whitney is a designer, live action director, multimedia artist, and the cofounder of Beehive. Originally a painter, she became one of the pioneering participants in the motion design industry, creating some of the first digital bumpers for *Saturday Night Live (SNL)* and animated logos for MTV. As the creative director of Beehive, she has led teams in building a body of work for the broadcast, entertainment, and live-event industries. "My passion for visual storytelling is fueled by my deep-rooted love of art, film, multimedia installation, design, architecture, music, and technology," she says. Beehive's main title design, network branding and promotion and theatrical media projects for HBO, Showtime, Disney, NY City Opera, and more, have been recognized by ADC, TDC, *Communications Arts*, The Academy of Arts & Sciences, and PromaxBDA. Their projects have been featured in numerous publications including reviews in *The New York Times*, *The Wall Street Journal,* and *Fast Company*, who described their experiential opera video as "an interactive, LED wonderland."

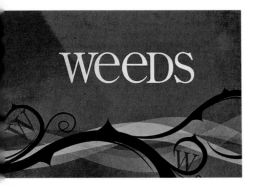

Showtime *Weeds*
Client: Showtime Networks
Creative Director: Ada Whitney
Designer: Marlie Decopain,
Marcelo Cardoso
Animator: Marcelo Cardoso

How did you become involved in making motion design?
My start in motion design was quite serendipitous. At the time, many of the early media companies were turning to artists, not designers, to work on the Quantel Paintbox, a precursor to Mac's. I started with painting SNL bumpers and fell in love with the collaborative and multimedia aspect of the work. The scene, a mix of writers, filmmakers, performers, musicians, editors, and artists, was intoxicating from a creative perspective.

You were a graphic designer, right?
I'm really a self-taught graphic designer. I relied on my background as an artist using my understanding of composition, color, line, and space to guide me. I found myself looking at letterforms as shapes when designing. I learned a lot on the job about typefaces, their form and character. I really loved that!

When you went from traditional design to motion, did you have to learn technologies that were cutting edge?
There is always a new technology to learn. To me that's one of the most exciting things about the medium. The cutting-edge tools at our disposal allow for new ways of thinking about the

ABC *Body of Proof*
Client: ABC Networks
Creative Director: Ada Whitney
Designer: Marlie Decopain,
Marcelo Cardoso
Animator: Florian Heger, James Bartley

form our messaging takes and the way we communicate. For instance, with all the advances in interactive animation, you can create dynamic responsive animation that is user generated and designer guided. I think staying in touch with technology is vital to communicating with a plugged-in contemporary audience.

What is necessary to know for broadcast quality that cannot be done today on the iPhone?
I'd say the most significant issues that arise with the iPhone are scale and readability concerns. Digital type and design choices that have expanded to include ultrathin, lightweight elements in broadcast HD are hard to read on the iPhone, as are very small images.

How is motion different from static design, other than the obvious?
Images are fleeting and change over time, so your message is not delivered instantaneously like a static image. It evolves and unfolds. The event becomes a timed experience allowing for emotional and cerebral arcs, not unlike theater or film. There is the opportunity to take the viewers and move them through space, over time and affect their perception through sound design, so that it becomes an immersive sensory experience.

Telling a story is key in your work. How do you structure stories?
I always think about the emotional arc and sensory journey we want to take the viewer on, and then, what information or content needs to be communi-

Defining the New
Animation: Popularity
By J. J. Sedelmeir

1. Animation is more popular than ever. Why is this?

2. Animation appeals to most people's "personal nostalgia." This began most prevalently with the "Baby Boomer"—the first media generation.

3. There's money to be made.

4. It has a universal appeal and appears to be in most people's DNA.

5. There's money to be made.

6. There are so many outlets (online, networks, etc.) looking for content, and animation often comes with subsequent marketing and merchandising potential.

7. There's . . . well, you know. . . It's just plain cool.

Defining the New Animation: Technology's Perks
By J. J. Sedelmeir

1. I no longer require a large studio of on-staff talent. All our work utilizes freelance artists and animators who come on board on a per-job basis and work closely with me online.

2. Any and all techniques (watercolor, airbrush, colored outline, live/animation combos) I want to use in my productions are possible through digital programs/software. It allows me to accept the responsibility of producing the work in any style without having to re-arm ourselves (specific equipment for specific techniques) for every production.

3. Project fees have unfortunately been negatively influenced by so much work being for an online/Web use. If it's online, the feeling is that it's not worth the same as if it's broadcast. This, of course, makes no sense since both the creative process AND the animation process is often the same for online as it is for broadcast.

4. Schedules are tighter because the time required is less.

5. The use of limited animation has increased. This only means that, again, I need to be careful that the technique matches the concept. . .

6. We hardly EVER use paper or any of the conventional materials of the past. I personally still draw with pen/pencil during the preproduction process, but the actual productions are all digital.

cated. Creating an opening scene that sets the tone and teases the narrative is imperative; it's what will hook the viewer. From there we build content that unfolds and leads us to the peak of the message.

Is motion the next big frontier for designers, or has it come and gone?
I think motion is already a big part of many designer's vocabulary. Not unlike still photographers, who migrated into the live action arena, I think many young graphic designers have embraced and added motion skills to their design acumen. With the explosion of tablets and smart phones, our culture's thirst for multimedia experiences has seemingly become insatiable. I think motion design is here to stay.

SNL Weekend Update Open
Client: NBC
Creative Director: Ada Whitney
Designer: Marcelo Cardoso
Animator: Marcelo Cardoso

When you hire someone for the creative side, what do you look for?
The first thing I look for is a person whose has a smart and unique perspective. I respond to a reel that doesn't look like the past 10 I've seen. I like to see work that is well thought out and speaks the language of its intended audience. I shy away from reels that rely heavily on current design trends and the latest visual effects plug-ins. I look for someone with a keen sense of communication, design, color, motion, [and] sound and who understands the meaning of less is more!

Jean-Louis Fréchin
Asking the Right Questions

Trained as an architect, Jean-Louis Fréchin teaches a course on digital prototyping and digital design at the prestigious Paris design school, ENSCI-les atelier. He is the founder of NoDesign.net, a French digital design agency specializing in innovative and human-centered design. For him, *human* is a key word. He believes that the digital age will give designers a chance to participate in the creation of a more ethical culture. He wants to turn his expertise—digital design and the conception of digital products, interactions, and interfaces—into a discipline at the service of a less materialistic conception of the world.

3-D Printing App, Sculpteo
Vases
Designers: Jean-Louis Fréchin
and Uros Petrevski
2012

How do you explain to your clients what you do?
For our clients—from global telecommunication companies to modest start-ups—we are forever attempting to enlarge the "scope of what is possible" and "desirable" without losing the basic values of design: meaning, simplicity, emotion, and above all human endeavor. For my partner, Uros Petrevski, as for myself, design is a state, a prism for understanding, and a tool for questioning the world. We thrive on new challenges and new territories.

Your agency is called NoDesign because you categorically reject conventional ideas about design?
In fact, the "No" in "NoDesign" is an abbreviation of "nouveau." In other words, new design—the new objectives of design. The name of my agency is meant to be a teaser, a way to start the conversation. People always comment on its name. It gives me a chance to explain to them that good design is

something you don't see, particularly when it comes to designing an interface, where the "feel" is as important as the "look."

For you, graphic design should be at the service of data visualization. Would you say that your passion in life is to create objects that allow users to better understand data and interact with it?
Indeed, I think of graphic design as first and foremost a formidable visualization tool. But, as a language, graphic design is not only objective; it is also subjective. It has a dual function. It can make you think and feel.

Twenty years ago, you were pioneering CD-ROMs. In your opinion, which digital innovation is most promising today?
As a communication tool, the Internet Protocol (IP) opens an infinite number of possibilities today. It's truly revolutionary. Nothing will ever be the same.

What sort of user experience do you try to create?

Today, we are developing an electronic format that will make it possible to create prototypes of objects, using the language of the Internet. These objects are in fact 3-D interfaces, like, for example, Sculpteo, an iPad or iPhone application that lets you create a ceramic vase shaped after a photographic profile of your choice. Or FabWall, a line of decorative wallpaper whose motifs are encoded in such a way as to give you access to personal information, family pictures, or favorite websites. We want to merge the functionality of traditional interfaces with that of interactive objects. We want to come up with meta design projects.

Should graphic designers be programmers as well, in order to be able to conceive truly innovative products, services, and experiences?

To be creative today, you have to use the most contemporary tools. In my opinion, being able to write programs is critical. Graphic designers who have an even rudimentary knowledge of coding will discover new territories of expression—from 2-D screens to 3-D interactive objects.

Some of your inventions are utopian—like the "dépendomètre," an instrument that is supposed to measure your level of dependency on social networking. Are you inspired by science fiction?

What we call utopia is usually an invention that has yet to be shared with others. The idea for the dépendomètre came about when we realized that, for

many people, dependency on social networks was a very real problem. Free services, free software, free applications, and free downloads are deceptive. They are not free. As the saying goes, "If you're not paying for it, you are not the customer, you're the product." Our intention was to invent a device that allowed Internet users to measure and visualize what is fast becoming a dangerous form of addiction. This device is a smart tracker, not unlike the body analyzer, Withings, a scale that monitors your weight and heart rate and sets health goals for you.

You are also an expert in digital design strategy. How would you describe this new discipline?

In the digital age, figuring out what to design is critical. Before you look for answers, you have to make sure that you are asking the right questions. Relevant design solutions will propose new and different products. They will come about as a result of innovative

thinking emanating from technologically savvy organizations with an unconventional approach. For me, digital design strategy is a process that yields a range of unexpected "possibles," usually based on the interaction of trans-disciplinary practices.

Interactive Tags for FabWall (opposite)
Designers: Jean-Louis Fréchin and Uros Petrevski
2010

"Cloud" Dependency, Monitoring System (below)
Designers: Jean-Louis Fréchin and Uros Petrevski
Prototype
2013

Alexander Chen: Working for Google

Since Alexander Chen, a creative director at Google Creative Lab in New York, was a kid, he studied everything from the viola to programming. "Even when I started working," he says, "I jumped around a lot, from interactive design groups to my own music and art projects." He heard about the Google Creative Lab through word of mouth, and it seemed like it might be a good fit for his background.

The Lab contains mostly a diverse group of makers, from designers, filmmakers, to writers, and more. They collaborate really closely with other Google teams by adding their skills. The Lab members like to work in "really small, scrappy

groups," Chen explained. "Of course, we all focus on certain skills that we're passionate about, but my favorite part is how we all teach each other new skills in the process. I've learned so much since I've started here."

Chen has made Google logos by integrating his personal projects with his work at Google. For example, he turned the New York subway map into a string instrument that can be played inside the web browser. It started as a side experiment, but once that bit of code was written, "I was able to hack a version of the Google logo as a playable musical instrument," he said. "I brought that prototype to the Doodle

team in Mountain View, and we collaborated on turning it into the Les Paul Doodle."He has also done things the other way around, bringing Google products into personal work. "I was working on films during the day at Creative Lab around Google Glass. But on the weekends, I decided to do something more personal. I used Glass to film myself playing viola and used the video clips to compose a song."

For Chen the Lab offers special moments, "when you can all huddle around something visual to react to, seeing something come to life."

15 Designing Apps for Mobile Devices

User Interface designers decide how users will have access to layers of information displayed on screens. They know how to adapt their designs to the size and format of the monitors. However, the difference between a computer screen, a tablet, and a smart phone is more than just the number of pixels.

The task of designers is greatly complicated when the screens are on mobile devices and when viewers are no longer sitting down in front of a computer or relaxing comfortably with a laptop on their knees. In terms of usability, touch-screen manipulations represent a quantum leap. As a designer, you have to figure out when, where, and how users interact with their handheld computer. Are they wearing headphones? Do they expect the images to be scalable? How important to them is a truly convenient search function? Issues of functionality are first and foremost, but just as important are layout considerations. The choices made by designers must integrate complex technological but also societal considerations.

Apps designers are usually self-motivated. In the digital age, creating a successful app is the ultimate fantasy, a popular rag-to-riches scheme. Granted, some people have become instant millionaires when launching small, dedicated, downloadable pieces of software—Instagram, Snapchat, Doodle Jump. Others have yet to stumble on an economic model to justify the expenditure of time, money, energy, and talent. Most exciting about designing applications is not the financial reward but the phenomenal appeal of this particular format as a popular means of communication.

Sean Bumgarner

Between Text and Images

Sean Bumgarner, at the time of this interview, was design director of platforms and devices for Condé Nast in New York. In other words, his job was to translate the editorial content of magazines to fit the format of various tablets and to develop new interactive features attuned to the mobile lifestyle of tablet users. However, adapting to the new technology was not enough; he also had to anticipate industry developments, refine purchase paths, and identify marketing opportunities. "Seven years ago, I was a print art director in the magazine world, getting restless and thinking, OK, what's next?," he recalls. These days, "next" is chief digital officer (CDO) at Galvanized, a global media agency that specializes in health, fitness, and nutrition.

Screen Captures of Preliminary Graphic Interface for iPad and iPhone
Men's Health magazine
Rodale
Designer: Sean Bumgarner
2009

Can you tell us how you pioneered your specialty—art director for platforms and devices? Surely you "invented" your job and are probably still reinventing it on a daily basis?
I had always been interested in media outside of print: the music world in particular. I went to work for an ad agency specializing in fashion, but I didn't really enjoy it. Then I had the opportunity to work on the first digital edition of *Glamour* magazine, for iPad only. That was five years ago. That first version was very clunky, home-brewed. I helped with its launch and then went back to my agency job.

I got called back at Condé Nast to work some more on a new and improved digital edition of *Glamour*. By then the technology had evolved and was already much more sophisticated—Adobe tools instead of HTML language. Next, I went to *Vogue* to develop an Alexander McQueen memorial iPad edition. I had access to incredible archives, videos, and documents. It felt more like art directorship.

From there on, I worked briefly at *Vanity Fair* and at some other CNP titles before switching to Rodale, where I was put on the launch of *Men's Health* for iPad. I was really excited because it was such a perfect title for that medium, with so much information and so many opportunities to tell stories in a different way.

What is the main difference between an edition for a tablet and one for a smart phone? Is it just a matter of size, or is the editorial content of each magazine affected by its format?
First, we were Apple focused: iPad and iPhone only. Back then, using the Adobe tools on Android was not as satisfying. Now it's better. But

Apple was truly innovative, and you wanted to be there. The phone was an incredible opportunity, because you had to reinvent the way you read and interacted with the content. On an iPad, you sort of duplicate the layout of a magazine, the typography, the sidebars, and the spread mentality, whereas on an iPhone, you have to completely reinvent the presentation.

Most critical was trying to understand the interface between image and text. That's really what defines a magazine: While the images are affecting your experience of the text, ultimately the headlines, heads, subheads, captions, and quotes drive the experience. Figuring out how to make typography impactful on such a small screen is critical.

Could a magazine like *Vogue*, which depends on images, work on an iPhone?
There is soon going to be a phone version of *Vogue*, even though, in that format, text-heavy magazines like *The New Yorker* and *Vanity Fair* work best. They are, by and large, about the stories. For them, there was no real need to reinvent the magazine for the smaller screen. The same Abobe tools used for the iPad could be used for the iPhone. But now, because of the latest improvements in technology, a magazine like *Vogue* can at long last consider going for the iPhone format.

In term of user experience, is it possible to clearly define the difference between a magazine on a tablet and a magazine on a phone?
On a phone, you usually wear headphones. So there is an opportunity for

someone to read you a story while you walk. We also can create a lot of frame-by-frame animations with voice over. In some sections, we can insert splash pages to let readers know what else is going on in the issue.

One of my criticisms of Web design on the phone is that it is not scaled for the device. What I like to do with magazines is give each headline its own screen. Let the user decide whether to scroll down to read the rest of the text.

A big question mark for our industry is how important it is to give readers the functionality of the touch-screen-scalable images and texts on the iPhone. There are many technological advantages and disadvantages to consider. And there are benefits to HTML versus Adobe, vector versus rasterized images, and so on. It is a little bit of a Wild West right now, with everyone trying to figure out what works with what.

An even bigger question mark today is whether a magazine on the phone is a delivery system for content—or some other medium that still remains to be defined.

And what's the difference between a magazine app (on a tablet or a phone) and a magazine website?
A website is a portal to more information—like *The New York Times* website–that gives you access to all the breaking news and latest updates in an endless stream of headlines and articles. But fewer and fewer people go to the *NYT* homepage just to read the news. They go in search of specific information, from how to fix pears for dessert to how to understand the latest development in the Middle East. They also get a chance to survey readers'

Screen Captures of Preliminary Graphic Interface for iPad and iPhone
Men's Health magazine
Rodale
Designer: Sean Bumgarner
2009

comments, check the "most-emailed" section, watch video clips, or be captivated by a live photo streams.

A magazine is different because it has a beginning and an end. There is something nice about being able to say: "I am done. Now I can do something else." A magazine is very directional; there is a hierarchy—you know where you are. And you are not endlessly distracted. Magazines are for people who do want to read without dealing with all those extra conversations so ubiquitous on the Web.

Magazines on iPads and iPhones can develop their own social network if the stories featured in the devices are also on their websites, like *The New Yorker*. But for the most part, e-magazines do not let you search the Web for related stories.

For the time being anyway, they are their own enclosed entity. Supporting a truly convenient search function on mobile devices is still dicey. It is a conundrum that the industry has yet to solve.

On smart phones, with headlines being more appealing than images, is the status of photographs and illustrations about to change?
A change is noticeable in the relationship between text and images. *Men's Health* is a good example. The information-rich content, with description of fitness routines, workout techniques, and nutritional facts, lends itself to a new sort of interaction. It can be very exciting, with frame-by-frame animations in some instances. Imagery no longer merely illustrates text—its role is to reinforce comprehension, enjoyment, design, brand, user experience, and so on.

With *Vogue*, it's a little different because fashion photographs are always retouched, and it's more complicated to retouch animations. What works best are video interviews of fashion designers. Readers can spend 10 minutes listening to celebrities talk about their personal views and philosophy. These videos are not in-and-out, one-minute clips, as is so often the case on the web, but leisurely conversations that can yield more information and insight than a printed interview ever could.

How do you define excellence on the digital frontier?
To define excellence, the overall digital experience would have to be reevaluated. We art directors in e-pub have been too quick to accept less than perfect design and typography: bad

hyphenation, orphans, widows, and so on. The conversation we need to have now is about programming tools, so that we can demand better control of the quality of the texts and the images. We must get back what we have lost in our eagerness to convert to the digital format.

It's interesting to see that Web designers are now embracing wide screen and luscious layouts—sometimes called "flat design"—with a more thoughtful design approach. E-magazine designers should do the same. But how can we convince the powers that be—the people who decide what e-pub is—that quality is important and that it's not acceptable to settle for less than perfect standards?

What sort of tools do you have to measure the quality of the user experience?
I can get reports on who reads what, when, and on what device—all that kind of stuff. That information is easily accessible. But in the end, how you interpret this data is a matter of intuition. What is clear is that on the iPhone, people don't want to shop or watch videos or movies anymore—they want to read. So, how do we make this reading experience really, really great? And how do we accomplish this across devices? Today, there are no guidelines on what that experience should be or could be.

The problem is that before anyone has time to figure out what works best on the iPhone 4, the iPhone 5 comes out. There is a level of fatigue there. One thing remains true: Readers will spend time with beautiful, well-researched, well-designed articles. And

time spent on a device can be measured. Though advertisers still evaluate magazines in terms of circulation, they soon will wake up to the fact that what counts is engagement.

You are now Chief Digital Officer at Galvanized, a media firm that provides digital content and audience engagement. What is your role there?
I am focusing on overall strategy. Only 50 percent of major magazines have digital editions. Among them, some are just putting PDF versions of their pages on tablets! Needless to say, most magazines are a long way from adapting their editorial content to iPhones. At long last, I am in a position to help people launch digital magazines— something I love to do. And because I am still basically an art director, I can ask the question, "How would it look? How could you present your information in the smartest possible way?" As an advocate of e-publishing on mobile devices, I believe that it is possible to preserve what we love about magazines in this new form.

Michel Chanaud

Always Learning

Michel Chanaud is editor-in-chief of *Etapes* magazine, a French publication on graphic design and the visual culture. He is also president of Pyramyd, a company that offers seminars and workshops for professionals in the publishing, advertising, graphic, and communication fields. "We've managed to remain a relatively small structure," he says. "At *Etapes*, on the 3rd floor, we are about 20 people altogether. On any given day, I might act as the publisher, the editor-in-chief, and the art director. We all do everything. We are practicing our profession as if it were a craft." However, at Pyramyd, on the 4th floor, the 10 classrooms are abuzz with people eager to keep up with the latest multimedia tools, digital technologies, and software upgrades.

Etapes Magazine Cover #218
Art Director: Michel Chanaud
2014

Can you explain your role at Pyramyd?

Twenty years ago, when I created Pyramyd, my ambition was to "form and inform" the design community in France. No one at the time knew what graphic design was, even though it was ubiquitous. I wanted to make its presence known!

Today, my company does just that: We "form and inform." We offer workshops and seminars to "form" designers and creative types—to help them keep up with the latest trends and software upgrades. We also "inform" them by publishing books on topics that range from calligraphy to codes, and from grids to graffiti. We publish a magazine, *Etapes*. It features the works of young designers and emerging talents. We print essays, interviews, and critical pieces. *Etapes* is in France what *Eye* magazine is in England.

An important piece of this puzzle is "e:," an application for the iPhone and iPad, which you introduced about four years ago. Weren't you ahead of the curve?

Technology is what drives my passion. Even when computers were big clunky machines, I thought of them as creative tools. In the 1980s, I was a designer, but I also imported hardware and software—I was a Mac dealer of sorts. Ever since, I have kept up with innovations. Early on, we developed an interactive website for *Etapes*. For a while, we published CD-ROMs featuring animations. Turning a blog into an application was the next thing, but in 2010, when I launched e:, I had no idea whether I would be able to make money with it. No one did. We yet had to explore the concept of "free" download and understand how it could be economically viable.

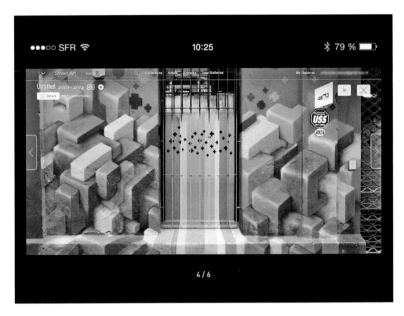

Screen Capture of e:
Application for iPhones
and iPads
Art Director: Michel Chanaud

And today?

Today, I still do not have a viable economic model for it! I am still in the red—even though more than 50,000 people have downloaded the app. These people are not *Etapes* subscribers; they do not buy our books or attend our workshops or seminars. They are a breed apart. It's not surprising. Readers in general expect different information from different devices. You don't want to find the same stuff on your tablet, your phone, your laptop, [and] your computer screen.

Did you know that 50 percent of people access the Internet from a mobile application? It's a little bit like getting your news from the radio. It all adds up—without the source of the information being identifiable as such.

Would you agree that the technology defines the form and content of a message?

You bet. New products and technological breakthroughs will create new forms. One example: the Push Pin style. It would never have existed without the new adhesive-colored films developed by 3M that allowed illustrators to obtain brilliant, flat, color surfaces.

Technology influences the form but also the content. The sort of information you'll find in our app is unlike what you'll find in your magazine: We seldom feature the same designers in both media, and when we do, our approach is totally different. On the app, we offer a service: easy access to news. In the magazine, we propose a mixture of eye candies and food for thought.

In the app, we have streamlined text to a minimum to deliver visuals in a more intuitive fashion so that you can navigate up and down and sideways with one thumb instead of two. We have learned that people seldom use links on an app. If they want to explore a topic in depth, they'll go to their tablet or laptop.

Are you exploring different economic models for your app?

Yes, of course. We eliminated the idea of using it to create a social network and capitalize on our membership. We simply don't have the manpower or the financial resources for this strategy. Meanwhile, there is a new generation of Web surfers out there who are willing to pay to get better apps, without advertising. We could simply sell our app to them. Quite a few people in the

Screen Captures of
e: Application for iPhones
and iPads
Art Director: Michel Chanaud

creative field might be willing to pay to get it.

There is also another option, called "Freemium," a contraction of "free" and "premium." More and more online newspapers have adopted this formula. It consists of giving free access to basic information, but then requiring readers to become paying subscribers to get the full story.

Has *Etapes*, the magazine, evolved as the result of the application?

Yes. One of the challenges has been to make the magazine more like the application: Make it part of the digital information stream. We are experimenting all the time. Recently, we have printed at the bottom of some pages a visual code in the form of a button that can be scanned by an iPhone or a laptop to open up links to Web pages.

What is fascinating for me is to try to understand how each device—a tablet, a phone, a magazine, a book—

requires its own specific form of communication because of its specific technology, but also because of the synergy between all of them. However, it's never what you expected. Take the magazine, for instance: Sure, we want to make it "interactive." We try. But is it really what it's all about? A magazine is precious because it fixes your memory in one place. Truth be told, you don't want a magazine or a book to be interactive; quite the contrary. You want it to be a thing on a shelf.

So you think that there is definitively a place for print in our digital culture?

Yes. More and more, printed matter is looked upon as a physical object. Designing a magazine is not unlike designing a table, a chair, or a lamp. Creating a book is not very different from designing an exhibition or a gallery show. That's why we are toying with the idea of expanding the maga-

zine into an actual space. It would be a cross between a gallery, a pop-up store, a gift shop, an artist's studio, and a performance space. Such a project would make perfect sense. The only problem is that it would require we learn yet another profession!

John Kilpatrick

Designer as Accelerator

John Kilpatrick has spent his career building new digital products and teams for both start-ups and large media organizations. He is CEO of an online app called Cabin, a Samsung Accelerator Company. Prior to that he was senior vice president and executive creative director for News Corp's iPad app, The Daily, for which he helped launch the company and ran the creative team. He was also vice president and group creative director for AOL Media, where he led the interactive design team, developing new digital media products and content for more than 80 websites. In his current position, he oversees many quick-hit prototypes. "We build, refine, test," he says. "After we land on a solid MVP candidate, we then shift to building a product that we can go to market with." The process continues with a framework that we could go live with, leveraging a mix of both open-source tech and custom-built capabilities."

Cabin App
Executive Director: John Kilpatrick
Creative Director: Ramon Espinosa
Art Director: Dami You

How did you develop Cabin, a remarkable app that allows members of a family to stay in touch with each other all day long, seamlessly, simply, and comfortably?
From the very beginning, we were a company founded by three designers—myself, Frank Campanella, and Ramon Espinosa. We worked together to develop the initial design and created the initial concept.

In the beginning, we designed and rapidly prototyped several concepts, and we used our personal experiences of interacting with our own families to shape the idea. We continued to work and refine the product. But, most importantly, we listened and watched others use Cabin.

Like any good designer, I'm very influenced by my environment. And in this case, my environment was my wife and two kids. They all had a huge hand in shaping the final product and helped us create a tool for the most important network in our lives: family.

Your background is in graphic design. What makes your start-ups different from those that do not have designers as founders?
There's such an eclectic mix of start-ups these days, solving a wildly diverse range of problems. So I don't think it's necessarily mandatory for start-ups to have a designer as a founder. However, it does offer some definite benefits. As designers, our brains are just

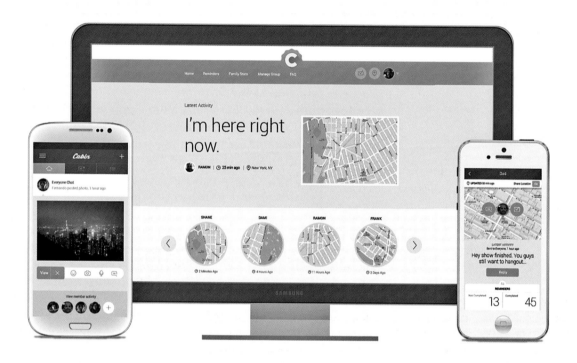

Cabin App
Executive Director: John Kilpatrick
Creative Director: Ramon Espinosa
Art Director: Dami You

trained to approach problems in a really unique way. We can't help ourselves but to dig for the simplest, easiest, most frictionless route to a solution. And with today's consumer tech start-ups playing in such a visual space, that kind of eye can be very, very useful.

When you're dealing with the precious real estate of a phone screen, every pixel has to count. It forces hard decisions to be made. And those decisions are hugely important to the way consumers interact with the product.

Design is important to you. But why is it important for the start-ups you are working on?
New technology is getting easier and easier to create. With today's user-friendly publishing tools and robust open APIs, and so on. it's easier than ever to make your own application or Web product. And with all this added competition, it becomes that much more important to design a user experience that stands out in this crowded landscape.

Also, what is the role of the designer (or, in some cases, designers) in your accelerators?

At most companies, designers sit in a dark room with their heads down. But at the Samsung Accelerator and on each team working within, designers have a seat at the table. They have the opportunity to not only shape the look and feel of the product but also to help steer the overall product and company.

What are the attributes you look for in designers joining your team?

Samsung Accelerator is built around being nimble and reactive. So anyone joining our team needs to be ready to turn on a dime and take on the jobs that need to be done—even if those tasks don't fall under their official "job description." We're a very multidisciplinary team and everyone wears a lot of hats around here. We also look for people who are self-directed. People who don't need a direct assignment to take action, but can recognize a problem and take the steps to solve it.

How do you identify these designers?

Through the years, I've been lucky enough to work with some of the best thinkers and designers out there. So that's the first place I look for talent: my network that I've created in my career.

But I also believe that the best recruiting tool you have as a CEO is your own team. Your employees are a deep well of talent—talent that's already been vetted. Not just vetted based on their skills, but vetted as a solid culture fit for your existing team.

Do the designers take part as workers or founders?

At the Samsung Accelerator, we keep our teams very small on purpose. So everyone does the work, designers and founders alike. I spend as much time answering customers' e-mails as I do making larger product decisions. And everyone on our team, regardless of their title, has a say in the direction of our company. I like to build consensus amongst the team anytime there's a major decision to be made. That's just my style.

Do you believe that designers are more or less in demand in today's start-up world?

I think designers are more in demand today than ever before, not just in the start-up community, but in every industry and at every level of business. And the role of designers within a company is changing as well.

Ten years ago you'd be hard pressed to find a CEO who came up through the design ranks (just like myself). But now I'm just one of many. Today, some of the world's most powerful and influential companies are headed by designers and creatives. And that isn't a trend I see changing anytime soon.

How much of your role is on the design side?

I'm still very active in the day-to-day design process, when I can be, though I definitely remember what it's like to have a design director looking over my shoulder, so I try to give my designers the distance and breathing room that they need to do their best work. But I still have a lot of love for design, and I try to get my hands dirty as often as possible in nitty-gritty design work.

Nicolas Ledoux and Pascal Béjean

Digital Books and Magazines
by Contemporary Artists

Nicolas Ledoux and Pascal Béjean are principals of a small Paris branding and graphic design agency called ABM Studio—short for "Art, Book, Magazine"—the name of their e-bookstore app. With Oliver Körner, they design books, catalogs, publications, and brochures for their virtual publishing house as well as for a number of French cultural institutions, including the famous Théâtre Nanterre-Amandiers. "Like most of our friends and colleagues, we worried about the future of print, the dumbing down of intellectual content, and the greed demonstrated by distribution channels," they say. So they have gone ahead and created an online alternative to high-quality, paper-based publishing.

How did you come up with the idea of publishing artist books for iPads?
Over the years, we have launched and published quite a few experimental magazines, each one exploring a different facet of our involvement with cutting-edge graphic design and the contemporary art scene. All along, we have been in touch with a network of designers and artists with whom we share information, resources, and projects. We are distressed when we see bookstores promoting cookbooks rather than art books.

At the same time, we are fascinated by new technological breakthroughs and have in our studio a savvy program developer with whom we collaborate to create apps. We saw an opportunity to fill a gap by designing an application that proposes books by artists online. Our goal is to set high standards of quality. We wanted to prove that the Web could give independent publishers access to readers who want something different, original, and exclusive. Our artist books are for sale, at prices that are frankly affordable.

Why is your app only available on iPads and not on other tablets?
The introduction of the iPad was truly a breakthrough, but the thing that attracted us to this revolutionary device is the fact that Apple users are design-conscious, more so than most people. We were pretty sure that our application would appeal to them.

However, this is just a first step, as we would like eventually to break our "Apple dependency" and explore other delivery systems. The App Store is indeed a convenient tool for beginners like us, but it imposes a price structure that is too restrictive when it comes to artist books.

Art Book Magazine App
Catalog: L'incident
Art Director: ABM Studio
2013

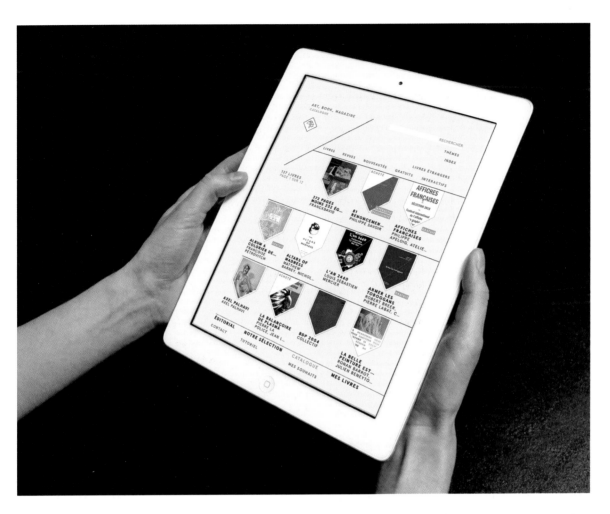

Art Book Magazine App
Vertical Interface
Art Director: ABM Studio
2013

You have designed an interface for your app that is perplexing at first: It doesn't use the graphic codes that Apple users have grown accustomed to. Why did you choose to disorient your readers?

We were reacting against the Apple aesthetic of the last few years, with its rampant "skeuomorphism"—fake wood shelves, fake on-off buttons, and fake torn paper and leather for the calendar, and so on. Even though iOS7 cleaned up all references to Formica,

vinyl, or paper products and replaced it with colorful flat icons, the navigational vocabulary of Apple's interfaces is still old-fashioned in our estimation.

What we wanted to do is reinvent the experience of buying books online so that it would be in synch with the digital realm rather than the analog world. One of our concerns was to create a comfortable and serene graphic space, far from the noisy visual environment of so many online bookstores.

Typography on the Web
By Jason Santa Maria

Typography is absolutely essential. The vast majority of the Web is text, and where there's text, there's an opportunity to communicate through typography. It's transportable, translatable, and the very stuff we use to talk to one another across time and space. And typography is at the very core of that experience on the Web.

The constraints of a boundless Web page may seem difficult to wrap your head around, but it really comes down to the absence of rigid control in typographic presentation. Methods for typesetting on the Web have come a long way in recent years, but more importantly, they rely most heavily on suggested typographic style than a fixed experience. The fluid nature of what a Web page can even be is what makes things so exciting. The ability to tailor typography for a situation, even beyond a desktop or a mobile device, means you are designing to be flexible for myriad potential experiences.

The biggest challenge I face is helping people understand that the Web is not print. It sounds like it would be obvious, and the two mediums do overlap in areas, but they are very different in terms of the user experience. People interact with a Website differently than they do with a fixed medium like print, and the design of a Website needs to be understanding of that fact. At the same time, centuries worth of design principles don't immediately transfer to the Web in the same ways. Many graphic designers think the Web is a barren place for design, when the reality is they are proclaiming they lack an understanding of the medium.

Art Book Magazine App
Catalog: Our House in the Middle of the Street
Designer: P. Nicolas Ledoux
2013

Did you think that your potential readers were people who were critical of the quasi-universal visual standards established and enforced by Apple?
It wasn't a consideration, really. However, we were aware that the Apple graphic guidelines had been created to accommodate all sorts of constraints having to do with the codes of marketing and global communication. We didn't have to worry about that graphic nonsense. We believed that our readers were ready for a challenge that would stimulate their imagination.

Are you involved in the conceptual, graphic, or technical development of the books you are publishing?
Yes, quite often. We get involved wherever our expertise is needed. Sometimes we create our own books from scratch. We collaborate with some artists to conceptualize their editorial project. For others, we suggest ways to create interaction. We can have an impact graphically, or we can act as editorial consultants, art directors, or production managers.

The real challenge today is to define the difference between a printed book and a digital book. You need to exploit the new opportunities, blur the boundaries, stimulate contradictions—in other words, you need to reinvent the experience of the book as such.

We learned from the demise of the CD-ROMs. We are convinced that digital books must not break away completely from publishing traditions but, on the contrary, must capitalize on our historical heritage, know-how, and savoir faire. Sure, you can publish an ordinary digital book in a few clicks and for practically no money. It would look basically like a Word file. But publishing a good digital book takes a lot of work! Those few clicks require that the content of the book be completely integrated with its form in a way that is both technologically relevant and ergonomically correct.

There are no norms yet for what constitutes a good digital book. Readers who are nostalgic about the feel and beauty of traditional books are suspicious of digital books, and rightly so. Downloaded publications are standardized products that look alike because they are generated by the same software. The fear is that the online publishing industry, like the music industry, will only support highly promoted artists and only release the most conventional and profitable best sellers.

Some of the books you publish emulate, electronically, the pleasure of "turning" pages. Yet, let's face it, the tactile impression is not the same. What are the real advantages, for readers, of digital books?
They are many advantages! First, the navigational options: the ease with which you access text, chapters, notes; the way you can zoom in and out; the addition of video and sound, not to mention the quality of the HD images.

The tablet itself is a fascinating object. It gives readers access to specific books but also to entire libraries. It is a virtual space, one in which you can go to explore content as you

please. When you discover the work of a painter on one of our books, the impression is very intense because it's personal. The feeling of immersion is total. The tablet does not exclude enjoying traditional publications—it is just another way of being absorbed in the content of a book.

You have chosen to appeal to readers who appreciate contemporary art and, thus, are most likely to be curious about the power and possibilities of digital images. Do you know what motivates your customers to buy your books?
One of the reasons they buy our books is to express their support of our venture. They want to believe that it's possible, in our day and age, to develop independent publishing initiatives, and they express their point of view by collecting autonomous and unusual publications. They want to take part a real alternative.

Art Book Magazine App
Catalog: Our House in the
Middle of the Street
(above)
Designer: P. Nicolas Ledoux
2013

Art Book Magazine App
Catalog: Didier Courbot
(bottom)
Art Director: ABM Studio
2013

Frédérique Krupa

Games as Powerful Motivators

Frédérique Krupa is a Web and documentation manager as well as a partner at Simple is Beautiful, a start-up that creates software for touch-screen, handheld devices. SiB's first titles, DrumTrack8 and SpillPills, were released in 2009. A former editor at *I.D.* magazine and assistant professor of industrial design at RISD and University of Art, she is now Chair of Communication Design at Paris College of Art. "That was a two-decade long progression during which I learned to focus on the user's experience," she says. "I consider that the designer's role is to be the advocate for the end user."

You were trained as a product design and design critic. How did you go from being an assistant editor at *I.D.* magazine to developing apps for games on touch-screen, handheld devices?

I have a personality that enjoys managing complexity, theorizing, optimizing, and analyzing structures and systems, but it took me a while to realize this was a valuable (and relatively uncommon) skill. I ventured into Web design in the late 90s for a company called Virtools, a game-industry software developer, and evolved in new media from there.

Simple is Beautiful's app development business evolved about five years ago from a mutual frustration with traditional software development. We took advantage of the opportunities that arose, thanks to Apple's touch-screen devices and the iTunes App Store. This made small-scale, independent software development economically viable for the first time by handling the tedious business end (i.e., sales and distribution). I consider myself a designer in the widest sense of the word, and my work encompasses aspects of product design, graphic design, user experience design, service design, and game design.

You are also Chair of Communication Design at Paris College of Art. Does your interest in game design relate to the fact that you teach system design methodology and understand complex processes?

I've always split my time evenly between industry and academia. I became chair of the department because communication designers have an important contribution to make to the field of new media, and they need to understand how this differs from the print industry. You usually work in multidisciplinary teams using core technology that evolves very quickly on system-level projects rather than on linear

MugguM Photography App
Side-by-Side Symmetrical Portraits
Designer: Taylor Holland
Developers: Aymeric Bard and
Frédérique Krupa/Simple is Beautiful
2011

processes. It can be a tough sell for students who are very "hands-on" or prefer working alone from start to finish. But it's important for students to understand that there are design methods for managing complexity.

My personal interest in games really stems from wanting to understand user motivation. Games are powerful motivators, provide a great deal of satisfaction, and teach social cohesion. Understanding why someone plays can give great motivational guidance when developing other types of software, such as for educational or training purposes.

What role does "graphics" play when designing a game? Is the quality of the visuals a very small part of the equation?

Aesthetics, in general, is an undervalued part of the equation. "Visual quality" has been so caught up achieving photo-realism as a technological feat that a game's aesthetics was seen as less important. Now we see that the next-generation consoles are no longer playing that card. So the game's visual quality will shift from technological achievement to aesthetic experiences. I can't think of an "ugly" game that sells well. Even games like the Sims or

Minecraft (which I don't appreciate, but my kids love) take an aesthetic stance and follow it through. There are some amazing games like Limbo that are just gorgeous, even if the gameplay is macabre.

What sort of misconceptions do students have regarding a career as a game designer?

When most people hear the word "game design," they picture AAA titles for the major game consoles to the detriment of everything else. The industry is much, much broader than that. First of all, there are nondigital games like boards games, card games, hybrid games, and so on. There are video game for PCs, phones, tablets, handheld consoles. There are casual games, serious games, MMORPGs, educational games, and so on.

Teams, expenses, and production schedules can vary enormously in scope. Casual games for touch-screen devices can be created in weeks by very small teams. Their gameplay is obviously very limited. On the other end of the spectrum, Grand Theft Auto V has been in development for over five years and has been one of the most expensive productions ever, surpassing budgets normally devoted to blockbusters. You play for 120 hours, and its script is better than a Hollywood movie.

Students don't really know what's involved in game development, often confusing game artists, game designers, and programmers. Game designers spend more time writing than anything else; they develop the gameplay—including rules, structures,

Smack That Gugl
Action Strategy Game for iPhone
Developers: Aymeric Bard and
Frédérique Krupa/Simple is Beautiful
2010

Girls and Games

An increasing number of women are graduating from art schools with degrees in graphic design, communication, Web design, and design management, yet they are still significantly underrepresented in most design fields—and particularly the male-dominated game design field.

Frédérique Krupa is doing PhD research in sociological causes, particularly negative stereotypes and self-esteem issues. "There's been amazing research done here, but I regularly get told 'girls aren't interested in video games' or 'boys are better at math' when I tell people I am working on correcting this gender imbalance," she says.

These are gross stereotypes. Girls have now surpassed boys' SAT math scores; it was a 200 point difference when Krupa was in high school 25 years

ago. Girls have caught up as consumers of digital media, but this belief that by creating women comfortable with using technology, we would be creating more female content producers really has not panned out.

"I'm choosing to focus my research on the early years because we lose probably half of the female demographic by adolescence," Krupra adds."By the time they get to college, most women will not even consider a SET career (Science, Engineering, and Technology) because they believe it is not 'natural.'"

So Krupra is working on video games for young kids because games are excellent vehicles for critical reflection. She wants them to question stereotypes and discover skills they may not have suspected. "If I can get more girls and boys excited about technology, all the better."

DrumTrackHD App,
Drum Step Sequencer, Toolbar
Developers: Aymeric Bard and
Frédérique Krupa/Simple ss Beautiful

goals. . . Game artists give visual form to the gameplay set up by the game designers. One of my students was a walking bible of video game knowledge, and I suggested that she think about going into the profession. She said to me, "I couldn't. I'm not good at math." To which I responded, "Can you write?" Public perception of software development is that it's 95 percent programmers on a team. It's usually closer to 35–50 percent.

Would you say that most students discover an interest for game design as they progress in their design studies, or is it something they always knew they wanted to do?
As it stands now, the people who go into game development are usually people who grew up playing video games and have their sights squarely set on that industry. It is highly

competitive, since it is one of the more "glamorous" technology industries. And since video games have been mostly designed and targeted for a male demographic, the profession is overwhelmingly male.

Why is the game design field male dominated? Is it changing?
The technology field has always been male dominated, and statistically, it's getting worse pretty much all over the Western European and Anglo-Saxon countries. There's been a tremendous amount of attention being focused on this gender imbalance for at least 20 years, described as a leaky pipeline problem whereby women are abandoning or losing interest in science, engineering, and technology (SET) starting in elementary school, throughout their education, and into their early professional careers.

More and more women are graduating from design communication schools and entering the workforce. As teachers, how do we prepare them to become leaders in the various fields where communication is critical?
It's important for women to develop self-confidence, which is easier said than done, and to learn to take risks— even if it means failure. Failure is not a bad thing if you learn from your mistakes. Feminine qualities that are reinforced in education, that is, discipline and perseverance, in the end make them better employees than engineers. Women have a different relationship to technology, one that is more cooperative than dominating. Girls need to be encouraged and rewarded for risk-taking.

16 E-Commerce with a Soul

Understanding how a brand lives in cyberspace is the first thing. However, getting involved with e-commerce also requires that you figure out how to translate the virtual brand image into its analog dimension. Sure, you can propose great products online, but the "unboxing" of the goods happens in the real world. The designers interviewed here are comfortable creating digital content, but they are also aware that the quality of the thing they sell makes the difference. Ethical and environmental factors, as well as aesthetic values, are very much on their mind.

The good news is that you don't need to sell the farm to explore the possibilities of this new form of commerce. An increasing number of graphic designers create distinctively branded "indie" products they sell directly on their website. T-shirts and posters, but also fanzines, fonts, toys, and home accessories are routinely available in their virtual gift shops. The ventures may not bring in revenue, but they always enhance the identity and credibility of their creators, many of them championing the idea that graphic design can and should project itself into the third dimension.

In some rare cases, these online stores become the raison d'être of the websites. The mini-outlets slowly morph into a full-fledged commercial venues. Burö Destruct in Bern, Switzerland, sells designer toys and hip art supplies. Vier5 in Paris, France, publishes a men's fashion magazine and a very smart line of clothes. Aaron Draplin in Portland, Oregon, features Action Caps, Field Notes Pencils, and Dock Beanies on his carefully curated list of populist "merch."

The next series of interviews features graphic designers who have jumped ship and embraced e-commerce as a full-time job.

Randy J. Hunt

Growing into a Job

Randy J. Hunt, a graduate of the SVA MFA Design/ Designer as Author + Entrepreneur program, calls himself a designer and author. He leads design at Etsy, the global marketplace for independent creative businesses. He proudly announces that the community of Etsy sellers sold more than $1.3 billion of merchandise in 2013. The products they sell range from handmade items to craft-manufactured design products, vintage goods, and supplies for making. Hunt came to Etsy as an interaction designer. By working alongside other designers, engineers, and people throughout the company, he evolved the role of interaction designer into what Etsy calls "product design" —a combined role of interaction design, UX design, interface design, and front-end engineering. He is responsible for ensuring the Etsy brand is not static.

Holiday Seller Campaign 2013
Designers: Melissa Deckert,
Nicole Licht, Jeremy Perez-Cruz
Photography: Aaron Cameron Muntz

What does Etsy mean?

The true meaning of the word "Etsy" is a secret known only to our founder, Rob Kalin. Any stories you may have heard about it are probably wrong. Or maybe they're right.

How did you get your position?

I grew and evolved into my current position at Etsy. I was given the opportunity to grow that team and eventually started what is now called our "brand design" team as well—communication design, art direction, illustration, and design for advertising and marketing needs. Along the way, I led and grew our product management, user research, and product marketing teams as well. It was helpful that as the company was growing, so was I. Also, the company's growth drove the need

for design team growth as well. Thankfully, other leaders at Etsy respected both design and my point of view, and that allowed me to use resources and have their trust in developing design inside the company and the community.

In your role, what are your responsibilities?

As the voice of design for and within Etsy, I work to make sure design is part of our strategic discussions and informs and supports our decision making. This manifests itself most clearly in the digital products we build and in our brand communications, though it's often integral to many other parts of the company in less obvious ways. As a manager, my role is to make sure that designers have the

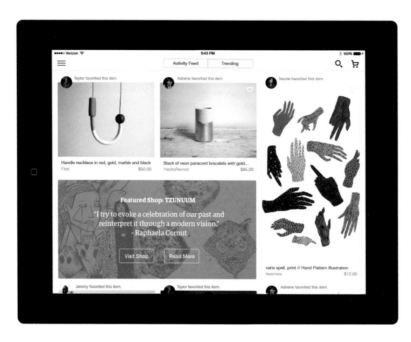

Etsy iPad App
Designer: Chesley Andrews

Holiday Seller Campaign 2013
(opposite)
Designers: Melissa Deckert,
Nicole Licht, Jeremy Perez-Cruz
Photography: Aaron Cameron Muntz

information, resources, trust, and collaborators they need to get great work done. As leader inside the company, I work to set a great example and offer inspiration and guidance—often employing design to help make that happen—to help us fulfill the company's mission to reimagine commerce in ways that build a more fulfilling and lasting world.

Does "leading" give you enough opportunity to design?

I work from the point of view that anything can be approached as a designer. These days I design high-level strategy, and I design teams. From time to time, I have the chance to engage in more elemental design work at Etsy, and also in projects I do in my leisure time. I'm equally satisfied and fulfilled with designing all along that spectrum.

When designing for an online company like this, what are the major responsibilities to the client?

One: preserving and amplifying the values and value of the brand. Two: facilitating scalability in both concept and execution of design work.

You have a large staff, and growing. What do you look for in designers?

I look for designers with strong fundamental design skills, typography most of all. I find the people who understand good typography also understand systems thinking, information organization and hierarchy, and it's a good way to judge their taste level. Beyond that, I'm looking for people who can communicate very well in written and spoken venues and who have an interest in problem solving more than beauty making. The elegant designs tend to come out of

elegantly solving problems. Also, I'm always looking for what we call "world class and quietly awesome." That means stellar work and low ego.

Are there different kinds of design skills that come to the fore in the digital age and space?

There are three skills that tend to be increasingly applicable:

1. Time-based design: Interaction and user experience design is designing for experiences that take place over time. Understanding the arc of an experience over time is crucial. "Flows, not pages" we like to say.
2. Systems thinking: The context of our choices are often complex systems. Being able to understand and design kits of parts and process that adapt to various inputs and circumstances is crucial.

BREAK EAK NEW GR OU ND

3. Software engineering: much of what we're designing is powered by and enabled by software. Being able to manipulate software is a powerful skill.

These aren't the only skills that come in handy though, and so perhaps the most valuable of all is the interest and willingness to learn new skills.

For those looking to work in this online world, what should they show to get hired?

Great typography, a willingness to learn, entrepreneurial spirit, and designs for complex systems that they've put in front of real audiences and then iterated based on feedback and learnings.

Because we work in complex systems and address complex problems, designers who can write and can share their process are most prepared to succeed. Fundamental communication skills apply.

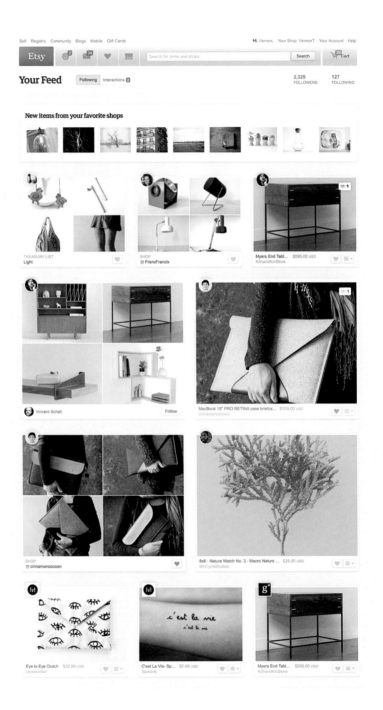

Activity Feed
Designer: Jung Park

Lucy Sisman

Online Editorial Ventures

Lucy Sisman is the principal of MiddleBlue, an online store that sells shirts, bags, accessories, and scarves made from saris by rural women from a small town near Bolpur in the Birbhum district of West Bengal, India. She also launched wwword, a website for all "readers, writers, illiterates, browsers, time wasters, mavens, and bores, and all those who use, abuse, love, and hate the English language." Prior to becoming an entrepreneur, she was an award-winning creative director (for *Allure* magazine, *Mademoiselle*, and *Details*), an advertising art director, a brand and corporate identity designer, and a packaging designer.

Allure Magazine
"Highbrow Eyebrows"
Client: Conde Nast
Art Director: Lucy Sisman
1991

What did you like most about being a magazine art director?

I loved working in magazines. I loved the pace, the drama, the discipline, the diversity of my job—from quiet moments working on layouts; crazy deadlines and all-nighters; bullish, rowdy competitive meetings; long collaborative hours in the studio or on location inventing images—and all with someone else picking up the bill. I knew I loved design. My father had been a designer, and as a child I used to help him, so I knew something about the way a designer worked. What first appealed to me about design still intrigues and delights me: I like the tidiness of a well-thought-out design solution, the simplicity when everything falls into place. I've always believed that, if a designer does thorough and exhaustive research at the beginning of any job, then it will work out well. Research can mean anything

from asking the right questions to using the right pencil.

Yet, somehow, you never "signed up." Even as the founding art director of *Allure* magazine, you remained a freelancer. Why?

There is something about working for somebody else that I just don't like. I wanted to feel that I could just walk out if it got too unreasonable or unbearably punishing. Of course, I never did, but all the time I worked at *Allure* I kept my own office. So when I finally left Condé Nast, I went back and built it back up.

I was determined not to be pigeon-holed into one area of design: I liked working on editorial, advertising, books, corporate identities, branding, logos, packaging, TV, and video—and I wanted young, energetic people around me who enjoyed working on a wide range of things, too.

Paper: Sixties Issue
Client: *Paper* magazine
Art Director: Lucy Sisman
1984

During that time, you became quite successful as a branding consultant. Why did you eventually turn your back on this profession?

It wasn't so much that I turned my back on branding, it's just that I felt I'd got far away from design. I had great clients—The Limited, Express, Victoria's Secret, Abercrombie, Sony, Shiseido, P.S.1, Revlon, Bruno Magli, Lilly Pulitzer, Sears, Diesel, Johnson & Johnson, Clairol, Ralph Lauren, LVMH—but one of the downsides of success is often that it takes you away from what you really love to do. At a certain point, I got tired of marketing directors, negotiating contracts, deal-ing with temperamental employees, struggling when times were hard, and I thought how nice it would be to go and read all the books that I'd always wanted to read.

So, again, I gave it all up and went to Oxford to study English for a few years. I didn't really know what I would do afterwards, but I thought that would just take care of itself.

Did it?

Yes, but it wasn't straightforward. After Oxford, I came back to New York to work on a "green" magazine with an old friend from Condé Nast. The idea morphed a bit—magazine turned into

MiddleBlue Website
Art Director: Lucy Sisman
2014

website and then into a store—but my partner wasn't really interested in commerce, so he bailed and I was left with this new interest in making things. Through a rather circuitous route, I found a woman in India who knew women who needed work, so we landed on this idea to make scarves from vintage saris, using a unique traditional stitching technique. Pretty soon we had over 30 women working for us. We called our e-commerce venture "MiddleBlue." We work on Skype.

Did your understanding of graphic design principles play a role in your entrepreneurial venture?

I'm not sure how anybody can start any kind of company if they aren't a designer, as there's so much graphic design involved from the logo onwards—labels, tags, press kits, promotional material, posters, website—it's never ending. But beyond that, designers are trained to solve problems, and being an entrepreneur is all about problem solving: starting at the beginning and then doing 500 things all at once, each one equally important and urgent.

As an entrepreneur, I also had to grow as a designer. One of the key things has been learning that new technology and keeping up with it: retouching my own pictures or mocking up some dummy packaging myself, for instance. Independence is vital. In the old days, I had people to do this kind of thing for me, but the world doesn't work this way anymore.

How would you define the very special visual characteristics of your product line?

What I sell is handmade, so I thought it was important to make the site feel as friendly as possible. The other thing is, I didn't want to spend money on photography, particularly at the beginning when everything was an outgoing expense. It then seemed obvious to shoot my friends wearing what I sold, so, in effect, I'm constantly updating the photography. It's very straightforward—daylight, no hair or makeup—but that's the kind of photography I like anyway.

In your experience, what are the most critical design features of a website that sells goods online?

A good website—for anything—has to be simple and work quickly. It's

hard working on your own site, where you're the client as well as the designer. It's important to have conversations with yourself, so you can criticize the work without the inner designer getting offended and ignoring practical needs altogether.

Nancy Kruger Cohen

Addicted to Start-ups

Nancy Kruger Cohen is chief creative officer (CCO) at Mouth, a Brooklyn startup that sells indie gourmet products online. A former art director of *Metropolis* magazine and *ESPN* magazine, she eventually went into advertising, creating campaigns for Polo Ralph Lauren, while at the same time developing her writing skills (one of her stories was published in *The New York Times*). "But all along, I wanted to feel more of a sense of ownership," she says. "I wanted to take a risk myself. That's why Mouth feels like an inevitable destination for me."

Mouth Packaging
Art Director: Nancy Kruger Cohen

How did you go from being an art director (*Metropolis* magazine, and more) to getting involved with an e-commerce venture, and what lessons have you learned along the way?

I was always interested in both writing and design, so I was drawn to magazines from the start. I was lucky to land at *Metropolis*, and then at *ESPN* magazine. Although not a sports fan, I realized that I could develop strong opinions about any subject, as long as I cared about the mission, process, and people.

After a few more magazine stints, I shifted into advertising at the agency Carlson & Partners. My client was Polo Ralph Lauren. My job was to create what was then called a "magalog"— a cross between a magazine and a catalog—for which I oversaw everything from photography to writing to design. From there, I became a consultant, creating print and TV ads, books, and identity branding for all sorts of clients. All of these work environments, by the way, were essentially start-ups. I'm addicted to a certain type of intensity and tend to gravitate to challenging projects like redesigns and new brands—basically, creating something from nothing.

Is that why working at a start-up appealed to you?

Yes. I was ready for it. From Ralph Lauren, I had learned about the importance of "the brand"—of a clear and consistent message. It was invaluable. But it got a little frustrating and soon I was ready to move into the business side of a creative project. As much as I had loved diving deep into photography (I had worked with Bruce

Yes, we're opening an online spirits and wine shop!

Why? In our search for the tastiest indie food, we've discovered a parallel movement happening in spirits! Passionate, inspired makers are working around the clock in small, craft distilleries across America.

Our team has put together the most distinctive whiskey, bourbon, rye, gin, vodka, rum, brandy, liqueur, moonshine, vermouth, absinthe, bottled cocktails and wine out there.

Sign up right here and we'll let you know as soon as the online shop is open for business.

YOUR EMAIL ADDRESS   OK

In the meantime, if you live in NYC, come by our brick-and-mortar shop! It's in DUMBO, Brooklyn at 192 Water Street. Cheers!

Mouth Website
Art Director: Nancy Kruger Cohen

breakfast in bed!*

ANARCHY
IN A JAR
STRAWBERRY
BALSAMIC JAM

LOVE

BROOKLYN
ROASTING CO.
COFFEE

BUMBLEBERRY
MAPLE HONEY
CREME

BLACKBIRD
FOOD CO.
SALTY SWEET
GRANOLA

QUEEN CITY
COOKIES
CINNAMON
ROLLS

MAGPIES
BLUEBERRY
POPPED TART

*IN A BAG

Mouth Breakfast in Bed
Art Director: Nancy Kruger Cohen

Weber and witnessed a true artist up close), I knew I needed to get back to words and concepts.

At the same time, your understanding of graphic design principles must have helped you establish the visual presence of Mouth.
Absolutely. I was brought in to help create a brand, which began with establishing a clear point of view about who we were: friendly, witty, and . . . hungry! Image and words needed to work together to form an accessible, conversational voice. So our site design is clean and makes use of the grid and white space. The colors are vibrant, and

the photography is visceral. The typography is simple and unfussy (I am a sucker for a classic sans serif paired with a hit of retro script). And the logo is a vernacular object, a hand-branded wooden tasting spoon.

What are the most critical design features of a website that sells goods online?
The brand experience needs to be consistent from start to finish, from website home page to the checkout to the final bag of goodies that arrives by mail. The user experience, at the same time, must be easy, without too many layers of clicking.

You also developed original packaging to ship the products you sell. Why is this so important, and did you need special skills?
The "unboxing" is a key brand moment. So this was just another design challenge of a different sort—coming up with a creative yet functional way to wrap and ship the products so that our voice would carry through.

Photography plays an important role in establishing the Mouth brand. How would you define the very special visual characteristics of your site?
Above all, the site needs to be mouthwatering. Most online food

stores just show packaging, but we make it a point to show the FOOD itself. Our photography tries to replicate the experience of being at a market, opening the jar, and having a taste. Our CEO, Craig Kanarick, is our photographer, and I pinch-hit as food stylist!

So you write in your spare time, you are the mother of two girls, and you are involved in a number of community projects. Is there a connection between all your interests and talents?

The connection is me. These are all the things I love and care about. And I put 100 percent into anything I'm doing. Whether I'm writing an e-blast, designing a home page carousel, art directing a pro bono invite for the local school, or assembling a birthday party goodie bag—it's just me being me, interested and invested in the ideas and people I care about. I no longer compartmentalize my interests and skills. Graphic designer, writer, mother—I'm not sure I see a need for these labels anymore. I'm not in a box.

What is the most interesting part of your day?

I love the diversity. Working with our tech people to improve site navigation. Creating marketing postcards or new tote bags. Writing and designing e-blasts. Curating new gift collections. Brainstorming promotions. My partners are brilliant and make me laugh, daily. And, of course, I love the food. Snacking is a job requirement!

Mouth Website
Art Director: Nancy Kruger Cohen

MEET YOUR MAKERS

EASTER TREATS (SEE ALL)

MOUTH
THE HOP - INDIE EASTER BASKET
$33.75 • PUT IN BAG

MOUTH
THE HOP HOP - INDIE EASTER BASKET
$52.50 • PUT IN BAG

MOUTH
THE HOP HOP HOP - INDIE EASTER BASKET
$82.50 • PUT IN BAG

ALMA CHOCOLATE
CHOCOLATE BUNNIES
$4.50 • PUT IN BAG

17 User Experience Specialists

User experience (UX) is today something of a buzzword. Those involved in this relatively new practice are not "touchy-feely" but aspire to make it an exacting discipline based on research and data analysis. Universally recognized as part of "best practice" standards, UX is the study of how to enhance customer satisfaction and loyalty.

Paradoxically, putting the user first is a new idea. For decades, graphic designers were focused on delivering their client's message in the most efficient and persuasive manner, forgetting the consumers in the process. Nowadays, thanks to the fluidity of the digital language, the communication between a brand and its audience is a two-way street. In fact, innovations are often customer driven: the way people experience a product or a service is very much part of the brand equation.

Designers who make a profession of UX are the first to admit that it is still an amorphous, multidisciplinary concept, incorporating aspects of psychology, sociology, ergonomics, and computer science, just to name a few complementary disciplines. In other words, user experience designers are not specialists but polymaths. They are the Renaissance men (and women) of the digital age. As such, they find their place in software development, but also in fields where fast-paced technological advances threaten the user's sovereignty.

Bruce Charonnat

Understanding Human–Computer
Interaction

Bruce Charonnat is a partner at Tangible, a consulting firm in San Francisco that specializes "in helping clients create intuitive, branded user experiences for applications, websites, and handheld mobile devices." He brings to each project more than 20 years of graphic design experience across multiple media, including interface design, information architecture, usability testing, and site strategy. In 1983, he was the first art director of *MacWorld*, which he designed on one of the first prototypes of the Macintosh 128K. Back then, it was called "desktop publishing." "In the 1990s, user experience design was a whole new world that opened up to those such as myself who grew up in the world of graphic design," he explains. "However, graphic design is just one of the many streams that flow into the world of user experience design."

Premier Issue of *MacWorld*
Art Director: Bruce Charonnat
1984

Can you tell us what the relationship is between graphic design and experience design—as practiced today?
I see user experience as a much broader term than graphic design. Its roots go deep into the history of communication, human-computer interactions, imagery, and technology. In our work now at Tangible UX, user experience design requires such diverse resources as the researcher with a PhD in cognitive psychology, the library scientist, the interaction designer, the visual artist, the engineer, the analyst, the marketer, and many others.

When it comes to developing user experiences, is there a difference between "designing" and "engineering"?
Absolutely. To the same degree as there is a difference between the architect of a house and its builder. Of course,

collaboration between design and engineering is critical to the success of any user experience. And in order to be a successful user experience designer, one must be aware and up to date with engineering trends. But, ultimately, the designer and the engineer have different responsibilities. These two skill sets are not mutually exclusive, of course, and many people today are fluent in both. I see more and more of that with younger designers, and less so with the designers from an earlier generation who migrated out of the world of print.

Successful interactive devices today always have a strong social network component. How come community building is such an important part of "interaction design"?
I would say that community building is an important part of the world

of mobile design—that is, design for smartphones, tablets, and so on. Interaction design is a process that is equally applicable for social and nonsocial experiences. As an example, designing Pinterest and designing Microsoft Excel are both exercises in interaction design. But one has a much more dominant social network component than the other. While I would say that "social apps" are becoming more and more dominant in our daily lives, they do not obviate (yet!) the need to design products with less of a social component.

Tangible UX helps clients gain strong user acceptance of their products. Is it a well-known fact in the industry that users have trouble "embracing" the functionalities of interactive devices? What users have trouble "embracing" are poorly designed products and experiences! As well they should. Embracing a well-designed product or experience should be fairly effortless. I have heard stories of children aged 1 to 2 that can call their parents on a smartphone.

Do designers today have to acquire a solid knowledge of programming to be able to develop more "user-friendly" experiences and interfaces? I would not say that programming skills are required as much as they are extremely advantageous to the user experience designer. Some people who gravitate to user experience design have more of a combination left-brain/right-brain fluency. As I mentioned before, knowledge of engineering trends and solutions, and the ability to speak to that world, are more critical to the designer than the actual ability to code.

The User Experience on Tangible Website (Top)
Art Director: Bruce Charonnat
2014

User-Friendly Macintosh in *MacWorld* (Bottom)
Art Director: Bruce Charonnat

Michael Aidan

Using the Audience as Media

Michael Aidan is in charge of digital brand platforms for the Danone Group. In his position today, he develops the digital framework for Danone, a company whose products include bottled waters but also fresh dairy products, baby nutrition, and medical nutrition. "Oddly enough, I have always worked in companies whose main products are liquid," he says. "Before Volvic, Badoit, and Evian waters for Danone, I worked on shampoos for P&G, perfumes for YSL, and beverages for Pepsico." Maybe it's not a coincidence: He is fascinated by the concept of fluidity—the free-flowing transversal communication between contents and audiences.

Can you tell us what evolution in mind-set you've witnessed in the last 20 years?

The most striking change is cultural, not technological! The digital age has completely transformed the relationship between people and companies. Dialogue has replaced one-way street communication. Captive audiences are a thing of the past. So are techniques of persuasion. Brands today are seeking engagement with users. At Danone, this new mindset forces us to rethink the way we approach marketing. We focus on storytelling—and high-quality content is the key.

Even innovations have changed: Whereas in the past they came from companies with money to invest in R&D, today they come from customers, individuals who are often more technologically savvy than the marketers themselves. As a result, instead of trying to be "on message," brand managers are now focusing on the user experience. More power to the people!

Do you know that today, according to the latest polls, only 16 percent of the brands out there are considered truly relevant by most people? In other words, over three quarters of the existing brands are in a take-it-or-leave-it limbo.

Specifically, what is your role at Danone today?

I am in charge of accelerating the digital revolution! This means working on the tools, the technology but, more importantly, the mindset and the contents. The marketing culture needs to adjust to all the changes we mentioned before. I'd like to develop tools and provide sources of inspiration so that we can progressively switch to a more intuitive connection with consumers. Linear thinking doesn't produce results anymore. We need to work the way start-ups do: take risks, stay agile, dare to do the things that have yet to best tested.

evian.
Live young

Evian Live Young
Print Campaign
2013

Evian has been successful at this. In 2009, we launched the "Roller Babies" campaign on YouTube. It went viral immediately. We got 2 million clicks in three days. It was one of the first YouTube-exclusive campaigns by a major brand, with now over 200 million total views—the *Guinness World Record* for the most viral video advertisement of all time. The heart of this campaign was on the Web, not on TV. And it was a first for us.

In 2013, still on a roll, so to speak, we followed up with the "Baby & Me" campaign. We also developed a Baby & Me app for Facebook, Android, and iPhone. Right from the start, we got 1000 downloads a minute. Our servers kept crashing. A nightmare, but also a marketer's dream: people willing to be part of your brand story.

How do you define your philosophy in terms of brand strategy?
I like to think of myself—and all marketers—as storytellers. This is neither science nor art. We need to tell a story that generates enthusiasm for our brand and surround ourselves with the best talents to make it happen; that is to say, create the "chapters": advertising, packaging, innovations, promotions, or services.

How does one develop the "digital language" of a specific brand?
The digital language is not the language of "persuasion" but the language of emotions. Your job as a marketer is to generate enthusiasm for your brand. How do you do that? First, you tell a story about the brand. Then

Evian Baby and Me
Mobile App
2014

you invite the public to enter into the narrative, to interact with it, to become "engaged" with it—digitally, of course—in a way that was not conceivable 20, 10, or even 5 years ago.

So, the very concept of interactivity is being redefined as we speak?
Yes, you have to inverse the traditional relationship with your audience. The way consumers experience a brand is the brand. And that brand is "relevant" only if it provides a way for people to engage with friends, colleagues, and

loved ones. And to do that, you have to be entertaining, upbeat, amusing. You can't be didactic. You don't sell a product, a service, or a lifestyle anymore: You provide a delivery system for emotions.

Can you train marketers to think "digitally"?
The best way to think digitally is to communicate digitally. We have developed an in-house app—Danone iBrand—to encourage our staff to look around, to be inspired by other mar-

keters do, to learn from each other, to see what works and doesn't work, and to share ideas and information. Instead of being trained, our marketers will train themselves. Using the app across the board will provide the common experience we need to understand the new paradigm. To survive, brands must learn to navigate the digital flow.

Hugh Dubberly

Mapping the Relationship
between Ideas

Hugh Dubberly is the proprietor of HD: Dubberly Design Office, a 12-person software and service design consultancy in San Francisco, "focused on making hardware, software, and services easier to use, more effective, and more fun, through interaction design and information design," he says. At Apple Computer in the late 1980s and early 1990s, Dubberly managed cross-functional design teams and later managed graphic design and corporate identity for the entire company. While at Apple, he cocreated a series of technology-forecast films, beginning with *Knowledge Navigator*, that presaged the appearance of the Internet and interaction via mobile devices. At Netscape, he became vice president of design and managed groups responsible for the design, engineering, and production of Netscape's Web portal. In 2000, he cofounded DDO. Dubberly edits a column, "On Modeling," for the Association for Computing Machinery's journal, *Interactions*.

iPad Repair App
Design: Michael Gallagher and
Jane Brown
Creative Direction: Robin Bahr
2013

You've been in the design business for many years, specializing in design services. What are the key changes or shifts you've seen in graphic design over the years?

I graduated from college in 1983, a year before Apple introduced Macintosh. A couple of years later, I joined Apple, and about 10 years later, I joined Netscape, when it was still a start-up. I was lucky to "grow-up" professionally as the technology matured. This process involved several large shifts:

1. From "pasting-up" "mechanical art boards" (my first job at a design firm the summer after high school was doing pasteup) to using com-puter-based phototypesetters and then laser printers. (In a summer job at Xerox during grad school, I developed font specimen sheets for Helvetica 300, the first laser version of Helvetica.) Ten years after the Mac intro, most printed material was being prepared entirely on Macs.

2. From print to online communica-tions. Corporations used to spend hundreds of thousands of dollars each year to produce glossy annual reports, in addition to brochures and other printed "collateral." In 1987, Apple released HyperCard, and we created the first interactive annual report, sending a floppy disk along with each printed report. A

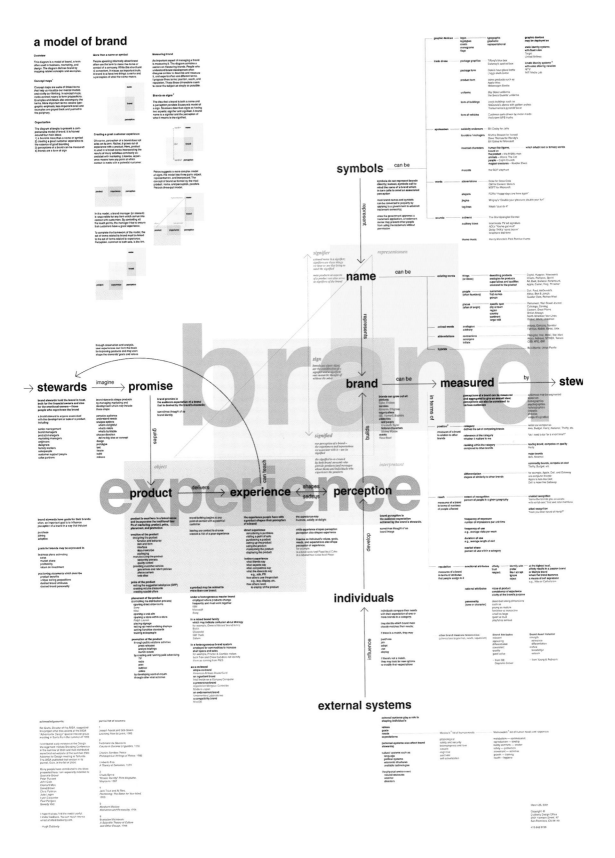

few years later, my team produced an online annual report to accompany Netscape's printed report. Today, financial information is available online, and glossy printed annual reports are a thing of the past. When I worked for Apple, the San Francisco Bay Area had four world-class printers; today, it has none.

3. From communicating about products to designing communications products. Graphic designers used to work primarily for folks in marketing communications, who worked for folks in marketing, who served engineers, who ran the company. Today, many graphic designers work directly on products and report to product managers. In addition to helping the people who create communications about products, designers are now just as likely to be creating the actual products.

The term "service design" is emerging of late. What is the methodology and goal of this?

As design emerged from craft during the nineteenth century and through much of the twentieth century, designers focused on the form of objects. Good designers have always had a broader view, and design managers often have had to consider not only form but also meaning, structure, and context. HfG Ulm introduced the concept of "environmental design" (meaning the design of everything), and the Dutch firm Total Design and the U.S. firm Unimark also promoted a holistic approach. These were early precursors to the idea that a brand

experience is built through a series of "touch points," which form a customer journey. Of course, the journey can be planned or to some extent designed. Thus, interaction at a series of touch points along a customer journey may be thought of as service design—or design for service. Service design also recognizes a shift in our economy from a manufacturing basis to an information and service basis.

Today, hardware products, such as iPod or iPhone or Kindle, exist largely as windows into services. So, the focus of design has expanded from the form of objects to the behavior of systems. The introduction of the term "service design" acknowledges this shift, and organizations like the Service Design Network seek to build knowledge about service design and help designers improve in this area.

Concept maps may have been part of the design toolkit in the past, but it is another emerging component and central to your work. What is it and its relationship to design?

Concept maps are tools for organizing ideas. They "map" relationships between ideas. At the simplest level, concept maps are node-and-link diagrams, where the nodes are nouns and the links are verbs. In English, node-link-node forms a sentence—subject-predicate-object. Concept maps are similar to mind maps, except that the links have labels. A concept map is also very like an outline, except that many branches or leaves at the edge of the outline are connected.

Since much of our work deals with software (which is intangible) or services (which unfold over time),

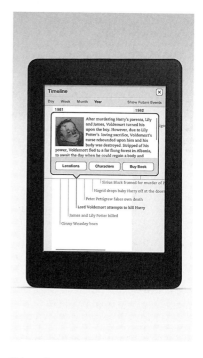

Fisheye Browser
Design: Ryan Reposar
Creative Direction: Hugh Dubberly
2012

we need ways to understand existing systems, confirm our understanding of others, and create and share prototypes. That means we need tools for modeling systems, which is one of the main ways we use concept maps.

Your firm creates products. Among them is one of my favorites (because it works), the Alere Diet Tracker. How was this developed in your hothouse?
Design proceeds through iteration. The Alere Diet Tracker was no exception. We had designed a couple of diet applications earlier. One version was for use in a blood glucose meter. It included a database of more than 500 food-calorie pairs, cross-referenced in a complex hierarchy. It also enabled users to perform calculations based on calories eaten and blood sugar level to determine suggested insulin doses. Needless to say, it was complicated—and thus cumbersome to use. Still another diet app we developed used calories, food type, and amount of exercise to suggest meal combinations that would help users reach weight goals. Again, a complex product concept.

We also surveyed existing diet apps—Apple's app store offers more than 100. Most of them are complex, in part because food is complex (official food classification schemes list seven or more dimensions); metabolism is also complex (the body resists losing weight as a defense mechanism); and unlike hardware, complex software costs no more to manufacture than simple software—in fact, more features can be a selling point. All these things lead to complex diet apps. From our frustration with this complexity, we asked, "What's the simplest possible

MyAlere iPad Diet Tracker
Design: Ryan Reposar
Creative Direction: Hugh Dubberly
2013

diet app?" That led to a challenge: "Could we design a diet app that is essentially one screen?" That became the product concept and the basis for the design.

I am very impressed by a project you conceived to show *National Geographic* how to refocus its energies. Is the role of the designer now to be a strategist?

Steve Jobs said it well: "In most people's vocabularies, design means veneer. It's interior decorating. It's the fabric of the curtains and the sofa. But to me, nothing could be further from the meaning of design. Design is the fundamental soul of a man-made creation that ends up expressing itself in successive outer layers of the product or service." Of course, designers can practice quite usefully at any of these "layers." It's fine to practice at the layer of form. It's also true that the inner layers, at least to some extent, constrain the outer layers.

An interest in form leads naturally to an interest in meaning, structure, and context—to understanding related systems and the ecology in which a product or service will operate—to wanting to influence the success of the product or service in the broadest possible way. That leads naturally to discussions of the organization of the product team, the team's process, larger product development processes, and then to the organization's larger structure, processes, goals, and, ultimately, to how the organization fits with and adapts to its environment. All these things are design questions, and

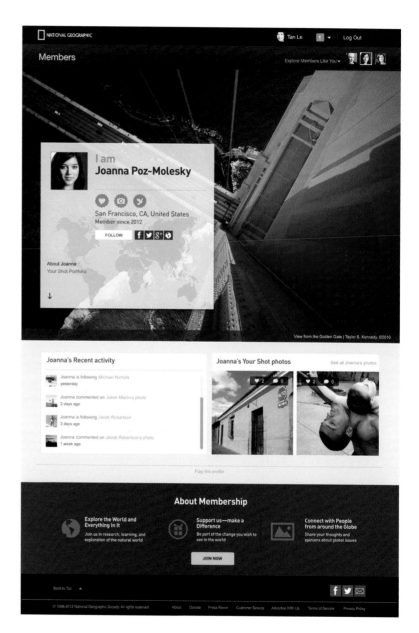

National Geographic Member Center
Design: Michael Gallagher and Jane Brown
Creative Direction: Robin Bahr
2012

discussing the answers benefits from design thinking, prototyping, and the involvement of designers.

The skills needed for strategic and systems thinking are different than those for pushing type around. How are these skills imparted to your employees?

Typography remains vital for design, in part because so much of the product of design involves type (even in architecture and industrial design) but also because design is a conversation, involving teams, which benefits from shared models, which inevitably require typography. Typography, well taught, includes a kind of systems thinking—rules-based systems, such as style sheets (CSS), proportion, grids, and signage systems. So, there's already a basis for systems thinking in typography.

However, other disciplines have developed approaches to systems, which should be part of design education, for example,

Formal Systems: information structures and network topologies

Dynamic Systems: stocks + flows, resource cycles, lags + oscillations, explosion + collapse, dynamic equilibrium + homeostasis

Control Systems: feedback + stability, goal-action-measure loops, requisite variety

Living Systems: self-organizing, dissipative systems, autopoiesis, positive deviants, coevolution + drift, biocost

Conversation Systems: observing-understanding-agreeing, learning-coordinating-collaborating, goal-task ladders, bootstrapping, ethics+responsibility

What do you look for when hiring for DDO?

We like to hire people who are curious—people who are not only interested in learning but also taking an active role in their own learning. Ideally, a designer would have great formal skills, deep experience with the patterns of interaction, basic coding skills, writing and presentation skills, and experience in product management.

Not only are physical products being integrated into systems; so, too, are online products and services.

The simple act of connecting products changes their very nature. Apple's iPod is more than a music player. Amazon's Kindle is more than an e-book reader. They are integrated systems of hardware, Web-based applications, and human services. Facebook is more than an online social network. Google is more than an Internet search engine. They are product-service ecologies—networked platforms creating opportunities for organic growth.

The networked platform revolution requires us to rethink our assumptions about products—and about design. We must think about integrated systems in new ways, define new ways to measure their progress, and organize new development and design processes.

Matthew Stadler

To Publish: To Create a
Public for Books

Mathew Stadler is the founder of Publication Studio, a small Portland, Oregon, DIY publishing venture, which he established in September 2009 with Patricia No. Their business model was simple: Print, bind, and sell books, using cheap, widely available, low-tech, print-on-demand technologies. Even though their involvement with the digital culture was minimal, their approach was exemplary in terms of user experience. The way they actively went about creating an audience for each book published was remarkable. They brought together potential readers by arranging lectures, meals, picnics, outings, and lively discussions. "I love the social life of books," says Stadler. "I thought about it a lot before opening Publication Studio. It was the rhetoric around which we shaped our venture."

Revolution: A Reader
by Lisa Robertson
and Matthew Stadler
2013

In an interview, you once said that selling books on demand was like selling loaves of bread in a bakery. Is it possible to make a living by selling books on such a small scale?

The idea was that book production should be tied more tightly to interest in the book, like the daily provision of bread from a bakery. New efficiencies in digital and handmade production made it possible to do so and still sell books at a competitive price. The most important recent change then was the availability of cheap, perfect-binding machinery. Cheap, but high-quality, digital printing had already been around for awhile. And there was a lot of great, unpublished literature already available.

You bought a small digital printer, a hand-operated book-binding machine, and went into business with practically no experience and no investors—yet you made it work. What was your most important asset?

The most helpful thing was our poverty. We had to sell books or stop making them. That motivated us to insist that our work was valuable, should be paid for, and not to tolerate the "everything should be free" ethos of many progressive cultural experiments. All work should be paid for. If more people would stick to this radical stance, I think we would have a healthier culture and economy.

How did you choose which book to publish?

We (Patricia No and I) published any book we thought was great. Since we made them one at a time and were obliged to sell whatever we made, it

Maple Bacon Strip Tease
by Rudy Speerschneider
2009

This is The Same Hillside
by Shawn W. Creeden
2011

Vertex
by Tim Roth
2013

What is the most compelling reason to buy a book, in your opinion?
Because you want to read it.

For the most part, the books you published were not by well-known authors, had not received reviews, were printed digitally, and didn't have illustrated covers. Why were people willing to pay $20 of them?
I'm not sure why anyone buys books. Each time I was party to such an exchange, it seemed obvious to me that the work involved—the writing, the book production, the social interaction of selling—were quite obviously (to everyone) worth well more than the price paid. If you think about the sorts of things we routinely pay 20 euros or 30 or 50 euros for (music, food, a night out, clothes), it isn't surprising to find that a great book is among them.

You rubber-stamped the titles of your books on ordinary stock from recycled file folders. Yet the result was oddly beautiful! What inspired your aesthetic choices?
Again, our poverty. The best choices we made, aesthetically, were all the product of trying to articulate, rather than obscure, our poverty and our passions.

Did you design the inside of your books as well, or did authors give you print-ready files?
For the most part, we designed the books, inside and out. Later, as we began to work with more visual artists, they took on the task of designing the insides of the books and sometimes also the covers. As a general rule, books of literature published by PS are usually designed by PS, and books by artists are usually designed by the artists or by book designers they or we choose to work with.

Can you explain why promoting a book to the right audience can be assimilated to "a political act"?
No. But I think every economic interaction is already political. So it makes sense to me that anyone trying to sell books in the market is already engaged in a political campaign, of sorts.

Would you recommend book publishing as a venture for people who want to try to live creatively outside the conflict of art versus commerce?
I don't understand the dichotomy. I suggest you publish books if there are books that do not have publics but you believe they should have.

You left Publication Studio. What is your next project?
I left a long time ago, because I am a writer first, a publisher second. I was interested in helping conceive and activate this infrastructure so that I, as a writer, could benefit from it. That has been my work for about three years now—just writing, and getting to use PS for publication where it fits, as the correct tool for me.

Latitudes and Longitudes
(opposite)
by Lyndl Hall
2012

was important to only publish books we thought were great. There were many of them.

The first print-on-demand book I published was one year before Patricia and I opened PS. It was a reader I had edited and annotated called *Where We Live Now.* That fall I gave a talk in Vitoria, Spain. I spoke about "the social life of the book" and about the logic and the meaning of the word *publication,* which I described as "the creation of a public." It's then and there that I figured out what I would do next. I would create a public for the books I would publish. This idea became the central focus of Publication Studio.

Do you agree with French author Charles Nodier, who said: "Only second to the pleasure of owning books is the sweet satisfaction of talking about them"?
Yes, we used any means possible to host and enrich the social life of our books!

LATITUDES AND LONGITUDES

OF THE

PRINCIPAL PORTS, HARBOURS, HEADLANDS, ETC.,

IN THE WORLD

18 Geeks, Programmers, Developers, Tinkerers

Designers today do not have to be able to write strings of codes to thrive in the digital environment, but it helps. While programmers are seldom designers (their work is so engrossing, they tend to lose track of the big picture), designers who master the basic principles of computer language are at an advantage. They are the folks who think in terms of possibilities instead of mere solutions. They can navigate effortlessly between print, digital, dimensional, interactive, motion, and environmental media.

For this next generation of design thinkers, the breakthrough design process is generative design. It is a computational modeling system that generates three-dimensional patterns through a series of repetitions (iterations), replicating the way forms grow in nature. The main application of generative design is data visualization and the simulation of architectural structures, but its sci-fi aesthetics makes it the perfect visual language for special effects. A small number of graphic designers use it to create interactive installations in the context of special events or contemporary art shows.

In general, geeky graphic designers and programmers are in demand everywhere, in every design studio, ad agency, or brand consultancy. Not only can they "fix" computer bugs and restore the functionality of various peripherals; they also think in term of systems rather than short-term design solutions. Hired as the "IT" individual on the team, they are often offered a partnership in small organizations, so critical is their technical but also intellectual contribution.

Frieder Nake

Controlling Computers
with Our Thoughts

Frieder Nake is professor of computer graphics and interactive systems at the University of Bremen, Germany. His involvement with digital art goes all the way back to 1963 when he was studying mathematics. Many of his art pieces, created by strings of mathematical codes, are held in museums in Germany, England, the United States, and Japan. Now 75, he is still a pioneer in programming and an active player in the field of generative design. "What keeps me going is the excitement that comes from being able to apply algorithmic thinking to problem solving," he says.

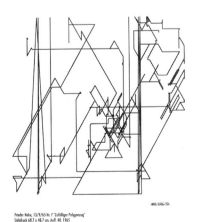

Frieder Nake, 13/9/65 Nr. 7 "Zufälliger Polygonzug"
Siebdruck 68,7 x 48,7 cm. Aufl. 40. 1965

Random Polygon
Frieder Nake
1965

What is algorithmic thinking?

In algorithmic work, the most important parts of a design are done in thinking—in the mental domain. It's as if, before you do anything else, you stop and try to determine which specific features your design should have—even though you don't know yet how these features will interact with each other. You must anticipate all the options and possibilities but then leave it to the program to proceed with the actual execution. The excitement is right there: in the discovery of how, where, in what manner, and to what extent the predetermined features will appear.

Of course, nothing will happen if I only "think" about it. I must shape my thoughts, wishes, intentions, vague ideas, and half-baked decisions into a program—into algorithms. So I must make my aspirations explicit, but not so explicit that only one option is left. I must really think in terms of possibilities (in the philosophical sense of

the word). The program becomes the description of things and events that may (or may not) happen. There is no certainty.

Also exciting is the fact that you must think in terms of entire classes or sets of design, not in terms of a single work. Algorithmic work can generate designs that are "art," even though they contain elements that we do not control.

Can you clear up another thing: What is the difference between generative design and digital art? Are the two terms interchangeable?

No, they are not interchangeable—not in the sense that any piece of digital art is also an example of generative design.

If you use a rich—or not so rich—piece of software to generate design on your screen, it is, by definition, "digital" (and may even be considered "digital art"). However, it is not necessarily "generative." In order to be "generative," some parameters, procedures, and "decisions" must be left to the program.

Granted, it is a little confusing because, in some way, all design is necessarily "generated" or else it is not design. When we talk about generative design, the term "generative" is not used in its broadest sense but in a specific interpretation: when the preparation for the actual material production of the work involves, to a large extent, algorithmic thinking.

Graphic designers are applying analog thinking to "find the best design solution." Instead, should they use algorithmic thinking to explore the possibility of infinite solutions?

That's a good formulation. The only difference I would see is this: I am not suggesting that graphic designers "should" explore all possible design solutions instead of trying to find the (almost) absolute best one. More modestly, I would say that since the "best" design solution is so unlikely to be found, the experimental and explorative attitude may be more promising.

What would be the best use of generative design in a contemporary design practice?

I am afraid, I do not know. It is a matter of attitude. As I mentioned earlier, the notion of "best" is ill defined. We kid ourselves when we believe that we know what's best. The space between better or best is so vast that we should be content with something good, agreeable, okay, nice, and so on.

Today, the majority of graphic designers are merely computer "users." They don't question the choices that operating systems and software programs make for them. This situation saves time, but is it dangerous?

It seems, indeed, that it is as you say: that a great number of (young?) designers use all these incredibly powerful software packages, and accept the results. These packages are powerful—they deliver acceptable results day in and day out. Nothing in the experience of most graphic designers tells them not to trust their software.

I don't like to speak of such a situation (to the extent that it is true) as "dangerous." But, in some way, the word is okay. The situation is particularly dangerous for experienced designers who have more to lose when they defer to software. Their expertise and experience seem less valuable, somehow. Young designers, on the other hand, have more to gain from trusting their software. Often, they come up with quite agreeable design solutions that they would not have imagined otherwise.

However, I am afraid to say, time constraints cannot be ignored when it comes to work that is assigned or commissioned. An automatically generated, pretty good (though not quite "best") design solution will often suffice.

Fields of Random Cross-Hatchings
with Vertical Random Lines
Frieder Nake
1965

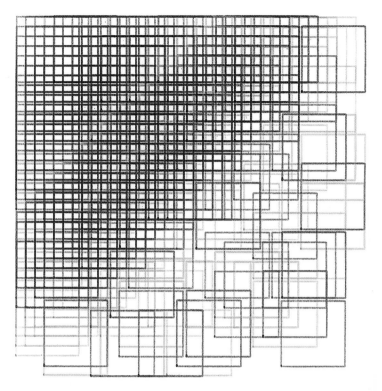

Random Walk Through Raster,
Series 7.1–3
Frieder Nake
1966

and observe the results generated by the computer. Paradoxically, though designers are not touching anything, they are in more control than if they were actively intervening. A funny dialectic, isn't it?

As you were talking, one thought occurred to me: Should we reevaluate mathematics as a new art form?
A lovely question, allowing for only speculative answers. Indeed, there is a broad trend currently to bring together mathematics and art, or science and art—many projects of this kind, almost in a torturous way. I am hesitant, waiting, skeptical.

Mathematics has, of course, strong aesthetic components. For example, the expression "mathematical elegance" is used to describe simple and effective theorems. The aesthetics of math is in the actual carrying out of math. And that's not new. It has always been with us, but we have not noticed and have ignored it. If there is now some more attention, that's nice.

But the "artistic" part is not so much in the way computer can be made to visualize some mathematical processes. Algorithmic thinking should remain different from aesthetic thinking, and that's good and welcome. La différence is important for us to notice and preserve.

Generative design proposes a totally different approach, one not compatible with the realities that most graphic designers encounter. You cannot tell a client, "Let us define the outcome of this project only to some extent. Let us explore it algorithmically. Let us be content with what we get because we do not believe in best solutions any more." That would not be comfortable!

The issue here is the collaboration of man and machine. What's human and what's mechanical? I call this question the "machinization of human work." I use this un-English word on purpose to describe the transfer and transformation of human work into "machinic" form.

Do you mean to say that when human beings program machines to generate forms, the result is necessarily "human"—even though machines did the work?
Yes. A lot of design work that is now shifted over to the machine (the computer) is actually performed in the interactive mode. This means, indeed, that a great number of actions and decisions are left with the human designer. Insofar it is "more human."

In some instances, designers set up the entire environment, with all the parameters and automatic procedures (algorithms) they want to control without necessarily intervening interactively. Then they can sit back

Mark Webster

Iterations and Algorithms

Mark Webster's principal line of work has been in the field of graphic design, but his main activities over the past five years have been focused on how programming can enrich the practice of graphic design. In line with this, he created in 2011 the nonprofit organization FAB, Free Art Bureau. Its mission is to promote programming practices in the arts and in an open and sharing manner. Through a variety of activities, events, and lectures, he tries to empower and build creative communities that are free from the restraints of closed systems. "Code and programming have become a major part of my thinking and understanding as one plausible approach to creativity," he says. "I am passionate about how to find ways to distill new practices with other disciplines."

Dessin via processing Code poster
Designer: student
Client: Mark Webster
2014

What do you say when people ask you what you do?

Creativity is manifest in many fields of work I practice—writing, designing, teaching, musical composition, and thinking! But I have no specific job title per se. I prefer to describe what I do and often answer that I teach designers to program computers to do things that will help them in their everyday practice. I help designers define the rules that generate possibilities.

In plain English, I would say that you teach designers programming skills. But I often wonder, what is the main difference between a graphic designer and a programmer?

The very act of designing can be viewed as a form of programming. Designing implies a logical and systematic approach to creation. When we design, we are often undertaking what

one could call, essentially, the making of a program.

Where graphic design and programming find a common ground is in their process. Both can follow what I have come to call over the years a "systematic approach"—often referred to as computational or algorithmic thinking. Whether you use a ruler and pen or write code to draw up a grid system, the process is inherently similar on a purely conceptual and mental level.

So, designing a program is not different from designing a grid?

There are a lot of overlaps between the designer and the coder. What is important to realize is that a system—a grid or a program—helps establish a coherent process from which is born a vast possibility of creative applications.

A grid is a tool set that enables the designer to position elements in space

"Art Design Code,"
Poster for a Conference
by Mark Webster
Designer: Mark Webster/
Free Art Bureau
2013

and establish a formal coherence as a whole for the final composition. Likewise, a program is a set of instructions based on a number of rules and a set of parameters. When we follow these rules, we produce an outcome. In both the grid and the program, there is scope for possibility built on an underlying logical system. It is the unique interaction of these rules, the tweaking of parameters and the media used, that will give forth to a wide variety of results.

Will knowing how to code make your students better graphic designers?
Beyond the technicalities of teaching designers to code, my task is much greater in ambition. Learning to program is more than just learning a technique for making things. It is

not simply a tool as such; nor is it just another means for creating dynamic websites, interactive tools, or data visualizations. Learning to program is learning an essential set of skills that opens up to a new way of thinking–"algorithmic thinking." I believe this knowledge can help the graphic designer reinforce his or her conceptual approach in the designing process as well as open up new and exciting possibilities in their practice.

What is the difference between "algorithmic thinking" and "generative design"—another term that attempts to define this relatively new approach to graphic design?
The two are obviously interlinked, although, there is a subtle difference.

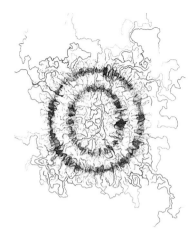

Algorithmic thinking refers to computational problem solving. Generative design is what algorithmic thinking produces: an infinite number of design solutions.

However, I don't like the expression "design solutions" very much. I'd rather think in terms of possibilities than solutions. Instead of solutions for problems, generative design proposes "programs for possibilities." This idea extends Karl Gerstner's seminal work described in *Designing Programs,* written in 1964.

Another way of thinking about generative design is as a means of designing through iterative processes. These processes are based on strict rules. The rules are "algorithms."

What do you mean by "iterative process"?
Iteration is a powerful means for prototyping ideas quickly and generating a myriad of possibilities. The creative process is always one of exploration and experimentation. There are no fixed, strictly defined solutions as there are no absolute ideas. Code is a flexible medium that enables one to express and implement many

possibilities. Generative design is the outcome of working with iteration and algorithms.

How can graphic designers learn more about programming?
There are a lot of resources on the Internet about programming, and there are increasingly more scripting languages and tools. It can be quite overwhelming at first to delve into this subject without some clear and concise references.

I would highly recommend reading *Processing for Visual Artists*, by Casey Reas and Ben Fry, to learn the fundamentals of coding practice. If you want to get an idea of code as a tool in its various applications, then *Code & Form in Design, Art and Architecture*, by Casey Reas, Chandler McWilliams, LUST are an informative introduction. At this time in writing, there is no book that explains this new approach specifically aimed for graphic designers. I am currently working on that.

Can you explain the main advantage of the Processing programming language as a tool for thinking?
Processing was conceived specifically

with visual artists in mind. That is to say that it uses keywords in its language that are easier to relate to for these people. It also simplifies a number of more complex concepts that are more laborious to implement in other languages, such as C++, for example. Processing is a simplified version of the more complex language, Java, which is still a highly influential and powerful programming language.

In terms of a tool for "algorithmic thinking," Processing introduces and uses the major concepts of programming that are found in so many other languages. It is these concepts that are at the basis of beginning to think with code.

There is an international community of people working with Processing and from many fields of work: interaction design, animation, art, architecture. It is widely used in research and as a pedagogical tool in art and design schools around the world. So, Processing is the perfect language in my opinion to start to learn about programming and code for creative practices. It is equally a great foundation for those who may want to move on to learning other languages at a later stage.

"Code"
Logo for a Conference on typography
as generative design, Bordeaux
Designer: Mark Webster/Free Art Bureau
2012

The Gerstnerizer

Another Open Source Design by th

"The Gerstnerizer"
Pattern Generator for
Graphic Designers,
the Silkscreened Version
Designer: Mark Webster/
Free Art Bureau
2011

Design Education

You can still get an education without formal design school—sort of. On-the-job experience can be an adequate means of acquiring necessary skills—after all, talent is inborn. Increasingly, however, the self-taught graphic designer is going back to school in a temporary or full-time capacity. Even with all the how-to books on the market, intensive training, if only to be fluent with the numerous programs, is essential. Yet in order to go beyond rote computer applications to make really smart graphic design, a undergraduate and graduate education is strongly recommended. Digital fluency starts in grade school. By middle or high school, students are making videos, websites, and even apps. But teaching theory and practice learning about aesthetics and functionality are best done in the class-room—at first. As this book reveals, there are too many niches and nuances to embrace and comprehend. A good undergrad program will provide a range of options; a good grad program will hone in on specialties. Even "distance" learning provides benefits that self-teaching is slow or never able to accomplish.

19 Making Choices

Education choices are never easy. Financial concerns weigh heavily. But there are some alternatives. Here is a guide: You should find a two- or, better yet, four-year undergraduate program at an art college or general university that offers a bachelor of fine arts (BFA) or equivalent degree. This is not to imply that a liberal arts education is to be ignored; liberal arts is a prerequisite that must be pursued in tandem with design classes. However, two years is barely enough time to learn the tools, theory, history, and practice of graphic and digital design, as well as to develop a marketable portfolio. Of course, as four or more years in art or design school may be impossible for some and excessive for others, continuing education is also an option.

For those with the desire and wherewithal, a graduate school education can be beneficial. A few people possess a natural gift for design and, with only a modicum of training, might turn into significant designers. But they are exceptions to the rule. Untutored designers usually produce untutored design. Although good formal education does not make anyone more talented, it does provide a strong foundation upon which to grow into a professional. While taking the occasional design class is better than no schooling at all, matriculation in a dedicated course of study, where you are bombarded with design problems and forced to devise solutions, yields much better results.

An estimated 2300 schools (two and four years) offer dedicated and ancillary graphic design programs and graduate about 50,000 students each year. Each year, more schools are adopting some kind of graphic or digital design program that ranges from basic instruction of computer programs (InDesign, Photoshop) to advanced typography to a range of complex digital media.

The investment is considerable, so look at many schools before selecting a two-year, four-year, or continuing education design program. Then create a portfolio that will make you an appealing student.

UNDERGRADUATE

Whether you decide on a dedicated art school or a state or private university art department does not matter (financial and location concerns often dictate this decision). More important is knowing the strengths and weaknesses of the chosen program. The fundamental instruction in the second year sets the tone for those to follow. Here are the areas to examine.

Computer. While some design courses offer instruction in computer programs after more basic conceptual and formal issues are addressed, others dive right into the tool as vital to design practice. It does not really matter at what point digital media application is taught (although most agree that it is better to understand the theory of design before attempting its practice), but computer skills must be keenly supported through individual and laboratory instruction throughout the program. Understanding what design is and how it works in both a philosophical and practical context may be more important than doing the work, at least at the outset. If a student does not know what design is and at whom it is aimed, then making marks on paper or screen is fruitless.

Graphic design is not a self-motivated fine art, and although the lessons of art may be integrated, communications theory in its various forms (semiotics, semantics, deconstruction, and so on) are the essential components of a well-rounded design education. The computer and everything it touches is not an end but the means. Yet it will become, if it has not already, the primary delivery mechanism for designed information and experience. If the program you are examining has too little or too much computer studies, find how design is introduced and taught.

Concept. Design is not decoration but, rather, the intelligent solution of conceptual problems; it is the manipulation of type, image, and, most of all, the presentation of ideas that convey a message. A strong design program emphasizes conception—developing big ideas—as a key component of the curriculum. Concept courses should include two- and three-dimensional design in all media. In short, a "trade school" education will not be as fulfilling as a design thinking course of study.

Type. This is one of the primary means by which civilization communicates. A type font is not just something that comes installed in your laptop. Classes in type and typography should, therefore, begin at least with the history of movable letterforms from the fifteenth century to the present—the art and craft behind them and the reasons that type, conventions exist. The application of type, past and present, in various media, and the purposes for which types and type families have been used should be covered. Type instruction should include a range of endeavors, from metal type founding to digital fontography. Once type has been fully addressed, typography—the design of typefaces on the page or screen context—should be thoroughly examined as both a reading and a display vehicle. Any study of typography should include intense debate about its function—legibility versus illegibility.

Image. Design is about image making (and storytelling), and a well-rounded program includes classes devoted to photography, typo-foto (the marriage of type and picture), and illustration. Certain courses emphasize computer programs such as Photoshop, and these are indeed necessary. But a good program makes the distinction between computer-generated art as style and imagery as essential to narrative.

Advertising. Some design departments segregate advertising from graphic design; others integrate the two. It is, however, useful for the graphic designer to learn the techniques that go into this very public medium. What's more, advertising agencies are employing large numbers of digital designers to execute new ways to reach the public. Learning advertising's requisites will stand you in good stead.

History. Most design departments are not equipped to offer more than survey courses on certain aspects of design history. Nevertheless, this is an integral part of design education that should continue throughout a design program (and not as an elective, either). It is essential to know that graphic design has a history, and to be familiar with the building blocks of the continuum.

Digital Media. The volume of cross-disciplinary endeavors that

affects designers today is only going to grow rapidly in the future. Training a student to design in the print or Web environment is necessary, but knowledge of other media—film, television, video for tablets, and hand-held devices—is not only imperative but also will open the student's eyes to the unlimited possibilities that design now offers.

Production. How can you design without knowing the means of production? For a designer, being detached from the output, whatever it is, is like being a doctor who never interned on a human being. Check on labs and workshops that provide production instruction.

Business. At the undergraduate level, few schools focus on the business of design in terms of starting a studio or firm, and all that it entails. Most design schools are concerned with developing the skills that lead to marketable portfolios, and energies are aimed at helping students get internships or jobs. Prudently, they do not encourage neophytes to start businesses immediately out of school. Nonetheless, business is an important aspect of a sustainable career, so even if developing business plans and spreadsheets is inappropriate at this level, courses that address general business concerns are useful.

Portfolio. The most important concrete result of a well-rounded education is the portfolio. Classes in how to develop portfolios usually begin in the senior year, when the student is given real-world problems in various media with the goal of creating a strong representation of talent and skill. A diploma is important, but the portfolio is evidence that a student earned it.

Placement. Schools with reputable internship programs are invaluable. Many programs have established relationships with studios, firms, and corporations throughout the United States and, often, the world. These schools place students and graduates in many working situations and monitor their development. Experience from these internships or temporary jobs (which may start in the sophomore year) is priceless, and, on occasion, they lead to full-time positions. Good placement offices also keep job-bank notices and help the students prepare for these opportunities.

Faculty. Let's not forget the teachers. A strong faculty is what makes all these programs work. Some schools maintain full-time faculty; others use adjuncts who are professionals (part-time teachers who work full-time as designers, art directors, creative directors, etc.). Both situations are equally good. The value ultimately comes down to the individual. Inspiring teachers make the difference. Find out who they are by reading their bios online. Google has become the primary reference source.

GRADUATE SCHOOL

Today, a growing number of two-year graduate programs address general or segmented design profession concerns. Graduate education is not for everybody, but it has become a viable means of developing areas of expertise that were ignored or deficient in most undergraduate schools. The master of fine arts (MFA), master of arts (MA), master of professional studies (MPS), and associate degree, which are the typical degrees from graduate programs, are not necessary to obtain jobs or commissions (although, if you want to teach at a university, the MFA and PhD degrees are usually mandatory), but they do indicate accomplishment: The designer has completed a rigorous course of study. For those interested in intensive instruction and networking, the graduate school experience can be highly beneficial in creative and practical ways.

Graduate school is, however, a major investment in time and money. The average tuition is between $19,000 and $35,000. Some schools insist that students devote the majority of their time to school-related work; others schedule their programs so that students can work at regular jobs or on commissions while attending evening classes. And new distance-learning programs are flexible enough for students to work at home at a reasonable pace.

Eligibility for graduate programs varies. All candidates must have bachelor or other degrees from undergraduate institutions (these need not always be design degrees). A few exceptions are made for work/time equivalency. Some programs accept all students immediately after graduating from a four-year undergraduate art or design school; others seek students who have been working professionally for a year or more prior to returning to school. Portfolios and interviews are usually required, and the portfolios must include school or professional work that shows distinct talent and aptitude. Some entry requirements are more lax than others, but if the portfolio is deficient—if the prospective student shows nothing, for example, but mediocre desktop publishing work—additional training and practice are recommended before reapplying. Graduate programs are open to applicants of all ages who meet the entry requirements.

Graduate school is a viable means for those who want to switch careers or to achieve greater proficiency and better credentials.

If a prospective student meets all the eligibility requirements, the next step is to explore programmatic options to determine which schools are best geared to the specific educational need. Possibilities are numerous. Some programs are fairly free-form, where teachers guide a student along a self-motivated course of study. Others are more rigidly structured, with a set of specific goals to attain by the end of each study period (which may be a semester or more). Some programs are geared toward specialties; others are more general in scope. Among the specialties are corporate design, advertising design, interaction design, product design, and branding, among others. A number of programs have philosophical and even stylistic preferences, while others avoid overarching ideology of any kind. Some are concerned with social activism, while others are devoted to the commercial marketplace and entrepreneurship.

Some programs are better endowed than others. Most programs have a cap on how many students are accepted annually. It is recommended that prospective students request literature from programs and personally visit those that are of most interest (some have open information sessions, whereas others grant individual tours).

Applicants commonly apply to more than one program, although each may require different materials.

The following are programmatic concerns that should be explored before applying.

Scope. A graduate program involves advanced study and is not simply an extension of undergraduate school. While a curriculum may include components that overlap an undergraduate or continuing education course, it must go way beyond what is provided at these lower levels. When looking at a prospectus or talking with a graduate school admissions officer, determine the scope and goals of the program and the expectations it has of its students.

Philosophy. This is related to scope but demands its own category. A graduate program may require that students adhere to a particular pedagogical concept. This can be anything from minimalist (modern) to complex (deconstruction) design, classical, avant garde, or any other approach. It can be based on a certain iconoclasm or eclecticism. Whatever the philosophy may be, decide by talking to former students and teachers about its compatibility with your own attitudes.

Tradition. While undergraduates are wrapped up in technology and processes that will allow them to get jobs immediately upon graduation, graduate programs should allow for greater reflection. A well-balanced program encourages students to work with their hands as well as with machines. Learn whether workshop or lab facilities are provided for this.

Technology. A graduate program should be state of the art. The design world is becoming inextricably connected to latest making machines. Advanced knowledge of the tools of production and creation is requisite. Most contemporary graduate programs spend at least 50 percent, if not more, of class time on technological concerns and have the hardware and labs to support thorough study:interdisciplinary studies. Graphic design graduate programs cannot afford to be specialized to the point of isolation. The more that relationships with other media and genres—inside and outside the design bubble—are carried out the better, even if only in survey courses.

Facilities. Graduate schools should provide facilities that encourage students to work in a more focused environment, both separately and in tandem with others. Facilities may include small studios or networked workstations in an integrated studio setting. It is important to know how you work best and in what kind of context. Some programs encourage the open studio; others simulate a design firms' environment. The location of the campus is also important—for example, its proximity to otherinstitutions or businesses.

Faculty. A program is only as good as its teachers. Some graduate programs pride themselves on employing the leading practitioners in the field; others rely on full-time professors. Balancing the two is usually a good solution. In most course descriptions, the faculty members are listed along with their credentials. These should be seriously studied.

Exhibition. Most graduate programs are concerned that student work be tested and, ultimately, published, exhibited, and even presented on stage before an audience. Although what a student learns is most important, the quality of the results is evidence of a program's effectiveness.It is useful to examine both the means of presenting student work and the work itself. Publications are available to applicants, as are schedules of student exhibitions.

Responsibility. A graduate program may be considered a cloistered existence. Increasingly, however, this is an opportunity for students to do the kinds of socially responsible projects that may less frequently be options in the workaday world. It is important to explore how a program contributes to the broader community.

Business. Even in a cloister, the real world must have a place, and the graduate school is indeed a good place to examine the business world. Graduate students are more likely than undergraduates to open their own businesses once they have earned their degrees. Design management and property law are important areas of concern at this level. Business plans are a must-have skill.

Thesis. The primary degree requirement is the final thesis. It is important to understand what the program expects of its students and how it goes about developing student thesis projects. What is involved in this process? Are there thesis classes, faculty advisors, review committees? Must the thesis be published? Will the thesis cost the student extra funds? Ultimately, the thesis can be a portfolio or a key to a new career.

DISTANCE LEARNING

The computer has changed everything in our lives, including the way we are taught. Home studies or "distance learning" is not a new idea. Correspondence schools taught students how to letter, draw, and otherwise do rudimentary and advanced graphic design. Today, with access to various computer-driven online classrooms, the ability to learn complex subjects in a virtual environment is easier every year. For the harried neophyte looking to change careers or the professional wanting to expand, improve, and elevate their skills, distance learning offers a wealth of options from scores of good old and new institutions. Some are entirely online, while others require a short annual residency as part of the degree qualifications. These virtual campuses also cost less than brick-and-mortar colleges and universities.

CONTINUING EDUCATION

Graduate school is not always feasible for those who work at full-time jobs or who choose to obtain specific skills as a means to widen their career path. Therefore, the most common method of developing additional skills (and receiving inspiration) is through continuing education, once called night school. Some general colleges and universities offer programs, but usually it is the province of the art and design schools and colleges to offer a wide range of professional courses, from introductory to advanced. In addition to a potpourri of professional courses, some institutions offer intensive weeklong workshops with master teachers. Abroad programs also fit this category.

Some of these programs are designed exclusively for working professionals (and require a fairly accomplished portfolio as a condition of acceptance), while others are open to a broader public. Enrollees in continuing education classes run the gamut from professionals who seek to better themselves (maybe to earn promotions in their current workplaces) to neophytes who want additional career options. Classes are available for any level of expertise and are useful in acquiring knowledge, experience, and, in some cases, job opportunities.

Obviously, reputable continuing education programs are best, and they are usually offered by art and design schools. Most computer tutorials are useful, particularly as insight into common layout, illustration, photography, and graphics programs (many older professionals use these sessions to learn or brush up on new skills).

Andrea Marks

Old School, New School

Andrea Marks, a design educator at Oregon State University (OSU), graduated from the Philadelphia College of Art (now called University of the Arts), where she studied the rationalist Basel approach to design. She studied typography with legendary Wolfgang Weingart when the first Macintosh computers were introduced. "They were like little jewels, and we were all enthralled with the ease of setting a paragraph of type," she says. Marks also learned to set type for letterpress, which allowed her to combine traditional technologies with a Swiss modernist approach. Oregon State is located 85 miles south of Portland, and when Marks went there for her interview in 1992, she said "I quickly realized the beauty of the Oregon landscape was as close to the Swiss landscape as I could find in this country." She says, "I was also fortunate to have found a university that valued design and wanted to create a high-quality program."

Do Good Index
(This page and opposite)
Designer: Christopher Shults
School: Oregon State University
Project: Undergraduate senior
project: a mobile app that allows
users to scan barcodes to see
how sustainable a product is.
After receiving the product
score, users can choose to
donate a total of the product
cost toward a portfolio of char-
ities that help offset some of the
adverse effects of consumption.
2013

How important is it for designers to attend a design school versus a traditional university?
I teach at a state university with over 26,000 students, more than 200 undergraduate programs, and over 80 graduate programs. This diversity with so many programs and activities on campus is great for the students and allows for many interesting cross-disciplinary collaborations. We are located in a small college town (population 55,000), so though the town is limited in terms of design studios to intern with, there are many on-campus internship opportunities, and students have to dig a little deeper and make more of an effort to go to AIGA Portland events, which, in turn, makes them really special.

You've been teaching for over 20 years. What curricula are different now than when you began?
In 2000, the graphic design faculty completely redesigned the curriculum and brought in many new classes, including a class on design process, a class on collaboration, and a senior capstone project class. We are currently in the middle of another curriculum revision, only this time it is with our new School of Design. In the fall of 2012, the graphic design program at OSU migrated from the art department and merged with apparel, interior, and merchandise management to form a school of design. The larger change is that we are now located within the college of business. The new curricula

we are developing has a design core with classes in collaboration across disciplines, consumer behavior, user-centered design, marketing, and entrepreneurship. Our new curricula have more classes in cross-disciplinary collaboration and systems thinking.

How have the students changed?

Fortunately, throughout the 20 years I have taught at OSU, students' enthusiasm and interest in learning has not diminished at all. We have a very competitive program (we admit only 25 students per year), and they become a very close community over the four years. They juggle much more than students did 15 or 20 years ago— keeping up with technology [and] part- and full-time jobs, and I am continually amazed at how much they can still give to graphic design.

How has your teaching evolved over the years?

When I began teaching, there were maybe one or two books on typography and no books on graphic design theory, history, or criticism. I love that there are more resources today, but it can be tricky to figure out how to teach a subject properly (history, context, etc.) in only 10 weeks. I have always looked at teaching like a design problem—I ask myself what is the narrative I want the students to come away with after 10 weeks (learning outcomes) and what types of projects will engage them and allow them to really engage in their learning? My role is to guide them through the subject matter and help them see the role of design in the broader context.

a bit allows students to see what they want to focus on next (and sometimes an employer will even pick up the tab for graduate school!).

What is most essential to learn in the twenty-first century?

It is essential for students to understand that design is a process and not only an end product. Design thinking and strategy are integral to the design process, and students need to be aware of audience and context for what they create.

What should students know when they leave school?

Students have to graduate with the idea that they will be lifelong learners. Our world is too complex and is changing too quickly to ever sit back and say, "Great, now I have graduated and can apply what I know." Some of what a student learns in school will be applicable, but much will not one or two years out. What will be relevant is how a student learns to dive deeply and creatively into a project (the process, methods, etc.) and the ability to adapt to change.

You can see potential . . . What do you see?

I look for much more than raw talent when assessing a students' potential. I want to see how they think, organize, write, and talk about their ideas and work. I also want to see how curious they are about the world and how resourceful they are. I am aware that all students communicate and process information in different ways, and it is my job as an educator to find ways to evaluate and motivate students to their full potential.

Brand People Story
Designer: Maschell Cha
School: Oregon State University
Project: Undergraduate senior project: A 36-page book about three individuals' relationships to brands.
2013

When you guide graduating undergrad students, do you recommend going directly to graduate school? Getting a job in a studio or firm? Taking internships? Or is there another alternative?

I typically do not recommend that path, as I feel students need to take a break and find out what they are really passionate about before heading back to school. Ten or 15 years ago, a graduate degree for a graphic designer was a more traditional MFA in graphic design. Today, there are many diverse grad programs, from MFAs in entrepreneurship and writing and criticism to MBAs in design management, strategy, and business, and online programs are also popping up. Waiting

Lita Talarico

Educating Design Entrepreneurs

Lita Talarico says that when she started developing the SVA MFA Design/Designer as Author + Entrepreneur program in 1997, "it was the beginning of digital technology, so although the founding concept was a master's in graphic design, it was quickly evident that it was going to be much more." Talarico is the cofounder and cochair of the MFA design program at SVA in New York City, which has consistently been listed in the Top Ten Graduate Design programs in *US News & World Report* and one of *Business Week's* "World Leading Design Schools." In 2009, she also cofounded the SVA Masters Workshop, an intensive summer typography program on design history, theory, and practice in Rome, Italy. She is coauthor of *Typography Sketchbooks: Design Firms Open, The Design Entrepreneur: Turning Graphic Design into Goods That Sell.* Building educational design communities is one of her missions as a founding board member emeritus of the Adobe Education Partners by Design program.

North
Design Entrepreneur: Donica Ida
School: SVA MFA Design
Project: A vacation-based
mobile application that locates
meaningful places in nature
through crowd sourcing.
2014

What do students require today as education fundamentals?
It is no longer acceptable to simply be a service provider, so we must educate students to not only create their own content but also to work collaboratively. This includes fluency in various visual languages and communication platforms.

Are MFA degrees truly necessary in achieving the fundamentals?
Not necessarily the fundamental skills, but definitely for more intensive research and exploration.

What else does an MFA degree provide for a designer?
In the past, one needed an MFA in order to teach, and that's what compelled most students to pursue one. This is no longer the case. An MFA now allows a student two years of focused study, not only on research and history but also on practice and viability.

What is the most unique quality of the MFA Design/Designer as Author + Entrepreneur program?
The MFA Design program is about getting students to create a project from idea to market and helping them with all the steps that are required in between. Students start off with their own concept, using various media to create and develop a thesis, or "venture," as we call it, for a marketplace of goods and ideas. They work individually and collaboratively for

Nagsha
Design Entrepreneur: Danah Abdal
School: SVA MFA Design
Project: Online cultural communication
between countries in the Mideast.
2014

!Lei Lei!
Design Entrepreneur:
Francisco Hernandez
School: SVA MFA Design
Project: An educational system
for Mexican-American children
and their parents.

two intensive years, to develop objects of value that are aesthetically sound and conceptually viable, guided by a network of renowned faculty—all practitioners.

Is there a possibility that entrepreneurship will become just another buzzword or fashionable trend?

Yes, the word perhaps but not the concept. This is not a new idea. In the nineteenth century, William Morris and designers who were part of the Arts and Crafts movement designed, made, and sold objects. The faculty and students at the Bauhaus created and manufactured products for the marketplace.

How do you teach students to stay current?

We don't have to teach them—they are current. They teach us. All we have to do is provide the education and tools so that they can realize their goals.

What does "maker" mean and imply?

It means thinking and creating and producing and delivering by filling a perceived need in society and hopefully making a difference and ultimately changing the world.

What do you look for in new students?

Someone who wants to commit themselves to two rigorous years of tapping into their creativity and dedicating themselves to finding a way to direct it into useful, meaningful, and sustainable products, whether social or commercial.

Chain Gang
Design Entrepreneur:
Tomás de Cárcer
School: SVA MFA Design
Project: An adventure-based
mobile app that rewards cyclists
for exploring New York City.

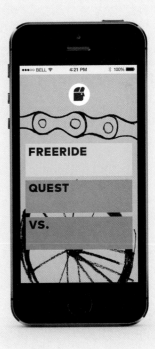

Rudi Meyer

Developing the Right Attitude

Rudi Meyer feels lucky to have been a student of Armin Hofmann and Emil Ruder at the Basel School of Design. He came to Paris in 1964, first as assistant to Swiss designer Gérard Ifert, then as his partner. Soon, he was able to set up his own independent practice as a graphic designer but also as a typographer, industrial designer, interior designer, photographer, and cartographer. For almost 40 years, he was on the faculty at the Paris Ecole des Arts Décoratifs. He taught typography, he explains "as an excuse to teach basic design principles: forms and counterforms, negative and positive space, hierarchy of information, grids—all tools for graphic communication but also for self-expression."

Poster, Theatre du Châtelet
(2004–2005)
Designer: Rudi Meyer

Just a quick question before we start: Was typography the cornerstone of your practice?

Typography was certainly important. I was for some time director of research at the Atelier national de création typographique. But I was equally intrigued by everything having to do with spatial representations—maps, in particular. I taught in a school specializing in the "sciences géographiques." I got involved with Roger Tallon and Massimo Vignelli when I redesigned trains and rapid transit system maps for the national French railroad company. I also got assignments designing exhibits and signage systems for museums. It was all related to typography, somehow.

You also did a lot of print work?

Yes—logos and corporate identity programs, books, catalogs, posters, and so on. I even designed watches.

In your opinion, are the teachings of Armin Hofmann, whose principles were adapted to the technology and design sensibility of the 1960s, still relevant today?

I find his principles more helpful than ever. He was not trying to be an expert; on the contrary. He believed that, in the long run, developing the right attitude would be more useful to his students than acquiring all the latest professional skills. He taught me to be steady in the pursuit of my goals—while, at the same time, keeping an eye on future developments and directions. He insisted we do not confuse communication with information . . . self-interest with general interest . . . knowledge with understanding . . . expansion with growth . . . or fundamental research with applied research. He also wanted us to differentiate between two approaches: appealing to the mind versus appealing to the emotions.

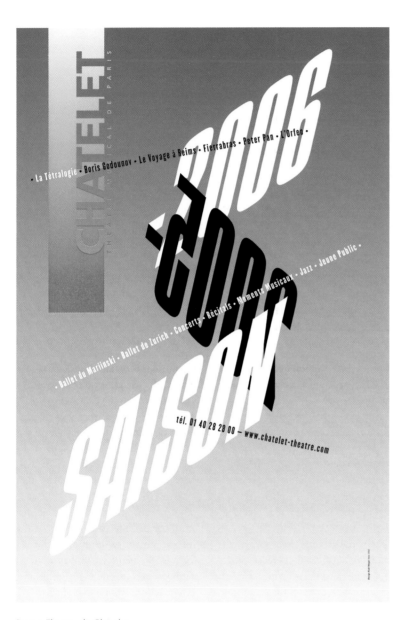

Poster, Theatre du Châtelet
2005–2006
Designer: Rudi Meyer

That's what you've learned from Armin Hofmann. What is the most important thing your students have learned from you?

You'd have to ask them! What I tried to instill in them is a sense of curiosity toward other disciplines and practices. I wanted to give them a design methodology they could adapt to other domains. Like Hofmann, I didn't present graphic design as an expertise but as a state of mind. Technologies and tools keep changing—and they do so at a faster and faster pace—but the creative process remains the same.

Still, graphic designers today have new opportunities—they have been liberated from the traditional constraints of print technology—but they must overcome new hurdles nonetheless. Would you agree that, paradoxically, it's both easier AND harder to be creative today?

Yes, I do. Back then, various constraints used to curb your creativity. But in the process of overcoming difficulties, you would be forced to explore an ever-expanding range of possible solutions. Each new invention was the result of having pushed the limits of technological restrictions. For example, traditional typography made it practically impossible for us to create curved headlines—yet we found a way to do it!

To go from the sketch phase to a full mock-up of a project took a lot of savoir faire, but it also required that designers and their clients use their imagination to visualize the final result. You also had to learn to translate forms from one medium to the next. Case in point, the original

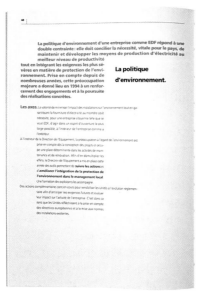

Annual Report, Interior Spread
EDF Electricité de France
Designer: Rudi Meyer
1990

gouaches Cassandre did as mock-ups for the lithographers. Just compare them with the final printed posters. What a difference under close examination! What you'd assume was Cassandre's unique rendering style is, in fact, the result of the work of some anonymous lithographer. Yet, if you compare the gouaches with the posters from a distance, they look absolutely identical. Cassandre knew how to ask for what he wanted.

Today, the situation is exactly the opposite. The images on our screens and the laser printed mock-ups are often more beautiful than the offset end products. In our day and age, the dematerialized digital language leaves no trace on the images it helps generate, as did pencils, paintbrushes, or calligraphic ink pens. The tools are no longer here to guide our hand. Not only do we need to be extremely vigilant when we design, but we also need to be on our guard when we try to come up with creative solutions.

Swiss graphic design, often identified as "International Style," has made a comeback under the name of "Flat Design." Is it a good sign, in your opinion?
Virtual "realism" had a raison d'être at the beginning of the digital age to help users connect with various functionalities. These "skeuomorphic" representations brought an emotional dimension—thus, the silly fake leather, the phony wood surfaces, and the hyperrealistic "push" buttons—not to mention the profusion of drop shadows so popular with the previous generation of designers.

At this point, Flat Design is first and foremost a reaction, but it is also a reinvention of abstraction—a good thing in my opinion. Information is taking precedence over baroque expressionism. Today, the International Style has acquired a nostalgic appeal, when, in fact, its codes are recapturing the spirit of Aesthetic Functionalism—of Form Follows Function. Will it last? Time will tell. In all likelihood, another style will soon replace Flat Design. You cannot stop designers in their constant search for the next thing.

Can you give us three typographic principles that could help young graphic designers today?
1. Think of a page or a screen as a space where forms and emptiness interact with each other.
2. Do not confuse hierarchy with differentiation.
3. Try to create startling results with as few elements as possible.

Lucille Tenazas

Idiosyncratic Contexts

Lucille Tenazas is the principal of Tenazas Design, a communication graphics and design firm with projects in the cultural, educational, and nonprofit sector. She has a distinctive typographic style and design methodology, yet she never pushes her own agenda on clients. At the same time, she always tries to surpass their expectations by taking them step-by-step through her design process. She is an educator at heart (she is currently the associate dean in the School of Art, Media, and Technology at Parsons The New School for Design). "My solutions never come to my clients as a surprise," she insists. "All along, they have been participants. I do believe in participatory design, not to be confused with collaborative design!"

You are the recipient of a 2013 AIGA Medal for your "role in translating postmodern ideas into critical design practice." It would be very helpful to our readers if you could explain the difference between a critical and a noncritical design practice.

I had to figure out for myself why I got the medal in the first place. I was unsure about my "role in translating postmodern ideas," as the AIGA put it. I felt that my greatest contribution was the way I had been able to be both a critic and a designer. I am most comfortable with the idea of a "critical design practice." By this I mean that I am critical of my own design process.

As a young designer, I worked much more intuitively. My design solutions were spontaneous reactions. I happened to be gifted; I have a native talent; I have a good typographical sense. It was too easy, perhaps. Once,

someone asked me, "Lucille, why did you do this?" and I couldn't answer. I had to learn to give meaning to my design.

But let's go back to the "postmodern" part of the AIGA statement about me. Postmodernism got such a bad rap. Truth be told, I was much more of a modernist at heart than a postmodernist—I went to Cranbrook in the mid-1980s, when postmodernism was exploding and the conservative, corporate design center of New York was being replaced by California. Originally, postmodernism had more to do with literary criticism than with design. Only later did it become associated with architecture and the other arts. Anyway, I was a postmodernist only in the sense that traditional design history wasn't part of my vocabulary. Being born and raised in the Philippines, I had no idea how to put postmodernism into a coherent historical perspective.

Barry Drugs: Street Signs
Project
Client: Cranbrook Studio
assignment
Designer: Lucille Tenazas
1981

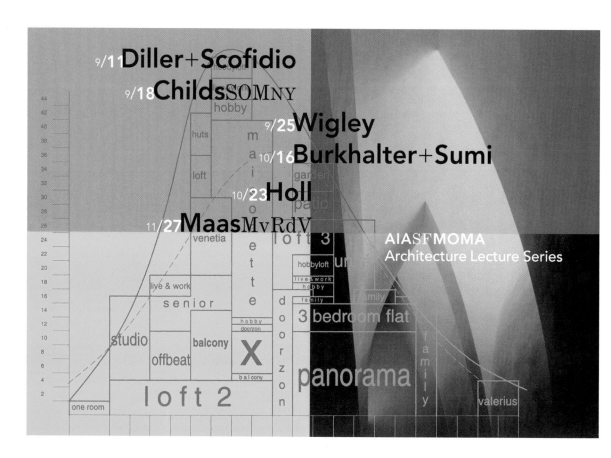

SFMOMA Lecture Announcements
in Collaboration with the
American Institute of Architects
(AIA San Francisco Chapter)
Client: SFMOMA
Designer: Lucille Tenazas
2000

In an interview, you said that for you, "form is easy." You are burdened with so much talent! How did you overcome this "handicap"?

Eventually, I came to question the way I intuitively used typography. Other designers, whose work I admired, were able to display levels of meaning in a singular image, whereas I layered letterforms, using words as texture or as background noise! I was cutting and collaging, which was the trend at the time. I created hybrid images and manipulated photography in a very uncritical way. I even thought that photography was at the service of design!

The result was pleasing, but was it provocative?

What is wrong with my methodology, I wondered. I became interested in the linguistic dimension of graphic design. I had been taught English in a very formal way in school in the Philippines, and it remained forever associated in my mind with academic exactness. This rigorous approach helped me reassess the relationship between content and meaning. I discovered semantics. I started to see words as "signs," as objects you can touch. The fact that I was teaching typography was an additional incentive to formalize my new interest in language.

Being Filipino, did you feel at a disadvantage, or was your multicultural education and your non-American design sensibility an asset?

I remember at Cranbrook, I felt clueless compared to my fellow students. For example, I used lots of colors in my work, whereas everyone else was doing tasteful black-and-white compositions, with just a red dot or a red line as an accent. I was asked: "Haven't you heard of Swiss design?" Well, not really. But I quickly absorbed what it was all about. Same with Russian Constructivism, Dada, or Fluxus. I had to educate myself in the art and design influences that practitioners were referencing.

I didn't know who April Greiman was! I had a different trajectory. I was older than my classmates. Coming from a developing country and feeling less experienced in design issues, I felt unsophisticated—yet, strangely enough, my work was better than the work of other students who tended to mimic design pioneers from the past. However, not belonging—not being able to explain why I did what I did—forced me to develop my critical thinking. I came to accept that my work would not look the way it did if I had been raised in the USA and if I had had a more comfortable relationship with the English language.

I wanted to learn to design like an American. It never really happened—

because I was different, I ended up influencing my American classmates. I am very proud of that: I could never conform, yet I am part of the American design history saga.

How does your personal experience influence the way you teach design?

I tell my students that there is a way that design can evolve from their own idiosyncratic context. Wherever they are from . . . the product of whatever . . . their yearnings . . . their need to belong . . . their specific urban sensibility . . . their mixed backgrounds . . . I want my students to be conscious of the filters through which they view their work. Their various lineages, strains, and ancestries should show up in their work. This is what gives their work a voice and a vision that will mark it as being unique. What a won-

derful gift it is to be from somewhere else. You do not have to replicate what has already been done. Instead of being "cultural tourists," you can be "cultural nomads." As such, you want to be fluid, adaptable, and alert to the needs and expectations of others.

Hot House: Expanding the Field of Fiber at Cranbrook Academy of Art
Client: Cranbrook Academy of Art
Designer: Lucille Tenazas
2007

Liz Danzico

Interfacing with UX

Liz Danzico is creative director for National Public Radio (NPR) in digital media, overseeing and guiding both the visual and user experience across NPR-branded digital platforms and content. She says she is part designer and part educator, being the founding chairperson of the MFA in Interaction Design program at the School of Visual Arts. She is also a strategist and advisor to start-ups, nonprofits, and global companies. Danzico's real job, however, is keeping ahead of the curve by monitoring and experiencing interaction design and user experiences. She has written for *Eye*, *Fortune*, and *Interactions* magazines, and writes her ongoing blog at bobulate.com.

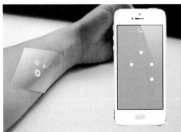

"Nuna"
Credits: Guri Venstad,
Class of 2013

How interactive are you in interactive design?
I'd give myself an 8 out of 10.

Fair enough, so what is UX?
UX stands for "user experience." But it's not as clear as that. Acronyms can be intimidating. I was recently asked to give an hour-long talk to a group of highly intelligent people on the difference between "UX," "IA" (information architecture), and "IXD" (interaction design). Shockingly, most of all to me, it was a pretty riveting talk.

How has UX—or whatever you want to call it—changed since you became involved?
UX, and arguably interaction design, 10 or even 5 years ago meant solving a very local problem—one of interfaces, one of interactions, one of feedback and usability. But today, that isn't the case. We consider those things across platforms and products, across ecosystems. In other words, systems design is much more often a concern than interface design.

How do you teach UX?
Throughout high school, college, and grad school, I waited tables. I worked my way from ice cream scooper to host, to server, to head server by learning how to understand customers and deliver what they wanted, when they wanted it. Through all the missed orders, dropped plates, angry customers, heavy trays, I had to figure out a way to make it all work out.

This idea of understanding customers came up again later during my first job as an information designer. Then again, when I began doing what is now UX, and when I started managing people, I started to think that perhaps the single best way to teach UX is to give someone a job waiting tables. Leave

"unVeil"
Credits: Tyler Davidson,
Class of 2014

"StickyJots"
Credits: Rachelle Milne,
Pam Jue,
Class of 2014

them on the restaurant floor with people who need things. Hungry people with no time. People with families. Mean people. Talkative people. The restaurant is really the best UX boot camp there is.

What do you expect students to learn?

What a happy customer looks like.

When hiring, what do you want to see in a UX designer?

I want to see someone who gets large systems and small containers, who has empathy, who can focus and scale, who has his or her head in the clouds and hands tinkering with something. And I want to see someone who can put together a focused, clear portfolio that shows not only finished products and services, but sketches and process.

Do you see any crossover between graphic and interaction design, especially UX?

There is a lot of crossover in the considerations of layout and engagement—they just happen across different spaces and tempos, like two songs as part of the same score.

What do you see looking forward in the next few years?

When we think about the future, we have a certain picture in our minds. It's a futurism that was built up in novels, in films, in TV shows, in modern mythology, in urban myth. It was a type of futurism we call "science fiction"—it represents some version of a future. But it's a speculative futurism about what could be. There is little to no thinking about how or when

it could be. Designing these types of futures becomes more of an aspiration, perhaps to inspire the design material we currently have to work with.

That was the past: the one in which science fiction was the unattainable future. But today is different. Today, science fiction can be the present. We are designing a pragmatic future. And the time when science fiction was the past has passed. Science fiction is the present. Today, futurism is usable; it's sensible. I think UX's next role is taking on pragmatic futurism.

Allan Chochinov

The Maker Generation

Allan Chochinov is the chair and cofounder of the MFA in Products of Design program at the School of Visual Arts in New York City, and a partner and editor-at-large of Core77, the design website for news and portfolios. He always took art, design, and shop classes as a kid. As an undergraduate, he studied philosophy, which he says is "very close to design in its demand for creative problem solving, lateral thinking, and strategic approach." He received his graduate degree in industrial design, specializing in improving the design of medical instrumentation.

That's enough for today.

Ice Cream Pint
Designer: Andres Iglesias

You've taught graphic designers how to design and make things in three dimensions. What is the biggest challenge that you've found in bridging the disciplines?

The biggest obvious challenge is that graphic designers are not typically taught to build things with their hands—they seldom have the shop skills or the hand skills required to create the three-dimensional prototypes that are so critical to the creation of innovative products. That said, they often have the drawing skills and, certainly, the illustration skills that are becoming more and more critical to sketching out user scenarios and storyboarding ideas.

What distinguishes a graphic from product designer?

That's an interesting question. I'd say a "love of stuff." Typical product designers grow up taking things apart, figuring out how they work, making things with their hands . . . that kind of thing. The reality that I've found,

however—and this became apparent the very first time that I taught a group of graphic designers a "crash course" in product design—is that though they may not have a history of building, graphic designers seem to have an absolute love of it once you get them started on their own projects. I think the gratifications that come with authorship—and especially with making something with your hands and holding it up in the air—are common to all people, regardless of design specialty. Humans are makers.

What are the necessary base skills or talents that an incoming student to MFA Products in Design must have?

We look for a deep passion for design, creativity, and problem solving. We seek a strong point of view and an acknowledgement that there's work to be done; that the failures and deficiencies of classic practices of design in our world have created as many problems as solutions, and that the consequences of industrialization and

Critter Bitters
Designers: Julia Plevin,
Lucy Knops

mass media have resulted in the systematic destruction of our planet and staggering inequalities between people. We look at artifacts through the lenses of systems, services, stewardship, and participation, and we want to fortify people to go out and create positive change.

Do you experience more students blurring the boundaries between two and three dimensions? Why?
Well, more than two and three dimensions, actually! I see a blurring between all dimensions—time is often referred as a "fourth dimension"—since most effective design happens over time,

and especially when we talk about the explosive growth and importance of interaction design these days. I think there is overwhelming pressure on classic graphic designers to build up their interaction chops and a similar pressure on product designers to make their objects "smart." We are now entering a period of "the Internet of things"—where microprocessors are embedded in more and more objects and the platforms that tie artifacts together are listening and responsive. There are massive sustainability challenges with such a world, but there are also enormous opportunities.

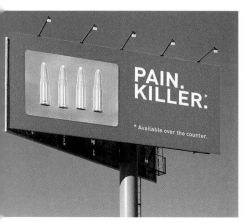

Pain Killer
Designer: Mohammad Sharaf

Must product designers be fluent in graphic languages, like type? Or is that delegated to others?

We push it pretty hard in the MFA Products of Design program, where we offer two graphic design courses that stress fundamentals like typography, grid, and hierarchy. Remember a few questions back where I talked about graphic designers falling in love with building models if you just give them the chance? Same thing with product folks learning about type. They universally adore it once they're turned on to it.

Collaboration is more common now than ever before. Would you agree that "teams" are surpassing "individual" efforts?

I was just putting together a few slides for a presentation I'm giving next week in which I talk about the requirement to acknowledge contemporary dichotomies in design and design

practice. And one of those dichotomies is exactly what you ask: "How do we fortify designers for a world simultaneously demanding individual authorship and collective effort?" We hear over and over that "design is a team sport" and that designers need to be team players. But in this era (and in this cultural moment), there is a supreme belief that "you are your own brand" and that authorship and entrepreneurship are now the coin of the realm. (It's a testament to your prescience, Steve, that you and your cochair, Lita Talerico, named your department "Designer as Author and Entrepreneur.") In any event, the demands on any designer are growing and growing, and certainly one of them is the ability to produce strong, unique, self-generated work, along with the ability to contribute significantly to group efforts.

The technology is changing so quickly; what do you see as flux and what do you see as static in product design?

I believe the ability to think strategically, empathically, and systemically are never going to change; those are central to any design process and they just make sense. How we bring technology into the mix is changing in a few ways: Where technology used to come at the end—to model with high fidelity or to manufacture an object for production—it is now coming more often at the beginning, since rapid prototyping, or "additive manufacturing," allows us to build and evaluate things so quickly and with such precision. The other revolution in product design has to do with the overlap of interac-

tion and artifacts I alluded to before. Platforms and languages like Arduino and Processing are allowing designers to embed circuits and smarts into their artifacts with a speed, ease, and affordability completely unheard of just 5 or 10 years ago. There are online communities of code to borrow and Instructables to teach that are vast and deep, and product design is benefiting from the maker movement and online tech communities in ways that are both generous and generative. It's an amazing time to be a designer.

Do you see your MFA program as a model for some more integrated design future?

I hope so. We organize our coursework along three interweaving strands: making grounds design and designers, and deepening the connection to craft and the preeminent role of "the prototype." Structures inform practice, immersing the students in the information and business structures that make effective design possible: research, systems thinking, strategy, user experience, and interaction/information design. Narratives respond to the reality that design demands stories—through drawing, graphic representation, videography, history, writing, and point of view. We like to imagine that the rubric of Making, Structures, and Narratives is a way to plan for the future as well; that we need to fundamentally "prototype" our possible futures, that we need to structure them based on cultural and marketplace realities, and that we need to understand that knowledge is most effectively spread and shared through the telling of stories.

David Carroll

Students and Surveillance

David Carroll is associate professor of media design at Parsons The New School. His research interests include interface design, mobile media, programming, social media, and transdisciplinary design. However, the focus of his studies is constantly shifting. Recently, he taught a course on surveillance design at Parsons Paris. "This is the nature of being in a field that is prone to radical innovations. Discoveries rapidly reach the marketplace and disrupt the disciplines of design and technology." One of these disruptions is the massive exploitation of personal data. But, he adds, "Designers increasingly need to tackle tough political issues in their education and careers."

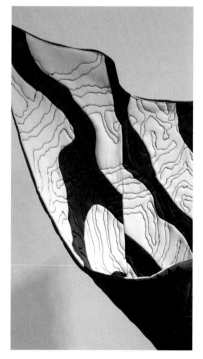

Antisurveillance Blanket
Student: Lucas Byrum
2014

How did you get interested in surveillance design as a focus of your studies?
I would have to admit that the Edward J. Snowden revelations had a profound impact on my thinking about the role of networked digital technology on our understanding of privacy and security as citizens and consumers starting to realize the magnitude of tracking technologies available to governments and corporations ("the investor-state") alike. We realized as well how contemporary designers and technologists, who are participating in this architecture of "dataveillance," have an effect on democracy and capitalism. As an interface or user experience designer, the minute you mock up your first login sequence or integrate social media features, you are doing your part to more fully enable the surveillance state.

I chose Parsons Paris as the ideal venue to launch this course. The language of this topic originates as French vocabulary, and important Parisian thinkers like Michel Foucault situate the topic within an originating milieu.

A silly question: Are the design students who sign up for your course on surveillance design fascinated by whistleblowers, secret agents, and spies?
Not silly at all. My students are part of a generation that was born into the Internet age. They don't know what it's like to live without being connected together through a highly designed digital technology. There's a myth that Millennials (Generation Y) don't care about their privacy because they share every part of their lives on social media. On the contrary, I've found in working closely with them that they are extremely concerned and savvy about how their choices affect their identity as they accumulate social currency.

They are fascinated by how the technology changes our collective behavior and how this is the conceptual basis of

Surveillance Selfie
Student: Diva Helmy
2014

surveillance itself. The fashion students, in particular, are interested in how the design and construction of garments can camouflage (there's the French vocabulary again) camera-based, computer vision tracking systems. They understand how there will be a market for privacy in the future and it will probably become a luxury good.

What could motivate a designer to embrace this specialty? Is a desire to expose unethical practices a big part of it?

The ethics of design have been recently focusing on sustainability and how we can make more environmentally and socially responsible products. However, the ethical design movement tends to eschew confronting even more difficult political problems head-on, preferring tactics that will remain friendly to corporate clients who

can climb aboard the sustainability bandwagon as a marketing message, for example.

Today's designers see the impact of how connected digital networks can both empower a democratic uprising and topple a cruel dictatorship, or conversely be used by a despot to quash unrest. They see the expanding use of drone warfare. These systems are all designed, and so the role of the designer to confront huge ethical and political issues is quickly becoming the new normal.

Presently, what artifacts, systems, or interventions are designed in response to the demands of the surveillance (and sousveillance) industry?

As designers and users become aware of how their actions on connected devices are datamined for consumer insights and intelligence operations, the market for new tools to manage identity and privacy is just starting to emerge, along with a debate over whether it will become a luxury good.

Some examples of important tools available to monitor and protect your privacy online include browser extensions like Ghostery and Lightbeam for Firefox that help users reveal and control the astonishing number of commercial trackers present on the websites we visit, which allows marketing agencies and customer identity brokers to assemble richly detailed profiles about us through our browsing habits. However, you need to be a serious IT geek or highly trained reporter to be able to use these encryption tools. Here's a great example where we need designers to take an interest in these issues to make protecting our privacy as easy as downloading a song.

In principle, should socially responsible designers refuse to contribute to the development of applications that encourage users to voluntary surrender their privacy?

This will increasingly become a personal decision designers will have to confront as they navigate their career paths. They will need to consider the business practices of the firms they seek employment from and understand how their business models generate the revenue that will supply their salaries. Furthermore, as security and privacy policies are articulated to users through the interfaces in the form of controls and settings, designers can play a very active role in being advocates for clarity to counter the attempts of lawyers to obfuscate these details.

Users are starting to accept that if a Web product is offered to you as free service, then we are actually the product. We do surrender rights to use these products, and in exchange we get to benefit from their affordances without spending our money. But we contribute massive value to these companies through our activity, and the immense return on these investments is showing that companies don't need to be profitable to be worth billions. They only need to show a critical mass of users willing to trade their privacy for a product.

Is it fair to say that the various participatory media (from *Wikipedia* to Facebook) are huge surveillance infrastructures?

I would say that Facebook is the most powerful and pervasive form of surveillance infrastructure ever created by humankind. It's beyond what Michel

Foucault or Jeremy Bentham could have imagined. It's a form of surveillance that we impose on each other on a service increasingly used as a passport that serves as an interchangeable commercial identity. In contrast, *Wikipedia* is anonymous and a nonprofit. It doesn't have shareholders, so it doesn't need to monetize user identity through data mining and advertising.

Today, how important to a design practice is a constructed criticism of the sociotechnical contexts of the Big Data phenomenon?
Given that design practice is increasingly pushed to deliver "results" based on analytics, Big Data is a big idea that all designers need to confront. People are so easily seduced by numbers because they supposedly represent objective truth. Big Data promises to answer the great questions of humanity by scaling statistical analysis toward a quantum set of correlations. However, what about all the aspects of life that aren't even measurable? How can we verify the claims of Big Data when the algorithms are a trade secret?

More specifically to designers, their practice is increasingly being driven by Big Data mechanics and its promise to provide analytical evaluations of design choices by measuring how designs affect specific user interaction outcomes. Designers will increasingly become accountable to quantitative results rather than mere aesthetic appeal. It's up to us to keep our machines and tools at the service of humans, not the reverse.

APPS That Track
By David Carroll

The concept of "The Quantified Self" might have started as a very pure graphic design project to explore data visualization vocabularies. However, it is now a cottage industry, with consumer products such as Nike+ and other athletic trackers widely available to consumers, accompanied with software that visualizes exercise data in a compelling and meaningful way.

Combine health consciousness bordering on fanaticism with the seduction of Big Data visualization in the context of self-empowerment and you have the perfect conditions for people to subject themselves to multisensor auto-tracking.

What's dangerous about Google Glass is how it allows the search giant to see the world as I see it when I wear them. (I do have a pair, yes.) For a company that wants to get into the mind of its users to control the presentation of the world's information to collect advertising revenue, Google Glass puts them as close as possible into our psyche as a point of view.

There have been multiple incidents of people with wearable computers being assaulted. A pioneer of wearable computers, while on a family vacation at the McDonald's on the Champs-Elysées, was assaulted in what some have termed the first hate crime against a cyborg. More recently, Google Glass owners in San Francisco have been assaulted while wearing the devices. These incidents epitomize not only the rejection of head-mounted cameras and computers, but perhaps more importantly, how people are becoming physically violent in resisting the invasion of surveillance trackers into every aspect of our lives.

However, there is an upside to ubiquitous monitoring and profiling. One of the promises of such immense tracking is an ability to learn about ourselves. For example, I use a product called Time-hop that shows me what I posted to my social media accounts on this day every year since I started posting. This means I see what I said four years ago today. It helps me remember my past more clearly. Some might say we're outsourcing our collective memories, but I would need to keep up with a personal diary discipline to have an equivalent experience, and it's not realistic. Here's an example where I'm willing to forsake control over my privacy to a third party because they offer me a valuable service for free.

As for whether surveillance provides increased security from violent attacks, I'm very doubtful it's effective. Privacy is a fundamental basis for democracy, so I don't understand how a surveillance state that imposes a Panopticon on us preserves our freedom for the sake of ubiquitous security. When people say, "I don't have anything to hide, so I don't mind giving up my privacy," a little bit of our collective liberty dies. It's very sad, and it's not the future I want my children to grow up in.

College Directory

UNDERGRADUATE

Academy of Art College
www.academy.edu

American Intercontinental
University
www.aiuniv.edu

The Art Institutes
www.artinstitutes.edu

The Art Institute of Boston
at Lesley University
www.aiboston.edu

University of the Arts
www.uarts.edu

Art Center College of Design
www.artcenter.edu

University of Baltimore
www.ubalt.edu

Boston University School
for the Arts
www.bu.edu/cfa/visual

Brigham Young University
College of
http://cfac.byu.edu/va

California College of the Arts
www.ccac-art.edu

California Institute of the Arts
School of Art
www.calarts.edu

California Polytechnic State
University (Ca l Poly)
art.design.libart.calpoly.edu

College of Design, Architecture,
Art, and Planning University
of Cincinnati
www.design.uc.edu

The College of Arts and
Architecture at Penn State
www.sva.psu.edu

The Cooper Union for the
Advancement of Science and Art
www.cooper.edu

The Corcoran School of Art
and Design
www.corcoran.edu

Digital Media Arts College
www.dmac-edu.org

Expression College for
Digital Arts
www.expression.edu

University of Florida
School of Art and Art History
www.arts.ufl.edu

International Academy
of Design and Technology
www.academy.edu

Kent State University
http://dept.kent.edu/art

Maryland Institute College of Art
www.mica.edu

Massachusetts College of Art
www.massart.edu

Minneapolis College of Art
and Design
www.mcad.edu

University of Minnesota
www.umn.edu

Montana State University
College of Arts and Architecture
www.montana.edu/wwwdt/

The New England Institute
of Art and Communications
www.aine.artinstitute.edu

North Carolina A&T State
University School of Technology
www.ncat.edu

Otis College of Art and Design
www.ojtis.edu

Parsons School of Design
www.parsons.edu

Pacific Northwest College of Art
www.pcna.edu

Pratt Institute
www.pratt.edu

Rhode Island School of Design
(RISD)
www.risd.edu

Ringling School of Art and Design
www.rsad.edu

School of Design College of
Imagining Arts and Sciences,
Rochester Institute of Design (RIT)
www.rit.edu

Ryerson University Graphic
Communications Management
www.ryerson.ca

Savannah College of Art and
Design
www.scad.edu

State University of New York
(SUNY) at Buffalo
www.art.buffalo.edu

School of Visual Arts (SVA)
www.sva.edu

Syracuse University College
of Visual and Performing Arts
vpa.syr.edu

Temple University Tyler School
of Art
www.temple.edu/tyler

Virginia Commonwealth
University
School of the Arts
www.vcu.edu

2-YEAR PROGRAMS

The Art Institute of Boston at
Lesley University
www.aiboston.edu

Briarcliffe College
www.bcpat.com

Brooks College
www.brookscollege.edu

College of Eastern Utah
www.ceu.edu

Community College ofv Denver
Art Department
www.ccd.edu/art

The Corcoran School of Art
and Design
www.corcoran.edu

Delaware College of Art
and Design
www.dcad.edu

Ferris State University
www.ferris.edu

International Academy of
Design and Technology
www.academy.edu

Palomar College
www.palomar.edu

Parsons School of Design
www.parsons.edu

Portfolio Center
www.portfoliocenter.com

School of Design, College of
Imagining Arts and Sciences
www.rit.edu

Spencerian College
www.spencerian.edu/lexington

GRADUATE PROGRAMS

Academy of Art College
www.academy.edu

University of Advanced
Computer Technology
www.uat.edu

Art Center College of Design
www.artcenter.edu

University of Baltimore
www.ubalt.edu

School for the Arts
Visual Arts Department
www.bu.edu/cfa/visual

Brigham Young University
College of Fine Arts and
Communications
http://cfac.byu.edu/va

California College of the Arts
www.ccac-art.edu

California Institute of the Arts
www.calarts.edu

College of Design, Architecture,
Art, and Planning University of
Cincinnati
www.design.uc.edu

The College of Arts and
Architecture at Penn State
www.sva.psu.edu

Cranbrook Academy of Art
www.cranbrook.edu

Digital Media Arts College
www.dmac-edu.org

University of Florida
www.arts.ufl.edu

IIT Institute of Design
www.id.itt.edu

Kent State University
http://dept.kent.edu/art

Maryland Institute College
of Art
www.mica.edu

Minneapolis College of Art
and Design
www.mcad.edu

Massachusetts College of Art
www.massart.edu

Montana State University
College of Arts and
www.montana.edu/wwwdt

New York University
www.itp.nyu.edu

North Carolina A&T State
University
www.ncat.edu

Otis College of Art and Design
www.otis.edu

Parsons School of Design
www.parsons.edu

Pratt Institute
www.pratt.edu

Rhode Island School of Design
(RISD)
www.risd.edu

School of Design College of
Imaging Arts and Sciences,
Rochester Institute of Design RIT)
www.rit.edu

Ryerson University
www.ryerson.ca

Savannah College of Art & Design
www.scad.edu

State University of New York
(SUNY) at Buffalo
www.art.buffalo.edu

School of Visual Arts (SVA)
http://design.schoolofvisualarts.edu

Syracuse University
vpa.syr.edu

Temple University Tyler
School of Art
www.temple.edu/tyler

University of Advanced
Computer Technology
www.uat.edu

Virginia Commonwealth
University
www.vcu.edu

Yale University
www.yale.edu/art

ONLINE SCHOOLS

The Art Institute Online
www.aioline.edu

Sessions.edu Online School
of Design
www.sessions.edu

MORE TO COME

For more schools, contact
sensebox, a graphic design
education source, at
www.sensebox.com

Additional Reading

PUBLICATIONS

Baseline
Bradbourne Publishing Limited
Bradbourne House, East Malling
Kent ME19 6DZ England
011–44–1–732–87–52–00 phone
subscribe@baselinemagazine.com
www.baselinemagazine.com

Communication Arts
110 Constitution Drive
Menlo Park, CA 94025
650–326–6040 phone
subscription@commarts.com
www.commarts.com

Design Issues
MIT Press Journals
238 Main Street, Suite 500
Cambridge, MA 02142
617–253–2889 phone
800–207–8354 toll-free phone
journals-orders@mit.edu
www.mitpressjournals.org/loi/desi

Eye
Eye Magazine Ltd
Studio 6, The Lux Building
2–4 Hoxton Square
London N1 6NU England
011–44–207–684–6530 phone
eye@ebsco.com
http://eyemagazine.com/

*Graphic Artists Guild Handbook
of Pricing and Ethical Guidelines*
32 Broadway, Suite 1114
New York, NY 10004
212–791–3400 phone
www.gag.org/handbook

Graphic Design USA
89 Fifth Avenue, Suite 901
New York, NY 10003
212–696–4380 phone
circulation@gdusa.com
www.gdusa.com

HOW
4700 East Galbraith Road
Cincinnati, OH 45236
513–531–2690 phone
www.howdesign.com

Metropolis
61 West 23rd Street, 4th Floor
New York, NY 10010
212–627–9977 phone
800–344–3046 toll-free phone
edit@metropolismag.com
www.metropolismag.com

Print Magazine
10151 Carver Road, Suite # 200
Blue Ash, OH 45242
Phone: 513-531-2690
Within the United States: 877-860-9145
Outside the United States: 386-246-3361
print@palmcoastd.com
www.printmag.com

INTERNET

AIGA
www.aiga.org

Big Cartel
www.bigcartel.com

The Book Cover Archive
www.bookcoverarchive.com

Communication Arts
www.commarts.com

Coroflot
www.coroflot.com

DaFont
www.dafont.com

Design Observer
www.designobserver.com

Design Taxi
www.designtaxi.com

The Dieline
www.thedieline.com

digg labs
www.labs.digg.com

Émigré
www.emigre.com

Etsy
www.etsy.com

Font Shop
www.fontshop.com

Hoefler Type Foundry
www.typography.com

MyFonts
www.new.myfonts.com

National Design Museum
www.cooperhewitt.org

Print
www.printmag.com

Rochester Institute of Technology
Design Archives
www.library.rit.edu/gda

Typographic
www.typographic.com

Typophile
www.typophile.com

Unbeige
www.mediabistro.com/-unbeige

Veer
www.veer.com

FURTHER READING SELECTED TITLES

Phil Baines and Catherine Dixon, *Signs: Lettering in the Environment*, Laurence King, 2008.

Marion Bataille, *ABC3D*, Roaring Brook Press, 2008.

Bo Bergström, *Essentials of Visual Communication*, Laurence King Publishers, 2009.

David Brody and Hazel Clark, editors, *Design Studies: A Reader*, Berg Publishers, 2009.

Seymour Chwast, *The Obsessive Images of Seymour Chwast*, Chronicle Books, 2009.

Timothy Donaldson, *Shapes for Sounds*, Mark Batty Publisher, 2008.

Brian Dougherty, *Green Graphic Design*, Allworth Press, 2009.

Michael Erlhoff and Timothy Marshall, editors, *Design Dictionary: Perspectives on Design Terminology*, Birkhäuser Basel, 2008.

Conny Freyer, Sebastien Noel, and Eva Rucki, *Digital by Design*, Thames & Hudson, 2009.

Milton Glaser, *Drawing Is Thinking*, Overlook Hardcover, 2008.

Steven Heller, editor, *Design Disasters: Great Designers, Fabulous Failure, and Lessons Learned*, Allworth Press, 2009.

Steven Heller and Gail Anderson, *New Vintage Type*, Watson Guptil, 2007.

Steven Heller and Mirko Ilic, *Handwritten: Expressive Lettering in the Digital Age*, Thames and Hudson, 2007.

Steven Heller and Lita Talarico, *The Design Entrepreneur*, Rockport Publishers, 2008.

Steven Heller and Lita Talarico, *Design Studios Firms Open for Business*, Allworth Press, 2012.

Steven Heller and Mirko Ilic, *Lettering Large: Art and Design of Monumental Typography*, 2013.

Steven Heller and Veronique Vienne, *100 Ideas that Changed Graphic Design*, Laurence King, 2013.

Tom Himpe, *Advertising Next*, Chronicle Books, 2008.

Wendy Jedlicka, *Packaging Sustainability: Tools, Systems and Strategies for Innovative Package Design*, Wiley, 2008.

R. Klanten and H. Hellige, *Playful Type: Ephemeral Lettering and Illustrative Fonts*, Die Gestalten Verlag, 2008.

George Lois, *George Lois: On Creating the Big Idea*, Assouline, 2008.

Keith Martin, Robin Dodd, Graham Davis, and Bob Gordon, *1000 Fonts*, Chronicle Books, 2009.

Lars Müller and Victor Malsy, *Helvetica Forever*, Lars Müller Publishers, 2009.

Michael Perry, *Over & Over: A Catalog of Hand-Drawn Patterns*, Princeton Architectural Press, 2008.

Rick Poynor, *Designing Pornotopia: Travels in Visual Culture*, Princeton Architectural Press, 2006.

Lucienne Roberts, *Good: Ethics of Graphic Design*, AVA Publishing, 2006.

Stefan Sagmeister, *Things I Have Learned in My Life So Far*, Abrams, 2008.

Adrian Shaughnessy, *How to Be a Graphic Designer Without Losing Your Soul*, Laurence King, 2005.

Jan Tholenaar and Alston W. Purvis, *Type: A Visual History of Typefaces and Graphic Styles, Vol. 1*, Taschen, 2009.

Jennifer Visocky O'Grady and Ken O'Grady, *A Designer's Research Manual: Succeed in Design by Knowing Your Clients and What They Really Need*, Rockport Publishers, 2009.

Armin Vit and Bryony Gomez Palacio, *Graphic Design, Referenced: A Visual Guide to the Language, Applications, and History of Graphic Design*, Rockport Publishers, 2009.

Index